The Chinese Party-State in the 21st Century

This book examines various mechanisms used by the Chinese Communist Party (CCP) in response to challenges raised against its claim to legitimacy. As the CCP continues to move away from traditional Maoism, it seeks to maintain its commanding role in Chinese political life despite a growing number of challenges, from political and non-political actors alike, to its claim that it is the most effective force to keep the country together. The contributions to this book describe some of these challenges and explain how the CCP selectively adapts to them in order to maintain its authority and relevance in China. Arguing that despite the severity of the challenges it faces, the CCP—and the Chinese state apparatus it commands—has not opted for retrenchment, but rather has found ways to adapt to contemporary political conundrums and dilemmas using a wide range of methods, the objective of this book is to describe how the CCP tries to succeed in these endeavours. Other studies of legitimacy in China have been produced in recent years, but this book proposes to look at it from a different angle: instead of looking at the forces in society that challenge the regime, it looks at the ways in which the regime adapts to them.

The Chinese Party-State in the 21st Century will appeal to students and scholars of Chinese politics, Asian politics, comparative politics and political sociology.

André Laliberté is Professor of Political Science at the University of Quebec at Montreal (UQAM), and Associate Professor at the Faculty of Graduate Studies, University of Ottawa, Canada.

Marc Lanteigne is Lecturer in the Department of International Relations at St Andrews University, UK.

Routledge Contemporary China Series

The Chinese Party-State in the 21st Century

Adaptation and the reinvention of legitimacy

**Edited by
André Laliberté and
Marc Lanteigne**

LONDON AND NEW YORK

First published 2008
by Routledge
2 Park Square, Milton Park, Abingdon, Oxon OX14 5RN

Simultaneously published in the USA and Canada
by Routledge
711 Third Avenue, New York, NY 10017

Routledge is an imprint of the Taylor & Francis Group, an informa business

First issued in paperback 2011

Typeset in Times New Roman by
Florence Production Ltd, Stoodleigh, Devon

British Library Cataloguing in Publication Data
A catalogue record for this book is available from the British Library

Library of Congress Cataloging in Publication Data
The Chinese party-state in the 21st century: adaptation and the reinvention
of legitimacy/edited by André Laliberté and Marc Lanteigne.
    p. cm. – (Routledge contemporary China series; 28)
    1. Zhongguo gong chan dang.   2. China – Politics and government – 2002–.
    3. China – Economic conditions – 2000–.   I. Laliberté, André, 1959–.
    II. Lanteigne, Marc.
JQ1519.A5C4679 2008
324.251'075 – dc22   2007028698

ISBN10: 0–415–45056–X (hbk)
ISBN10: 0–415–69218–0 (pbk)
ISBN10: 0–203–93327–3 (ebk)

ISBN13: 978–0–415–45056–0 (hbk)
ISBN13: 978–0–415–69218–2 (pbk)
ISBN13: 978–0–203–93327–5 (ebk)

Contents

Notes on contributors

Dr. André Laliberté is Associate Professor at the College of Political Studies, University of Ottawa, Canada. He has published the *Politics of Taiwanese Buddhist Organizations* at Routledge. His current research concentrates on the relationship between government and religious organizations in the PRC and Taiwan.

Dr. Marc Lanteigne is a Lecturer at the School of International Relations at the University of St. Andrews, United Kingdom. He is the author of *China and International Institutions: Alternate Paths to Global Power* (Routledge, 2005) as well as articles on Chinese foreign policy and Asian security.

Dr. Charles Burton has been borrowed twice since 1991 from Brock University by the Department of Foreign Affairs to work in the Canadian Embassy in Beijing. He is the author and editor of books and articles about China and North Korea, and continues to consult for the Canadian Government.

Dr. Susan J. Henders is Associate Professor of Political Science at York University. She specializes in human rights, "ethnic" conflict, and territorial politics. Her books include *Democratization and Identity: Regimes and Ethnicity in East and Southeast Asia* and the forthcoming *(In)tolerance and (A)symmetry: The Politics of Special Status Regions*.

Dr. Diana Lary is Professor *emerita* at UBC. She works on the impact of the War of Resistance on Chinese society and has also a strong interest in the borderlands of China. She has edited *The Chinese State at the Borders* and her most recent book is *China's Republic*.

Dr. Hélène Piquet teaches Law at Quebec University in Montreal's Law Department. She holds degrees in East Asian Studies (BA and MA) from McGill University and Law degrees from UQAM and McGill (DCL). Fluent in Chinese, she researches the Chinese legal reforms since 1978.

Dr. Jonathan Schwartz is Associate Professor of Political Science at SUNY New Paltz. His primary research focus is on factors influencing policy enforcement in transitioning regimes. He is currently conducting comparative research on environmental and public health policy enforcement in China, Taiwan and the United States.

Dr. Xu Feng is Assistant Professor at the Department of Political Science, University of Victoria, Canada. She is the author of *Women Migrant Workers and China's Economic Reform* (Macmillan/Palgrave, 2000). She is currently working on a project on unemployment, community/*shequ* building and urban governance in contemporary China.

Acknowledgments

The editors would like to first extend their thanks to the Social Science and Humanities Research Council (SSHRC) of Canada and the *Centre d'études sur les politiques étrangères et de sécurité* (CEPES), which generously contributed to the convening of a conference on the challenges of governance in China at the Université de Québec à Montréal (UQAM), which provided the impetus for this volume. We are grateful to all of the participants in the conference for their comments and ideas, which formed the basis for this project, and to those participants who later provided chapters which expertly reflected some of the many facets of modern Chinese governance. At the same time, we are also thankful for the support given by UQAM, McGill University, Montreal, and the University of St. Andrews, United Kingdom, for their support during the various stages of this book's preparation, and to friends and colleagues in North America, China and beyond who provided much-needed encouragement. We would also like to thank the anonymous reviewers who carefully looked at an earlier version of the manuscript and provided very helpful comments and suggestions, and Jean-Philippe Brassard, who diligently helped us prepare the final version of this manuscript in a very short time. Last but definitely not least, we would like to extend our thanks to Stephanie Rogers at Routledge, who helped shepherd this project from its beginnings. *Xiexie nimen!*

Abbreviations

AFC	Asian Financial Crisis
APEC	Asia Pacific Economic Cooperation
BEDI	Beijing Environment and Development Institute
BESTU	Beijing Environment, Science and Technology Update
BL	Basic Law
CCP	Chinese Communist Party
CCTV	Central China Television
CEEC	Center for Environmental Education and Communications
CLAPV	The Center for Legal Assistance to Pollution Victims
CNOOC	China National Offshore Oil Corporation
CPSU	Communist Party of the Soviet Union
CWI	China Welfare Institute
CYDF	China Youth Development Foundation
ENGO	environmental non-governmental organizations
EPB	Environmental Protection Bureaus (local)
HKSAR	Hong Kong Special Administrative Region
JD	1984 Sino-British Joint Declaration
MCA	Ministry of Civil Affairs
MII	Ministry of Information Industry
MITI	Ministry of International Trade and Industry
MOFCOM	Ministry of Commerce
MOFERT	Ministry of Foreign Economic Relations and Trade
NEPAD	New Partnership for Africa's Development
NPC	National People's Congress
PLA	People's Liberation Army
PRC	People's Republic of China
PTA	preferential trade agreements
ROC	Republic of China
SAR	Special Administrative Region (as in Hong Kong)
SARS	Severe Acute Respiratory Syndrome
SASAC	State-owned Assets Supervision and Administration Commission
SCLF	Soong Ching Ling Foundation

SCO	Shanghai Cooperation Organisation
SEPA	State Environmental Protection Agency
SETC	State Economic and Trade Commission
SEZ	special economic zones
SOE	state-owned enterprises
SRDC	State Development and Reform Commission

1 The issue of challenges to the legitimacy of CCP rule

André Laliberté and Marc Lanteigne

Introduction

News and analyses from China point to growing internal unrest, an increasing number of strikes, upheavals, protests and other signs that the authority of the Chinese Communist Party (CCP) is being questioned. Yet, there exists no credible alternative to the CCP and no signs that the Party is experiencing divisions or indecisiveness from within that could threaten its control of the country. On the contrary, the leadership transition in Beijing from Jiang Zemin to Hu Jintao has been successfully and smoothly completed, a significant change from such transitions in the past. Moreover, the performance of the Chinese economy, which has dazzled the world since 1978, once seen as an example of success in poverty alleviation is now perceived as an economic juggernaut about to dominate the world economy. In the wake of liberal economic reforms begun by Deng Xiaoping in the late 1970s, their continuation under Jiang Zemin, and their acceleration in the first years of the Hu Government, China is positioning itself as the potential "number one" in the twenty-first century's global economy.

Despite all the positive signs on the economic front, however, there is no sign of a political opening or the development of greater pluralism in China. On the contrary, since taking office, Hu Jintao has continued to limit the freedom of the domestic media as he has consolidated his hold on power. Furthermore, in a sign that the current regime does not feel entirely confident about the claim that its rule is accepted by most people in China, the CCP leadership has refused to use the passing of former premier Zhao Ziyang in January 2005 to reconsider the verdict handed down on the student demonstrations that led to the June 1989 Tiananmen Massacre. Zhao had been placed under house arrest for fifteen years for showing support for the movement, and his funeral took place under heavy security restrictions. In China today, outspoken intellectuals continue to face censure, underground Christian church devotees and adherents of *Falun Gong* spiritual movement, which Beijing has denounced as a destabilizing cult, continue to face persecution, and the authorities continue to impose severe limits on what the media can report, with the result that serious unrest is under-reported.

The government continues to try to regulate the flow of information despite the spread of communications, the Internet and wireless text-messaging technologies, throughout Chinese cities and even the countryside. It is becoming increasingly difficult to filter information, as more of it can reach more people than ever. Cracks have started to appear in the Chinese information monopoly, as was demonstrated during the 2002–3 outbreak of Severe Acute Respiratory Syndrome (SARS) in the country, which forced the CCP into greater openness about its health care and public safety policies. As well, there have been an increasing number of incidents of internal unrest being leaked to the international media, such as the June 2005 protests in Shengyou, which were captured on a digital camera and smuggled out of the country (Pan 2005: A12).

This raises questions as to the extent to which the CCP trust that the Chinese people believe in the fairness of its rule and the extent to which Party leaders feel the current regime is facing a crisis of legitimacy. In the wake of the reforms launched by Deng after 1978, values promoted by Mao have steadily eroded (although he remains a significant icon in contemporary Chinese political life) and many of the traditional communist ideals in Chinese society have given way to nationalism. The CCP positions itself as the only political actor with the ability to govern China; oversee its economic growth; maintain social stability; and ensure state coherence. The successive governments of China since 1949, well aware of the chaos and disorder which marked the last decades of the Imperial era and the Republican period, have remained very sensitive to instability from within, because of their fear that it could facilitate interference from outsiders and even threaten the integrity of the state.

Many cases of internal dissension in Imperial China, such as the Taiping (1850–64), Nian (1851–68), Panthay (1856–73) and Boxer rebellions (1899–1900), have shown how much this intersection of domestic challenges with external intervention can threaten a political regime. The Chinese governments since 1978 have all wanted to prevent a repetition of this fatal combination, and it is with great caution that they have adopted bold policies favouring economic growth, trying to ensure that the tremendous social changes they will generate will not threaten political stability. The fall of the Soviet Union in 1991 has provided a textbook example of what the CCP does *not* want to see occur as the result of economic reform. Therefore all CCP leaders since Deng have encouraged wide-ranging economic liberalization while preventing any push towards a corresponding degree of political democratization.

In the years that immediately followed the Tiananmen Massacre, there were fears that this conciliation between economic growth and political stability was impossible and that the regime could not survive this major crisis of legitimacy. The success of Deng's "Southern Tour" (*nanxun*) in 1992 and the "glorious decade" of the 1990s that followed, however, have suggested that this verdict was premature. The demonstration of the *Falun Gong* around

Zhongnanhai in 1999 seemed to reveal another challenge to the regime's legitimacy. The violent response from the government to this movement that followed a few months later appeared to betray a deep sense of insecurity Eight years later, in the run-up to the Olympic Games in Beijing, the regime remains nervous of any form of discontent and continues to clamp down on dissident religious groups, labor organizers, displaced peasants and other groups of people who seek redress. Yet, it would be wrong to conclude from this that China is on the verge of collapse. Economic growth has continued, there is no mass movement of protest threatening to overthrow the regime, and China is more respected than ever on the world stage.

This volume considers the diverse approaches the Chinese party-state has used to face the various challenges to its claims to legitimacy that have emerged in the last decade in the realm of economic growth, social stability, and national unity. The examples brought forward represent a range of issues directly tied to the consequences of the modernization processes which began in the late 1970s and have accelerated under Jiang and Hu. These issues represent direct and indirect challenges to the Chinese party-state which have forced the CCP to seek not only new forms of accommodation, but also adaptation to political realities, as the Chinese state oversees massive socio-economic change resulting from one of the most ambitious programmes of social transformation in the history of developing societies. Although it remains uncertain whether the CCP in its present form can address all these challenges, the case studies discussed in this book provide an opportunity to explore the ways in which it had successfully managed them at the turn of the century.

The challenges to the CCP claims to legitimacy since 1949

Twenty years ago, scholars used classical Weberian sociology to describe the transition from Mao to Deng and explained this evolution as an example of "routinisation of charisma" (Tiewes 1984). Ten years later, the 1989 student protests, which would lead to the Tiananmen Massacre, drew attention to a major crisis of legitimacy; a failure to achieve a transition towards a rational-legal source of authority (Ding 1994). Some observers contended that the events of 1989 marked the second crisis of legitimacy faced by the CCP; the first crisis emerging after the death of Mao, when the disastrous results of its policies during the Cultural Revolution were felt acutely. That first crisis was resolved by Deng Xiaoping and his allies, when they based the CCP's claim to legitimacy on economic performance rather than ideological conformity. However, this solution did not last long because the social tensions generated by the transition towards a market economy, in the absence of any political reform, became intolerable.

The resolution of that second crisis was the establishment of a new legitimacy based on economic nationalism, political conservatism, and the rehabilitation of the individual pursuit of personal happiness (Yang 1996: 217). At the end of the twentieth century, this approach appeared to have succeeded: no political opposition challenged the CCP. It was clear to outside observers, however, that a claim to legitimacy based on economic perform-ance was vulnerable to continued corruption and the possibility of an economic downturn (Burns 1999: 594). There have been serious concerns that the reform process has thrown open the door to increased levels of corruption (*fubai*) at various levels of the Chinese state despite the creation of the Ministry of Supervision and other oversight bodies after 1987, as well as government campaigns during the Jiang era to actively combat the problem. Although the Jiang Government did see some high-profile crackdowns on illegal government activities; including the ouster and arrest of former Beijing mayor, Chen Xitong, in 1998 and the high-profile smashing of the Yuanhua smuggling ring in Fujian in 2001, corruption and misuse of power remain a constant threat to both economic reform and the stability of party and state (Wedeman 2004). The degree of the corruption problem was further under-lined with the September 2006 removal of Chen Liangyu, CCP head in Shanghai, over accusations of widespread misappropriation of that city's social security funds (Kahn 2006: A10). Questions of party responsibility and accountability have continued to affect the reform process, especially as more people achieve middle class status and demand proper representation.

CCP leaders also saw, ten years after the Tiananmen Square massacre, another threat to their legitimacy emerging with the *Falun Gong*. The group emerged from relative obscurity in 1999 when ten thousand of its adherents descended upon the gates of Zhongnanhai, the government compound in Beijing, to protest their alleged harassment by authorities. The CCP saw that movement as an ominous sign of the social instability that could undermine the regime, and also as an ideological threat to the CCP's claim to embody patriotism (Ostergaard 2004: 216–17; Ownby 2001: 13). The movement has been branded as a cult by Beijing, and has since been curtailed both by government pressure and the after-effects of an incident in January 2001, later widely televised in China, of five alleged members setting themselves on fire in Tiananmen (Eckholm 2001: A1).

At the beginning of the twenty-first century, the regime continues to base its legitimacy on economic growth and the improvement of living standards on the one hand, and on the maintenance of stability on the other (Yang 1996: 217–18). The international context of the late 1990s, however, has seen the emergence of a third source of legitimacy: the appeal of nationalism, expressed in the calls to achieve national unity (Zheng 2004: 51). The increasing prominence of China's international presence, the crackdown on corruption, the improvement of government efficiency, and even, arguably, the clean-up of the environment are also evoked as major sources of legitimacy (Lin and Hu 2003: 121). A few even mention the ability to incor-porate local leaders into the government structure (Howell 2004: 238). Beyond the differences in these conclusions, however, a minimum consensus is emerging. No one believes that reference to the heroic narrative of the revolution can sustain a viable claim to legitimacy. Everyone agrees that economic performance represents the foundation of the CCP's continued ability to assert its authority. Opinions differ on the quality of that perform-ance and the limits under which it stops being effective. Another issue that generates consensus is the paramount importance of stability. This time, analysts vary in their assessment of the threats to stability or on the severity of instability. Finally, although they approach the issue from different angles, most analysts agree about the importance of nationalism as a powerful source of legitimacy for the CCP (Zheng 2004: 51; Lin and Hu 2003: 121; Ostergaard 2004: 218). These findings, we believe, justify the focus of this book on the different tools the regime uses to maintain its legitimacy along the dimensions of economic prosperity, social stability, and national unity. But before we get to that point, it is important to determine to what extent the Chinese authorities believe the legitimacy of their regime is threatened, and if they do so, how they can respond to this perception.

State responses to the challenges of legitimacy in China

At the beginning of the twenty-first century, the CCP entirely controls the state apparatus. Although there were some limited attempts by Zhao Ziyang in the 1980s to achieve a separation between the party and the public administration (*dang zheng fenkai*), such experiments ended with the events at Tiananmen Square. Despite the re-launching of reform in 1992, no subse-quent attempts have been made to separate party and state. However, as a result of Deng's reforms and ongoing economic liberalization and revital-ization under Jiang and Hu, the role of the CCP is being challenged from many different directions. As a result of the erosion of Maoist thought, the Party can no longer act as a guarantor of societal well-being for every Chinese citizen. Yet it wishes to remain the only option for governance in China. This has led to the question of how the CCP will be able to respond to the new ideas and pressures that have appeared in China as a result of economic opening and greater international engagement. The three options which the Party may face in the future are *retreat*, *retrenchment* and *adaptation*.

The idea of state *retreat* is not new, and has actually been a feature of many states undergoing a governmental transition (Strange 1996). Much of the former communist world, which, during much of the twentieth century, saw the state capture most if not all of the features of governance, has now had to address the withdrawal of the state in many social, economic and political areas, often giving way to the development of greater civil society. Not every reforming state, however, has experienced the same transition. While some post-communist regimes have settled into greater liberalism with relative smoothness (Czech Republic, Hungary, Poland) others have opted for selective state retreat (Russia, Vietnam) and still others have halted the retreat altogether (Belarus, Turkmenistan, Uzbekistan) by resisting pluralistic reform and entrenching single-party rule. China, by contrast, cannot be seen as possessing a state apparatus in retreat, and the CCP has demonstrated a remarkable resilience in the face of international change.

Some theorists, who have studied the development of globalization, have argued that the transfer of power associated with this phenomenon in a downward direction (to sub-regions, interest groups, and civil society) and upward (to international regimes, international law, multi-national corporations) suggests that power is inexorably being siphoned from the state. The abilities of a given state to set laws, economic policies, and international policy, argue the "hyperglobalist" school of globalization studies, are being chipped away as a result of ongoing economic and in some cases political interdependence (Camilleri and Falk 1992). State retreat, in this case, is seen as non-voluntary on the part of the state itself, and is instead viewed as "running ahead of the wave" rather than risk becoming completely swamped. As will be argued later in this volume, however, China has thus far been able to channel the forces of globalization and actually incorporate it within the state itself, as the CCP has endeavoured to establish itself as the sole political force able to channel economic globalization into economic benefits for the majority of the Chinese people. In that, the Party has been successful in overseeing the development of a small but growing middle class as part of "socialism with Chinese characteristics."

State *retrenchment*, by contrast, suggests a state realizing its growing limitations, purposefully ceding some areas of governance to the private sector, but retaining others in order to ensure stability and survival. Russia today could be considered an example of this phenomenon, albeit a flawed one. It can be argued that China may face this option in the near future as the political, economic and social issues of the Chinese state simply become too many for the Party, large as it is, to adequately address. However, despite these pressures there is so far no sign that the CCP is engaging in this option.

The third path which the Chinese state can take is one of *adaptation*, the act of evolving in order to meet the needs of the Chinese state. As Weiss noted, most states do have the ability to adapt to changing circumstances, and the inability to identify the adaptive abilities of a given state may lead some observers to inaccurately assume that the state is in decline (Weiss 1999: 10–11). That risk is certainly a factor in Chinese studies of governance. By casting aside much of traditional Maoist political thought and economics in favour of state-guided socio-economic development, the Chinese party-state has steered away from the fate which befell the Communist Party of the Soviet Union and has instead situated itself as the guarantor of state stability, safety and prosperity via selective importation of international ideas and goods, while continuing to associate challenges against the Party as challenges against the state itself. The CCP has been successful, in no small part due to China's growing economy, political power, and diplomatic presence on an international level as well as growing prosperity on the domestic level. Despite naysaying analysts at the beginning of the 1990s who argued that the CCP would have no better luck than the Communist Party of the Soviet Union (CPSU) in adjusting to governance in the post-cold war world (Waldron 1995: 148–53; Chang 2001), these concerns have been proven premature at best.

The adaptation of the CCP since the beginning of the century has taken many forms. In 2000, entrepreneurs and private sector workers, once the bane of the party ideologues, were formally invited into the party. At the same time, Jiang Zemin attempted to place his own stamp on China's political doctrine by unveiling the "Three Represents" theory, stating the future role for the Party would be to represent "the interests of the masses," "advanced productive forces," and China's "new advanced culture." After much political discourse, the Three Represents were added to the government's constitutional amendments in March 2004 and remain a focus of debate in Chinese policy circles. The 2004 amendments also included provisions that further recognized private property, as well as promises to protect the rights of self-employed and private businesses and establish a modern social security system to replacing the fraying net of the "iron rice bowl" (*tiefanwan*) structure of protected state jobs and basic needs. The party-state has also adapted other programs designed to adjust to modern realities, including an ongoing anti-corruption campaign in place since the 1990s, and a 1998 decree by Jiang Zemin calling upon the People's Liberation Army (PLA) to divest itself of all significant business holdings in exchange for regular annual increases in the military budget.

Although the CCP today is not facing the crisis of governance that had been predicted in the 1990s, its role nonetheless remains far from stable. Greater international engagement and economic reform has produced apathy towards the Party (especially in the richer coastal areas where many see the government as a potential hindrance to further prosperity) and in some cases outright resistance, including a growing number of protests in the interior over land appropriation, corruption, incompetence and environmental damage. The adaptation process has therefore been very difficult and the party-state simply cannot afford to relax its attempts to maintain its integrity and its relevance in China. After the Sixteenth Party Congress in November 2002, a turning point was reached not only in the adoption of Jiang's "Three Represents," but also in the entire Chinese reform regime (*tixi*) which Hu Jintao has inherited. The Hu Government has dedicated itself not only to continuing the modernization of China but also to maintaining a threshold level of stability in the face of overwhelming socio-economic change. The authors of the chapters presented in this book all agree that the Chinese state is not adopting strategies of retreat or retrenchment, but is instead exploring strategies of adaptation.

This argument has been made most forcefully by Yang Dali, who has argued recently that the Chinese state, far from facing a crisis of legitimacy, is becoming "more efficient, more service-oriented, and more disciplined" (2006: 312). He makes his case by demonstrating that, in trying to achieve the goals of economic growth through reform and opening, the government has had to adopt important measures. These he has regrouped into four different categories: economic constraints; intra-governmental discipline; constitutional constraints; and international engagements and obligations. The goal of participation in the global economy, he explains, imposes on the Chinese Government, at central and local level, the need to cultivate its reputation as a responsible stakeholder (Yang 2006: 304–5). Intra-governmental discipline, he asserts, serves to promote checks and balances in accordance with law (305–6). The effectiveness of constitutional constraints, he admits, remains fragile, but nevertheless the authorities pay increasing attention to governance according to law (306–7). Yang, finally, concludes that China's accession to many international organizations exercises a powerful effect on its government, which feels increasingly compelled to comply or adapt to international rules (308–9).

There is no denying that China is registering considerable progress in trying to address all these challenges. However, if the response of the Chinese state to the forces of the world economy may please bankers, entrepreneurs and outsiders, it is perceived very negatively within China by those who are left out by the formidable growth the country is experiencing (Perry and Selden 2006; Hurst and O'Brien 2002; Chan 2001; Bernstein 2000). The challenge to the CCP legitimacy thus remains entire. This book does not take issue with Yang's argument about the ability of the Chinese state to maintain a sustainable regime of authoritarian government. It seeks instead to examine further how the CCP tries to generate consent over its claims to legitimacy. These claims, in a nutshell, are encapsulated in the notion that only the CCP is able to ensure economic growth, provide social stability, and defend national sovereignty.

Three bases of legitimacy claims: economic performance, stability and nationalism

Economic performance

To preserve its control of Chinese society, despite the disillusions incurred by the policies of Mao, the CCP under Deng Xiaoping has turned to a strategy of eudaemonic legitimacy, that is, it has encouraged the individual pursuit of material improvement (Chen 1997). The success of this strategy represents one of the most enduring and remarkable achievements of the CCP. The celebration of individual success, encapsulated in the slogan "to get rich is glorious"; the creation of the special economic zones after 1980; and later on the de-collectivization of the countryside, all stood in stark contrast to the policies advocated by Mao during the Cultural Revolution. One of the most noteworthy aspects of this radical transformation was Deng's ability to claim that his bold policies represented a solution of continuity with the emancipatory goals espoused by Marxism-Leninism and Mao's own ideals.

Deng managed to convince his colleagues and opponents that his policies conformed to a historical materialist perspective. Although his own participation in the Long March probably lent him some of the charismatic authority from which Mao benefited, his most significant contribution was to ensure that his successors, Jiang Zemin, and later on, Hu Jintao, could continue his policies even if they had none of his revolutionary credentials.

In order to ensure some solid foundation to his policies and ensure that no successor could undo the reforms, Deng sought the institutionalization of his reforms and enshrined in the constitution some of its major elements. For instance, the enshrining of the Four Cardinal Principles has confirmed the leadership of the CCP, while the amendment, adopted in 1988, that the CCP recognizes the complementary contribution of the private sector in the economy has, in effect, given a legal sanction to the policy that rehabilitates a practice previously condemned by the regime. Thus, a major component of the legitimacy based on economic performance is the process of legal reform (Potter 1994: 325). The law is instrumentalized in order to give some legitimacy to a process where successive reinterpretation of the socialist ideology have gradually facilitated the use of capitalist methods to develop the economy that could, in turn, contribute to the erosion of the ideology (Chen 1995). This instrumentalization of law, in sum, means that China is not a society governed by the rule of law, as this concept is understood in the West. This limitation is especially obvious in situations where political dissidents, adherents to illegal religions, or other marginalized elements of Chinese society, see references to the law used against their activities, as is the case in the campaign launched by the CCP against the *Falun Gong* (Keith and Lin 2003: 642).

The reliance on economic growth as a source of legitimacy is problematic because this positive development, for an unprecedented number of people, has also led to a series of contradictions. Among the most serious of these problems is a widening gap between rich and poor. Yet, despite these limitations, the CCP under Jiang appeared determined to pursue a strategy of rapid development to bolster its legitimacy (Lewis and Xue 2003: 941).

One of the most important limitations to this strategy of eudaemonic legitimacy, however, remains the ever-present occurrence of a serious economic downturn (Burns 1999: 593–4), and the regime's capacity to deliver material resources (Chen 1997: 423). In 1978, Deng could ask the population to forego references to egalitarian ideals because of the exhaustion felt after a decade of political unrest and economic decline: the population welcomed above all the political stability that came with his program of reforms, and believed that they would provide an improvement of their living conditions with the dismantling of the communes, and the policy of opening and reform. These hopes were proven true during the 1980s, and student protests notwithstanding, the CCP regime was not seriously threatened by any outside force in that decade. In the 1990s, however, the weaknesses of the eudaemonic strategy were revealed. While the Chinese economy continued to experience formidable growth, the wealth generated had become unevenly distributed, corruption was increasing, and the reform of the state-owned enterprises was creating uncertainties, as an increasing number of workers were being laid off. These numerous problems, created by economic reforms, threaten the second pillar of the regime legitimacy: political stability.

Stability

The tragedy of 1989 and its aftershocks showed the limitations of the eudaemonic strategy pursued by the CCP. In particular, it had demonstrated that this strategy alone could not guarantee political stability (Chen 1997: 421). After Deng Xiaoping undertook his Southern Tour in 1992 and re-launched the policy of reforms, the CCP announced that it was returning to the same strategy but that it would enhance it with new and different mechanisms (Chen 1997: 422). In particular, the regime paid closer attention to civil order and peace. Arguably, the social stability that is ensured by the ruling party, allows people to pursue their own private objectives in the spheres of work, education, leisure, and welfare. To reinforce its claim to legitimacy, the ability of the CCP to maintain these conditions may matter more to an ordinary Chinese person than a good economic performance or even nationalism (Friedman 2000: 237).

Conventional wisdom holds that one of the consequences of the absence of any new moral order is the worsening of corruption from the beginning of the reforms (Wedeman 2004: 920). Yet, recent research holds that narrative on corruption produced by the regime in the 1990s has allowed the regime to recapture legitimacy, by presenting the fight against corruption as an effort to improve economic opportunities, raise living standards and bring social stability (Hsu 2001: 25).

The Party faces an uncertain future in its relations with five different groups: peasants, urban workers, minority religious groups, demobilized soldiers, and some intellectuals (Lewis and Xue 2003: 929–30). Peasant unrest shows the limits of an eudaemonic strategy for legitimacy: economic growth based on industrialization and urbanization has led to land expropriation (Guo 2001: 422). Workers have also experienced significant deterioration in conditions with the beginning of reforms, in the domain of health care and work safety (Wright 2004). The decline of the position in society of industrial workers, having represented for a long time the foundation of the CCP's claim to legitimacy, should have heralded a major crisis for the regime. Indeed, workers unrest throughout the country appeared to signal such a possibility. Pensioners' protests represent a case in point: their demands for redress in cases of unpaid pensions are seriously perceived as legitimate (Hurst and O'Brien 2002: 345).

Despite all these problems, the CCP has managed, during the 1990s, to convince the population that it represents the only force capable of preventing chaos (Chen 1997: 439). Surveys in 1999 showed that while urban residents deplore the too rapid pace of economic reform and the unwillingness of the

Party to encourage the expression of political views and participation, their conservative orientations and their nationalist sentiments provided a positive context to deepen economic reforms (Tang 2001: 908).

Nationalism

Many observers have asserted that without any credible claim that could generate spontaneous or voluntary obedience to the party, the CCP turns to nationalism as a source of legitimacy (Lam 2003: 255–6; Cheng 2001: 119; Chen 1997: 439). The study of nationalism in post-cold war international and comparative studies has undergone many changes, and beyond the idea of "sense of nation" this concept has been greatly open to interpretation, and in light of recent civil and international conflicts has been prone to be confused with "hyper-nationalism": the belief of the superiority of one nation over another, as was observed for example in Yugoslavia's wars of secession in the 1990s. Scholars studying the development of nationalism in China are not in complete agreement as to what forms of this phenomenon are developing both in the political centre and the nation itself as a result of the steady erosion of Maoism as political doctrine.

The assertion of sovereignty by the government to bolster legitimacy claims is certainly not something new: since the founding of the People's Republic of China (PRC), there has been a close link between sovereignty and regime legitimacy (Austin 1998: 31). The use of nationalism as a pillar of legitimacy has re-emerged through the stoking of anti-American sentiment during the May 1999 bombing of the Belgrade embassy by an American fighter jet during NATO military operations against Serbia (Wang and Zheng 2000). A similar anti-American nationalist outburst took place two years later when an American EP-3E surveillance plane was challenged by two Chinese J-8 fighter jets in the South China Sea. A collision between the plane and one of the jets resulted in the death of the Chinese pilot and the forced landing of the American aircraft on Hainan Island. The plane was boarded by the Chinese military and the crew of twenty four taken into custody for eleven days until Beijing received a satisfactory apology from the United States. In both cases, however, the CCP quickly saw the limits to this exploitation of nationalist sentiment, and rapidly tried to rein in demonstrations before they went too far. During the 1990s, other sources of friction, including Sino-American policy differences over China's long campaign to join the World Trade Organization, as well as concern in Beijing over American policy towards Taiwan, which took great steps in developing democracy and pluralism during that decade, also added to nationalist thinking in China (Fewsmith 2001a: 204–14).

The same scenario repeated itself in April 2005, when protests against the authorization of revisionist history textbooks by the Japanese education ministry were criticized by the state media, even though they first appeared to have been given tacit approval. The protests in Beijing and elsewhere, which saw Japanese businesses and government edifices attacked and vandalized (Kahn 2005: A6), demonstrated lingering hostility towards Japan for its historical legacy in China during the Second World War but also the willingness of Beijing to tolerate such outbursts to a specific degree. Uneasiness in China about Tokyo's application that year to become a permanent member of the United Nations Security Council and its emerging willingness to expand its military interests beyond its home waters have also contributed to nationalist sentiment towards Japan despite the growing prosperous trade relationship between the two states.

Those episodes of equivocation by the CCP demonstrated that while nationalism can constitute one of the new bases for legitimacy, it cannot represent a long-term solution because of its inherent instability (Chen 1997: 421). In that particular sense, legitimacy buttressed by nationalism does not differ much from charismatic legitimacy. In addition, nationalism may not be a sufficient substitute to offset the deleterious effects of corruption, as discussed before, nor can it compensate for economic mismanagement. Nationalism can also backfire: the leadership can be attacked for not defending the national interests with enough vigour, exposing the Party to challenges from the PLA, conservative factions within the CCP, or, as was the case in the two events discussed above, by students. As the events of the anti-Japan protests of April 2005 have shown, once nationalist sentiments are unleashed, they become difficult to contain and the government is faced with a complex choice: on the one hand, clamping down on patriotic protest may infuriate a segment of the population that has some clout, but on the other hand, stoking the fire of nationalism can frighten Japan and the United States into trying to contain China (Downs and Saunders 1998–9: 142; Gries 2004). Moreover, there is the concern that popular protests against an external actor can create "blowback" against the Chinese state itself, as was well-demonstrated in 1919 when the May Fourth Movement protests against the Treaty of Versailles and Japanese expansionism also contributed to the further destabilization of the Republican Government and to the development of the Communist opposition (Mitter 2004).

Another element of uncertainty in resorting to nationalism as a source of legitimacy is the nature of the nationalist sentiment itself. The reference to nationalism often conjures up the extremes of the anti-foreignism or anti-imperialism displayed during the Boxer Rebellion (1900) or the Cultural Revolution (1966–76). Yet, there are three other forms of nationalist sentiment that can be expressed in contemporary China. Joseph Fewsmith mentions the two traditions of nationalist sentiments described by Paul Cohen that emerged in the hinterland and the coast in the nineteenth century (Cohen 1974: 241–2), and adds a third one that sought to reconcile them. The "hinterland" tradition, which was associated with a conservative emphasis on Chinese traditional culture, was exemplified during the late Qing Dynasty by intellectuals such as Liang Shuming, who emphasized neo-Confucianism. Mao, with his emphasis on the peasantry and autarky, is also considered a representative of this hinterland nationalism. The "littoral" tradition of nationalism, on the other hand, refers to late-Qing reformers such as Kang Youwei and Western-educated intellectuals such as Hu Shi. Fang Lizhi, in his advocacy of "complete westernization" echoes the views espoused by this current thinking (Fewsmith 2001b: 21).

Deng Xiaoping and his program of modernization were reviving a third nationalist trend, exemplified by the "self-strengthening" movement of the late Qing, sponsored by Zhang Zhidong and other officials. This program blended elements of the two other perspectives: it borrowed from the "littoral" tradition by seeking to learn modern techniques from the West, but it also took from the "hinterland" tradition the idea of using China's cultural tradition as the foundation of legitimacy (Fewsmith 2001b: 20). This approach, which necessitates maintaining good relations with advanced industrialized countries and which favours a peaceful environment, facilitated China's relations with other states and international organizations and, in return, encouraged the massive injection of foreign direct investment in the country that would help in its economic growth. The first attempt to set up the "self-strengthening" strategy came too late. At the beginning of the twenty-first century, a second attempt has undeniably delivered remarkable results. Yet, as China becomes increasingly integrated in the global economy, and therefore, like other major states, vulnerable to international economic uncertainty, its leaders are navigating uncharted territory: if the economy is faltering and/or if social unrest increases, the reference to nationalism as a source of legitimacy might become more problematic. International crises may make economic recovery even more difficult; nationalist passions may turn against the CCP itself for not defending the state's interests with enough vehemence. As Hu Jintao and Wen Jiabao try to address the multi-faceted challenges China faces, the issue of legitimacy remains a difficult one.

The organization of this volume

The contributors to this book have assessed the issue of legitimacy and the evolving role of the CCP in Chinese socio-political life from widely different perspectives. Some of the chapters address the reliance on more than one source of legitimacy by the CCP.

Xu Feng considers the issue of social stability as the foundation for the CCP's claim to legitimacy and looks into the Party's strategy to address this concern head on. She examines the pragmatic efforts at the local level to implement this stability, by looking into the Party's effort at building a "harmonious society" (*hexie shehui*) through constructing "harmonious communities" (*hexie shequ*). She describes a new mode of urban govern-ance, the *shequ*—translated usually as "communities"—as the "most intimate and immediate level" of social organization in Chinese society. *Shequ* acts throughout the country as the equivalent of previously ubiquitous organiza-tions during the Maoist era, such as neighbourhood committees and "work units" (*danwei*). But although they are expected to deliver a wide range of social services, they are not acting like the People's communes (*renmin gongshe*) of the Maoist era, which integrated social and economic institutions. Xu explains that the *shequ* institutions do not mean community of interests, but simply describe social organizations within the boundaries of a local geographic unit. She argues that communities—or *shequ*—remain under the leadership of the CCP and as such, represent institutions that help the party-state reclaim legitimacy in a more participatory way

Shequ represents a remarkable example of adaptation to new economic circumstances and social conditions as well as another instance of the Chinese party-state's ideological shift towards a neo-liberal world view. This is especially striking, as Xu demonstrates, in the use of the slogan "small government, big society" (*xiaozhengfu, dashehui*), and the emphasis on "good governance" instead of a stress on politics. The modes of political participation in this context, not surprisingly, fall into the rubric of "democratic governance." This includes not only the practice of local elections but also the delivery of social services. These social and political practices, in the end, serve to reinforce the legitimacy of the existing political structure. Xu's chapter describes how far China has moved from the previous Maoist model, but also explains that the resilience of the CCP's hold on power owes a lot to its ability to mobilize pre-existing institutions without ever giving up on the necessity to exercise control.

Helene Piquet looks at another aspect of China's social stability as a foundation for legitimate governance that has gained considerable salience with the deepening of reform: the evolution of workers' rights. She argues that recent legislation for labor has been used as an instrument to bolster the CCP's claim to legitimacy as it pursues a controversial transition to a "socialist market economy." She also believes that the promotion of economic growth by the Chinese leadership was seen by them as a most important means to retain or regain legitimacy following the Tiananmen Massacre. The existing laws and regulations, she explains, have been criticized as outdated and unfit for the economic restructuring policies the government has been pursuing since the 1980s. Although the changes envisioned by the CCP, she notes, partially fit with the trends seen elsewhere of flexibility and efficiency, she argues that they are counterbalanced by important developments with respect to the protection of workers' rights.

The current legislation on labor, argues Piquet, reveals that the foundations of legitimacy based on economic growth and social stability can be difficult to reconcile. On the one hand, the Labor Law provides a framework that subjects workers to the pressures of efficiency imposed by the market economy, on the other hand, the improvements of the legal system paves the way for better regulations addressing the interests of the workers, thereby preventing social unrest. She notes, to that effect, that the Chinese authorities are developing, at the local level of government, a number of measures aimed at alleviating the effects of the lay-offs brought about by the reforms. Yet, she admits some of the limitations to that strategy, and points to a number of issues that need to be addressed to prevent abuses against workers, and which are also necessary to buttress the CCP's objective of social stability, ranging from improvements in the monitoring of the treatment of Chinese workers by their employers, to better legal protection for the organizations defending them.

In his chapter on trans-national philanthropic NGOs, André Laliberté looks into another mechanism through which the party-state seeks to prevent social instability, this time, in impoverished rural areas where the central government has difficulty in ensuring the delivery of social services. He points to one of the central dilemmas faced by Beijing as it seeks to reconcile the goals of poverty alleviation and economic growth: the potential challenges to the economic performance and social stability bases of its legitimacy that can arise when it lets non-state actors assume responsibilities from which the government has divested itself. For years, decision makers involved in welfare policy, as well as academics researching in China itself, have considered the positive effects on society that could accrue from the incorporation of NGOs to public policy in the area of social welfare. Such an approach represents a dramatic departure from the policies enforced under Mao, when the CCP used the state apparatus to intervene in all spheres of social life. One crucial aspect of this reliance on NGOs, which speaks this time to the nationalist credential of the CCP, has emerged in the 1990s: the acceptance of trans-national NGOs from Taiwan, whose status in the PRC remains a sensitive issue.

The significance of the state's official support for NGOs, and of the latter's proliferation, remains unclear: do NGOs represent the emergence of a civil society, as we understand this concept in the West, or do they signal the implementation of a more sophisticated strategy from the party-state to mobilize the population? Laliberté discusses this issue in the context of the programs for poverty alleviation put in place by the CCP during the 1990s. He looks in particular at one specific category of NGOs that seems to demonstrate the extent of the tolerance displayed by the regime: charity organizations and philanthropic societies, some of which have a religious background. These associations test the confidence of the regime and present it with an important dilemma: on the one hand, they are seen as useful in the strengthening of social capital and essential in the edification of a spiritual socialist civilization inspired by virtue (*daode*), but, on the other hand, their organizational skills, their appeal, and their independence, always represent a potential threat to regime legitimacy. The fact that some of these organizations come from Taiwan, whose political status remains controversial, suggests that to a degree the Chinese central government remains confident of its ability to withstand potential challenges to its legitimacy. Yet, as Laliberté concludes, confidence at the center is not always reflected in local governments.

Jonathan Schwartz's contribution stresses another obvious limitation to the economic justification of legitimacy as he looks into the disastrous environmental fallout resulting from unfettered economic growth. He argues that the Chinese state has sought solutions to the challenges of balancing economic growth with environmental degradation, namely by developing a broad array of environmental protection laws and policies, and by enhancing the powers of those institutions charged with environmental protection. Despite these efforts, however, he finds that environmental degradation has continued at an increasing rate and as a result the state has had to respond in part by looking to environmental non-governmental organizations (ENGOs) for assistance. This decision raises a significant question regarding possible challenges to the traditional role of the state in China: do ENGOs offer a solution to the environment challenges facing the state, or do they represent a challenge to the state itself?

To address these questions, Schwartz briefly illustrates both the costs to China of environmental degradation and the inadequacy of the state's institutional response to that degradation. The paper then draws on the "state-led civil society" model designed by Bernie Frolic to explain the assumptions underlying the Chinese state's decision to draw on ENGOs for assistance. This conception of state–civil society relations is then considered within the broader context of the role of the CCP in Chinese socio-political life from widely different perspectives. This examination leads Schwartz to ponder whether the Chinese state–civil society relationship is unique or follows developments in state–civil society relations elsewhere? Focusing on environmental NGOs as an advanced expression of Chinese civil society, the author evaluates the capacity and roles of ENGOs, suggesting that the pace of change in state–civil society relations is greater than is usually assumed in the literature about contemporary China.

Charles Burton also looks at the CCP's claim to legitimacy based on economic growth. He argues that although the specific elements of this foundation for legitimacy have changed considerably since the Mao era, it remains influenced by a normative dimension that reveals a nationalist agenda. That is, the CCP still proposes a model of governance that could serve as a source of inspiration for other societies looking for different paths to development. In examining the CCP's quest for legitimacy, Charles Burton's chapter examines the impact on governance of the search for a legitimating basis in the context of a neo-liberal society based on market economics and the rapid expansion of the private sector. The legitimating *raison d'être* of the CCP has been to represent industrial workers and landless peasants, and to lead them to a new society based on social justice and plenty for all. In the more than twenty years since the CCP *de facto* abandoned Marxist doctrine in the face of the failure of its Mao-era Stalinist economic policies— compounded by the tragedies of the Great Leap Forward and the Cultural Revolution—the nature of the Party's relationship with its core constituency of workers and peasants has become more and more ambiguous.

The Jiang Government sought to bridge this gap by promoting the "Three Represents," and his successor Hu has tried to present himself as a guarantor of the poor's rights. Yet, the "China miracle" has yet to be seen in the interior;

and the polarization of wealth between rural and urban China continues apace; workers in state-owned enterprises (SOEs) suffer from high rates of unemployment and the loss of their "iron rice bowl" of housing and social welfare benefits while CCP cadres enjoy a standard of living far in excess of the means of civil service salaries. Meanwhile the dramatic drop in agricultural commodity prices and crippling taxation by bloated and corrupt local bureaucracies has led to considerable discontent among farmers. These contradictions feed a pervasive cynicism about the currently professed policy priority of addressing the concerns of workers dispossessed by the failing state industries, the pervasive poverty of the floating labour population, and the despair in much of China's rural areas.

Susan Henders examines the intersection between the economic and nationalist bases of the CCP's claim to legitimacy from an original angle. She argues that the self-government regime for the Hong Kong Special Administrative Region (SAR) legitimizes laissez-faire capitalism and the nation-state model as the standard of legitimacy for political communities in the post-Cold War era, while revealing the underlying contradictions of both the norms of self-determination and democratic self-governance. Territorial self-government arrangements are widely used to manage political tensions in many states where sub-state territorial communities claim distinct identities, she argues. In China, territorial self-government has been a state-building and state-maintenance strategy in minority nationality areas as well as a means of managing market reforms and integration with global capitalism while resolving territorial disputes in the Han heartland.

Following the development of the "special economic zones" (SEZs) of the late 1970s and 1980s, the PRC authorities had proposed the "one country, two systems" policy to entice Taiwan back to the motherland and applied this territorial autonomy regime to Hong Kong and Macao. The aim was to end China's humiliation at the hands of European imperialists, while protecting communist party rule in China and Hong Kong-style capitalism, already the engine of China's post-Mao market reforms. The former British colony reverted to Chinese administration in 1997 and the former Portuguese colony, Macao, in 1999, but civil protests in Hong Kong; concerns about the role of Beijing in the former colony's political and economic affairs; and lingering governance concerns among the public, contributed to the ouster of the Hong Kong's first Chief Executive, Tung Chee-hwa, in March 2005. Anger over the Tung Government's handling of the SARS crisis, as well as a proposed anti-subversion law, Article 23, which according to critics would have greatly curtailed the right to free speech, has raised questions over the role of Beijing in Hong Kong and whether the "two-systems" idea can remain viable.

The chapter by Diana Lary looks into the role of nationalism in the assertion of regime legitimacy from a different angle by examining the retrieval of historical memories and its effect on the regional stage. She contrasts the different narratives adopted in China, Taiwan, and Japan, by different actors, to commemorate the achievements of a historical figure reclaimed today in these three polities as "their own son": Zheng Chenggong, as he is known in China (Cheng Ch'eng-kung, in Taiwan, and Kokusen in Japan) and also known historically as Koxinga in the West (1624–62). The narrative about his life speaks about a Ming loyalist who took refuge in Taiwan, but, as Lary writes, while much uncertainty remains about his real identity, the myths surrounding the circumstances of his life are used by nations with competing claims.

The evocation of Zheng's destiny is marshalled by Beijing to justify its claim for the recovery of Taiwan, while people from the province of Fujian, who have developed the Minnan culture, view him as a local hero. This view is shared by many Taiwanese, who look at Cheng Ch'eng-kung as the unquestioned hero of independence. Others in Taiwan have also looked at him as a symbol for the Nationalists who took over Taiwan from the Japanese in 1945, and "reunited" the island with the Mainland. The views of Cheng are contested in the present within the ethnic Chinese world, but until recently the contest was between Chinese and Japanese views: Kokusen was considered a hero, a move aimed at boosting Japanese claim to the control of Taiwan. Although in the West Koxinga was downgraded as an uninteresting pirate, Lary notes that stripping away myth from reality about the historical figure of Zheng/Cheng/Kokusen/Koxinga would certainly upset states' claims in China, Taiwan, and Japan about sovereignty.

The major challenge to the CCP's claim to protect the national integrity of China is perhaps the onset of globalization, especially since the 1990s, which affects severely the claim of legitimacy based on economic performance. The chapter by Marc Lanteigne examines the CCP's attempts to address the economic, cultural and technological dimensions of globalization, which are affecting Chinese state and society. The CCP has adopted Deng's open-door policy, encouraging foreign investment, the "walking out" (*zouchuqu*) of Chinese firms into international markets, as well as the development of commodity and service industries capable of competing globally. However, the CCP has also attempted to prevent the forces of globalization from undermining its legitimacy by adopting state-guided developmentalist economic policies. Partially as a result, China's economic growth has proven to be extremely resilient, shaking off both the Asian Financial Crisis of 1997–8 as well as the SARS epidemic, strongly suggesting that the state has been adjusting to globalization well enough to continue to post impressive annual economic gains. The question which must be asked, however, is whether the Chinese Government will be able to continue moulding globalization, as well as adapting to it, as a means to maintain its leading role in socio-economic life.

Altogether these chapters demonstrate how the Chinese party-state is responding to various challenges to its legitimacy through an ongoing process of adaptation in order to retain its roles and relevance during the ongoing reform processes. In stark contrast to other reforming communist states, the CCP has been able to "ride the tiger" with a high degree of success because of its abilities to channel and guide the forces of modernization in the name of enriching the Chinese state. Whether this adaptation process can continue with the CCP in its present form, and whether this grand experiment will have a successful outcome in the face of so many obstacles, is one of the most pressing questions in the study of Chinese politics today.

Bibliography

Austin, Greg (1998) *China's Ocean Frontier: International Law, Military Force and National Development*, St-Leonard, NSW: Allen & Unwin.

Bachman, Michael (2003) "New Leaders, New Foreign Policy Procedures?," in Lin, Gang and Hu, Xiaobo (eds.), *China After Jiang*, Palo Alto, CA: Stanford University Press, pp. 115–35.

Bernstein, Thomas (2000) "Instability in Rural China," in Shambaugh, David (ed.), *Is China Unstable?*, Armonk, NY: M.E. Sharpe, pp. 95–111.

Burns, John P. (1999) "The People's Republic of China at 50: National Political Reform," *China Quarterly* 159 (September): 580–94.

Camilleri, Joseph A. and Falk, Jim (1992) *The End of Sovereignty? The Politics of a Shrinking and Fragmenting World*, Aldershot: Edward Elgar.

Chan, Anita (2001) *China's Workers Under Assault: The Exploitation of Labor in a Globalizing Economy*, Armonk, NY: M. E. Sharpe.

Chang Gordon (2001) *The Coming Collapse of China*, New York: Random House.

Chen Feng (1995) *Economic transition and Political Legitimacy in Post-Mao China: Ideology and Reform*, Albany, NY: State University of New York Press.

—— (1997) "The Dilemma of Eudaemonic Legitimacy in Post-Mao China," *Polity*, 29(3) (Spring): 421–39.

Cheng Li (2001) *China's Leaders: The New Generation*, Lanham, MD: Rowman and Littlefield.

Cohen, Paul (1974) *Between Tradition and Modernity: Wang T'ao and Reform in Late Ch'ing China*, Cambridge, MA: Harvard University Press.

Dahl, Robert (1984) *Modern Political Analysis*, 4th ed., Englewood Cliffs, NJ: Prentice-Hall.

Ding Xueliang (1994) *The Decline of Communism in China: Legitimacy Crisis, 1977–1989*, Cambridge and New York: Cambridge University Press.

Downs, Erica and Saunders, Phillip C. (1998/1999) "Legitimacy and the Limits of Nationalism: China and Diaoyu Islands," *International Security*, 23(3) Winter: 114–46.

Eckholm, Erik (2001) "To Fight Sect, China Publicises a Public Burning," *The New York Times* (January 31): A1.

Fewsmith, Joseph (2001a) *China since Tiananmen: The Politics of Transition*, Cambridge and New York: Cambridge University Press.

—— (2001b) *Elite Politics in Contemporary China*, Armonk, NY: M. E. Sharpe.

Friedman, Edward (2000) "Globalization, Legitimacy, and Post-Communism in China: A Nationalist Potential for Democracy, Prosperity, and Peace," in Tien, Hung-mao and Chu, Yun-han (eds.), *China Under Jiang Zemin*, Boulder, CO: Lynne Rienner, pp. 233–46.

Frolic, Bernie Michael and Brook, Timothy (eds.) (1997) *Civil Society in China*, Armonk, NY: M. E. Sharpe.

Gries, Peter Hayes (2004) *China's New Nationalism: Pride, Politics and Diplomacy*, Berkeley, CA: University of California Press.

Guo Baogang (2003) "Political Legitimacy and China's Transition," *Journal of Chinese Political Science*, 8 (1–2) (Fall): 1–25.

Guo Xiaolin (2001) "Land Expropriation and Rural Conflicts in China," *China Quarterly*, 166 (June): 422–38.

Habermas, Jurgen (1973) *Legitimation Crisis*, trans. Thomas McCarthy (1975), Boston, MA: Beacon Press.

—— (1984) *Theory of Communicative Action*, Boston, MA: Beacon Press.

—— (1992) *Autonomy and Solidarity: Interviews with Jürgen Habermas*, London, New York: Verso.

Howell, Jude (2004) "Getting to the Roots: Governance Pathologies and Future Prospects," in Howell, Jude (ed.), *Governance in China*, Lanham, MD: Rowman and Littlefield, pp. 226–40.

Hsu, Carolyn L. (2001) "Political Narratives and the Production of Legitimacy: The Case of Corruption in Post-Mao China," *Qualitative Sociology*, 24(1) (Spring): 25–54.

Hurst, William, and O'Brien, Kevin (2002) "China's Contentious Pensioners," *China Quarterly*, 170 (June): 345–60.

Kahn, Joseph (2005) "Riot Police Called in to Calm Anti-Japanese Protests in China," *The New York Times* (April 10): A6.

—— (2006) "Shanghai's Party Leader, Mistrusted by Hu, Is Purged," *The New York Times* (September 26): A10.

Keith, Ronald C. and Lin, Zhiqiu (2003) "The 'Falun Gong Problem': Politics and the Struggle for Rule of Law in China," *China Quarterly*, 175 (September): 623–42.

Lam, Willy Wo-Lap (2003) "The Generation after Next in Chinese Politics," in Finkelstein, David M. and Kivlehan, Maryanne (eds.), *China's Leadership in the 21st Century: The Rise of the Fourth Generation*, Armonk, NY: M. E. Sharpe, pp. 251–70.

Lewis, John L. and Xue Litai (2003) "Social Change and Political Reform in China: Meeting the Challenge of Success," *China Quarterly*, 176 (December): 926–42.

Lin Gang and Hu Xiaobo (eds.) (2003) *China after Jiang*, Palo Alto, CA: Stanford University Press.

Lipset, Seymour Martin (1960; 2nd ed. 1981) *Political Man: The Social Bases of Politics,* Baltimore, MD: Johns Hopkins Press.

Mitter, Rana (2004) *A Bitter Revolution: China's Struggle with the Modern World*, Oxford and New York: Oxford University Press.

Ostergaard, Clement Strebens (2004) "Governance and the Political Challenge of the Falun Gong," in Howell, Jude (ed.), *Governance in China*, Lanham, MD: Rowman and Littlefield, pp. 207–25.

Ownby, David (2001) "Why China's Falun Gong Shakes Communist Rule," *International Herald Tribune* (February 16).

Pan, Philip P. (2005) "Chinese Peasants Attacked in Land Dispute, At Least Six Die as Armed Thugs Assault Villagers Opposed to Seizure of Property," *Washington Post* (June 15): A12.

Perry, Elizabeth J. and Selden, Mark (eds.) (2006) *Chinese Society: Change, Conflict and Resistance*, 2nd ed., London: Routledge.

Potter, Pitman B. (1994) "Riding the Tiger: Legitimacy and Legal Culture in Post-Mao China," *China Quarterly*, 138 (June): 325–58.

Poulantzas, Nicos (1980) *State, Power, Socialism*, London: Verso.

Shambaugh, David (ed.) (2000) *Is China Unstable? Assessing the Factors*, Armonk, NY: M. E. Sharpe.

Strange, Susan (1996) *The Retreat of the State: The Diffusion of Power in the World Economy*, Cambridge and New York: Cambridge University Press.

Strecker, Erica and Saunders, Phillip C. (1998–9) "Legitimacy and the Limits of Nationalism: China and the Diaoyu Islands," *International Security*, 23(3) (Winter): 114–46.

Tang Wenfang (2001) "Political and Social Trends in the Post-Deng Urban China: Crisis or Stability?," *China Quarterly*, 168 (December): 890–903.

Tiewes, Frederick C. (1984) *Leadership, Legitimacy and Conflict in China*, London: Macmillan.

Waldron, Arthur (1995) "After Deng the Deluge," *Foreign Affairs*, 74(5) (September–October): 148–53.

Wang Gungwu and Zheng Yongnian (2000) *Reform, Legitimacy and Dilemmas: China's Politics and Society*, Singapore University Press.

Wang Hui (2005) "The New Criticism," in Wang, Chaohua (ed.), *One China, Many Paths*, London and New York: Verso, pp. 60–2.

—— (2003) *China's New Order: Society, Politics and Economy in Transition*, Cambridge, MA, and London: Harvard University Press.

Wang Xiaoying (2002) "The Post-Communist Personality: The Spectre of China's Capitalist Market Reforms," *China Quarterly*, 147 (January): 1–17.

Weber, Max ([1921] 1978) *Economy and Society*, edited by Guenther Roth and Claus Wittich, Berkeley, CA: University of California Press.

Wedeman, Andrew (2004) "The Intensification of Corruption in China," *China Quarterly*, 180 (December): 895–921.

Weiss, Linda (1999) *The Myth of the Powerless State*, Ithaca, NY: Cornell University Press.

Wright, Tim (2004) "The Political Economy of Coal Mine Disasters in China: 'Your Rice Bowl or Your Life'," *China Quarterly*, 179: 629–46.

Yang Dali (2006) *Remaking the Chinese Leviathan: Market Transition and the Politics of Governance in China*, Palo Alto, CA: Stanford University Press.

Yang Zhong (1996) "Legitimacy Crisis and Legitimation in China," *Journal of Contemporary Asia*, 26(2): 201–20.

Zheng Shiping (2003) "Leadership Change, Legitimacy, and Party Transition in China," *Journal of Chinese Political Science*, 8(1–2) (Fall): 47–63.

Zheng Yongnian (2004) *Globalization and State Transformation in China*, Cambridge and New York: Cambridge University Press.

2 New modes of urban governance

Building community/*shequ* in post-*danwei* China

Xu Feng

Introduction

Economic reforms, now in progress over almost three decades, have changed the political, economic and social landscape of China. According to the Annual National Survey of Urban Residents, conducted by the Institute of Macroeconomics of the State Planning Commission, unemployment, corruption, and the increasing gap between the rich and poor have become, since the mid-1990s, the three most important issues challenging the Communist Party's legitimacy (Hu 2003: 267). The rise of urban and rural unrest, sometimes on a large scale, has further sharpened the Party's focus. As a consequence of these pressures, the Party has been preoccupied with a key question of governance: how to govern a consolidating market economy in an increasingly heterogeneous and polarized society, yet maintain the political monopoly of the Party? Jiang Zemin's "Three Represents" (*sange daibiao*) and Hu Jintao's "people-centered governance" (*weimin zhizheng*) are the Party's latest efforts to conceptualize the task of representing "the people" as a cohesive social body in the midst of social polarization and social heterogenization. These efforts are crystallized in the state project of building a "harmonious society" (*hexie shehui*).

The eighty-fifth anniversary of the founding of the Party on July 1, 2006 was another striking occasion to educate both Party members and non-members about the uniquely "advanced nature" of the Party (*xianjinxing*). In the days leading up to July 1, news media was saturated with Party-related news and entertainment. In its daily prime-time evening news, China Central Television (CCTV) has been running a segment called "Red Memories" (*hongse jiyi*). The purpose of this segment has been to reinforce a necessary link in the viewers' mind between the history of the Communist Party and the history of the People's Republic of China, and hence the necessary continued convergence of the Party and the state. It was the latest occasion for the Party propaganda machine to demonstrate to the Chinese people that the Party is the reason for China becoming strong, prosperous and proud. The highly symbolic opening of the Tibet railway on July 1 further enabled the Party to claim to the Chinese people that it is the only Party that could bring China to the point of being a strong, united and prosperous nation in the eyes of the international community.

In summary, the Party spares no effort, in the most extravagantly visible way, in making a causal connection between the Communist Party, economic growth, national strength, social stability and prosperity. As Laliberté and Lanteigne point out in the introductory chapter of this book, the bases of the Party's legitimacy are economic growth, stability and nationalism (pp. 8–13).

This chapter focuses on one of these legitimating bases: stability. But it moves sharply away from propaganda efforts at the national level to consider much more pragmatic efforts at the local level. Specifically, it aims to understand the Party's effort at building a "harmonious society" (*hexie shehui*) through building a "harmonious community/*shequ*" (*hexie shequ*).[1] This increasingly studied development constitutes new modes of urban governance at the most intimate and immediate level of social organization in Chinese society. Built up across the country as the functional successors of the neighborhood committees and workplace "work units" (*danwei*) of the Maoist period, *shequ* organizations are designed to stand apart from local state institutions as a form of participatory civil societal organization, even as a form of social organization some of whose offices are subject to competitive elections, all the while remaining firmly under Party leadership. Designated in national policy as the primary vehicle for the delivery of a range of social services, *shequ* institutions also represent a repudiation of the Maoist integration of social and economic institutions, while equally rejecting what it views as the failures of the Western welfare states. While typically translated as "community" institutions, it is important to stress that *shequ* organizations are above all "community" institutions in the specific sense of being a local geographic unit of social organization. The term does not first imply a communion of interests, whether or not those common interests are clustered in space.

This chapter argues that the Party's resilience lies in its ability to adopt such methods of governance, despite their seeming incompatibility with its founding philosophy. Some such institutions, such as steering people to govern their own affairs, closely resemble those found in neo-liberal societies in the wake of the crisis of the welfare state (Foucault 1991; Dean 1999; McAllister 2004).

Viewed in this light, *shequ* self-governance is not about democracy as an end, but rather as a means to strengthening "the Party's governing capacity" (*dang de zhizheng nengli*). In community/*shequ* building, self-governance is emphasized in the areas of delivering services to residents through the use of voluntary and professional labor, such as caring for seniors, and helping in the delivery of social services. (*Shequ* institutions also assist in finding employment for the unemployed, though not so much by the work of volunteers.) Further, self-governance in the form of direct (democratic) elections of members of the *shequ* governing bodies is promoted as urban grass-roots democracy (*chengshi jiceng minzhu*), which has become an integral part of China's effort at political modernization. But on the other hand, a strong Party organization network is being strengthened in community/*shequ* to ensure that the Party commands detailed knowledge of its urban population and exercises hegemony in the increasingly diverse and polarized Chinese society.

In *shequ* building, then, we see simultaneously a striving towards self-governance in areas that used to fall under the jurisdiction of government *and* an expanding and strengthening of the Party's power base in urban China amidst the decline of former *danewei* and neighborhood-committee surveillance institutions.

Materials for this chapter are drawn from fieldwork I conducted in Shanghai in the summers of 2004 and 2006, personal experiences of living in both *danwei* and *shequ* in China, and documentary research. This chapter is by no means aimed at generalizing grass roots *experiences* of community/*shequ* building on the basis of these localized sources alone. It does attempt to treat community/*shequ* building as a nation-wide *project* of revitalizing Party legitimacy in urban China. As the Party claims, community/*shequ* building is a long-term and complex social system project.

Shequ building

The rationale

China's transition to a market economy involved wide-ranging efforts to draw clearer boundaries between the ruling party and the state; between the state and the economy; and between the state and society. All these strengthened distinctions were made with the aim of facilitating economic growth, but none is meant to constitute a division or separation of power. In Chinese circles, these moves are considered essential to achieving a more efficient and effective way of governing, marking a shift to a macro-management (*hongguan*) approach, rather than micro-management (*weiguan*).

The deliberate "hollowing out" of the Chinese state has involved two main steps. First, the state retreats from the economic sphere (*zhengqi fenkai*), so that markets function with fewer outside constraints. Second, the state offloads social responsibilities previously assigned to state-owned enterprises to societal and market institutions, a process that goes far beyond laying off large numbers of employees. Social responsibilities such as medical care, pension, and employment are now deemed responsibilities *of society itself* rather than responsibilities of government alone. The "hollowing out" of the Chinese state has been explicitly carried out in the context of China's wider effort to "connect to the global track" (*jiegui*), that is to conform to internationally accepted (essentially neo-liberal) norms of domestic governance.

Reforming the Mao-era system of *danwei* epitomizes this effort at boundary drawing and offloading the state's social-welfare burden. Under the *danwei* system, *danwei* were virtually identical with society as a whole. Those few who fell outside *danwei* were called "socially idle people" (*shehui xiansanrenyuan*), and were subject to supervision by neighborhood committees. *Danwei* was as much a branch of government as a profit-making economic entity (Walder 1986), providing employees with everything from employment, through welfare benefits and political rewards, to social identity. In return, employees offered loyalty to the Party and government. The relationship between employees and their *danwei* was that of "organized dependence" (Walder 1986: 13). Further, people within a given *danwei* were relatively homogenous in social terms, even if *danwei* covered nearly the full range of urban Chinese society. Urban governance was thus achieved at the level of *danwei*.

In many ways, the reform of the *danwei* system and the substitution of *shequ* organizations has become necessary because the *danwei* system became decrepit amidst the logic of institutional separation implicit in the economic reform process. With reforms, more urban Chinese were outside the *danwei* system than ever before. To further complicate matters, the privatization of the housing market proceeded hand in hand with the coming apart of *danwei*. This meant that many people now lived further away from where they worked than was the case before, and that they lived less and less often with their neighbors as co-workers. The numerical growth of rural migrant workers in cities posed a further challenge to urban governance.

A post-*danwei* society calls for new strategies of urban governance. The relationship of "organized dependence" under *danwei* is disappearing, as the state no longer monopolizes the supply of economic and social resources. The state finds it more and more difficult to exercise social control over its increasingly heterogeneous urban residents through old-style disciplinary mechanisms and mass mobilization. Meanwhile, the state's perceived need for such mechanisms mounts, arguably as a direct consequence of the new social uncertainties brought in by successive economic reforms. Rising unemployment rates and forced relocation due to urban development led to urban residents' open confrontation with government in the forms of collective appeals to government, protests, and public disturbances. These collective actions, though typically targeted with care against local officials rather than against the Party as a whole, nonetheless pose a broad challenge to the Party's legitimacy as the paramount actor in urban governance, legitimacy that in the absence of legal-rational electoral grounding, is based on serving the interests of "the people."

This dilemma directly led to the national state project of building *shequ* self-governance to provide citizens with a sense of empowerment through formal political participation, and to achieve a renewed level of social stability. As Pei Minxin (2000), among others, has suggested, the Chinese state has been building formal institutions of political participation in order to ensure that collective actions against various levels of government do not occur on the street. Thus, *shequ* building is in effect a strategy of containment. It is in this context that we should view recent governance innovations such as public hearings, labor arbitration systems, village elections, and *shequ* self-governance.

The law, the policies and the programs

The 1989 *Law on Urban Residents Committee Organization* was the first legal framework for the development of community-building policy. As part of this framework, the law summarized the new government policy direction under the official slogan that *shequ* committees served three "self" functions: citizens' self-management, self-education, and self-service. As with the implementation of most central government policies in China, *shequ* building was initially carried out in a few experimental sites. Big urban centers such as Shanghai, Shenyang, and Wuhan were chosen to run the experiments. The experience of each site then became a distinct model whose relative merits were debated nationally in academic and policy-making circles (Wang *et al.* 2001; Xu *et al.* 2002; Wang 2006).[2]

Shequ building picked up speed and became national policy in 1998. This coincided with the serious push to reform the state-owned enterprises (SOE), which meant cutting large numbers of people off from employment and therefore from the social benefits provided by their *danwei*. To promote "grass-roots democracy" (*jiceng minzhu*), the Ministry of Civil Affairs (MCA) set up a Division for Grassroots Authority and Community/*Shequ* Building (*jiceng zhengquan yu shequ jianshe si*). In response to these developments, Hu Jintao issued direct instructions in March 2004 that *shequ* research be strengthened, specifically in order to build "harmonious communities" (*hexie shequ*). After those instructions, the MCA organized its first nation-wide survey on *shequ* initiatives. The purpose of the survey is to "get a feel" (*moqing*) for the following aspects of *shequ* organizations developing nation-wide: social organizations (*shehu zuzhi*); forms of organization (*zuzhi xingshi*); relationships among social interests (*liyi guanxi*); and social stability (*shehui wending*). According to the government, the study was aimed at the successful development of *shequ* and the implementation of working programs to promote the building of "harmonious communities."[3]

According to public government statements about these initiatives, community/*shequ* is about "people-centeredness" (*yiren weiben*).[4] This concept implies that *shequ* are concerned with handling affairs that affect people's everyday lives, such as local public security and public hygiene. The key reform is a transition to "humanistic management" (*renxinghua guanli*) in the form of self-governance, and efficient and effective service delivery. The contrast is with the prior "administrative management" (*xingzheng guanli*), by which neighborhood committees primarily handled government orders "from above," even if these orders did not necessarily improve people's lives (Lei 2001).

The break with the past should not be exaggerated. To act on the citizens' own initiatives is inherent (albeit in a substantially altered context) in the Maoist style of government, insofar as it is exemplified by mass-mobilization campaigns. The populist streak in mass mobilization also tended to be juxtaposed with top-down administrative measures that treated citizens as passive and submissive objects. This contrast was a major philosophical divide that served to differentiate China's Revolution from the Soviet planning experience. But subsequent resort to terms such as *yiren weiben* and *renxinghua* has broken with the Maoist tendency to call out a citizen identity that undertakes such initiatives in a collective, self-abnegating framework. Under Mao, Chinese people were mobilized to participate in public causes, but in a Maoist style of participation that inherently disavowed the self: one had to give up one's self-interest totally in favour of the public interest (altruism).

Since the sixteenth Party Congress, people centeredness and humanistic management have not only become key terms in official discourse, but also have entered the everyday parlance of ordinary Chinese people. *Yiren weiben* and *renxinghua* mean, among other things, that individuals are encouraged to be self-determined citizens, without coercive administrative orders telling them what to do and how to act. A deputy director of the bureau of civil affairs in one district in Shanghai summarized the new direction for me in this way: "building *shequ* self-governance is about how to change from what government 'from the above' wants you do, to your desire to do it yourself" (personal interview, May 18, 2004). But on the relationship between *shequ* self-governance and government, the same deputy director told me, "*shequ* should represent the masses' (*qunzhong*) voices, but it does not mean confrontation with government."

Self-governance is considered more humanistic than governance by the state because it focuses on people's needs in life, and it is also emancipatory because it frees up people's energy to solve their own problems.[5] In contrast, administrative order comes from the top, and necessarily from administrators who do not know (or care) about individual people's needs. Administrative order is portrayed more as a show of power, and therefore as unacceptably coercive. And the collective bottom-up populism of Maoism is similarly rejected as vulnerable to both administrative manipulation and to the potential loss of central control.

As the foregoing discussion already suggests, it is useful to track policy implementation in China on the basis of key priorities, typically listed in easily summarized slogans. The central government insisted that community/ *shequ* must govern based on the model of "self-management, self-education, self-service and self-surveillance" (*Law on Urban Residents Committee Organization* 1989, Article 2). Six tasks for community/*shequ* are laid out in the same article of this law:

1   publicize the constitution, laws, and government policies; educate residents to fulfil their obligation according to laws, and treasure public property;
2   take care of residents' public issues and causes;
3   mediate conflict between neighbors;
4   assist in societal safety and security;
5   assist the government or its agencies in public hygiene, family planning, relief, and youth education; and
6   report residents' opinion to the government or its agencies.

Not surprisingly, these tasks correspond to the main social problems the government sees in post-*danwei* urban governance, some of which have not yet been touched upon in this chapter:

1   aging populations where small families are increasingly the norm;
2   rising unemployment;
3   the declining importance of *danwei* for a large portion of the urban population, and hence the decline of a major social-control mechanism in people's lives;
4   growing social marginalization, exclusion, frustration, and therefore unrest; and
5   policing the growing migrant populations, who fall outside of existing urban social control (Wang *et al.* 2003; Lin 2003).

Programmatically, community/*shequ* self-governance involves institutional and behavioral changes that require delicate balancing in the Chinese context. Institutionally, community/*shequ* must be allowed its own autonomy from government intervention in running its own affairs. The hierarchical government structure of Chinese cities is this: municipal (*shi*) and district (*qu*) levels of government, followed by the street committees (*jiedao weiyuanhui*) as the lowest-scale agencies of government (*zhengfu paichu jigou*). Under the old system, the neighborhood committee (*juweihui*) was, in theory, an even smaller-scale mass organization under the leadership of the street committee; in practice, of course, it still acted as an arm of the government. Under the formula of community/*shequ* self-governance, which is the functional replacement for the neighborhood committee in the local formation of citizenship virtues, government (i.e. the street committee) now plays only the role of "guidance" (*zhidao*) rather than that of "leader" (*lingdao*).

In this respect, the aim of building community/*shequ* self-governance is to abolish the hierarchical relationship between the street committee and the neighborhood committee, and to set-up a self-governed and self-contained entity. It is also within community/*shequ* that democratic experiments in the narrow sense of elected offices can occur. But the Communist Party is still understood to lead any democracy, the scope of whose activities extend beyond those of the state to cover all of Chinese society. This shift to community/*shequ* governance is therefore both a change from the past (with respect to state omnipresence), and a development in clear continuity with earlier practice (with respect to party leadership or party guidance).

By drawing a clearer boundary between community/*shequ* and local government (municipal, district, and street-level), *shequ* proponents hope that the community/*shequ* can enjoy relative autonomy in running its own affairs. But the space for formal political participation is in the territory-bound community/*shequ* and matters affecting residents' immediate living environment (security, hygiene) and quality of life (specifically with reference to such issues as local service delivery). Self-governance is to empower residents to work actively towards solving their own problems, primarily so that government does not need to intervene in mundane matters relating to people's lives such as mediating disputes and, when conflicts do arise, government can act as "neutral" arbiter, instead of being blamed for wrong-doing.

Besides institutional change, changes to citizens' identity and behavior are also deemed necessary to build community/*shequ* self-governance. In terms of identity, urban residents are expected to shift from identifying themselves with *danwei* to identifying themselves with community/*shequ*, a "*shequ* person.*" The identity change also involves attitudinal and behavioral changes. To become a *shequ* person, one must, writings on this subject state, replace dependence (*yilai*) and submission to authority (in the sense of simply doing as one is told) with independence and active participation in community/*shequ* affairs. In other words, a community/*shequ* person is someone who is both independent and responsible for others in the community/*shequ*. This change of attitude from *daneweiren* to *shequren* is especially encouraged among laid-off workers from SOEs, who are used to their *danwei* taking care of everything (*danwei baogan*).

The Party and shequ self-governance

The Party is the initiating force in *shequ* building and its move towards self-governance. Why and how does the Party extend and consolidate its power; press forward with what amounts to a major reform at the local level; and yet, at the same time, promote *shequ* self-governance? The Party is concerned that *shequ* self-governance, if carried out on its own, might weaken Party's power base. The Party's worry about its power base in urban areas is not ungrounded. As Xu and his associates point out, the Communist Party historically established its branches in *danwei*, as a result, in the face of the decline of the *danwei* system, its presence in the urban grass roots is weak and disorganized (Xu *et al* 2002: 258–9). In the 1989 Law guiding community/*shequ* organization, the role of the Party and the relationship between Party branch and *shequ* committee are not explicitly mentioned, although the leadership role of the Party is constitutionally guaranteed.

However, in 2004, the Ministry of Organization issued an official opinion on how to strengthen and improve the Party's organization in *shequ*. The opinion promoted the idea of the *shequ* Party Secretary standing for election as the Head of the *Shequ* Committee (SMBCA 2006). The rationale, as Lin suggests, is that the Party must be intimately involved at the beginning of building *shequ* self-governance so that the Party can steer *shequ* self-governance to its desired goals (Lin 2003: 66–7). However, as Lin continues, this is different from the Party coming in as an outside force to intervene in *shequ* affairs. The Party Secretary is appointed "from above," and the Director of the *shequ* committee (executive branch) is elected democratically "from below." But as the 2006 Ministry of Civil Affairs announcement concerning the next round of *shequ* elections recommends: the Party-nominated Party Secretary shall be appointed Party Secretary only if first elected to the position of Director. If the recommended Party Secretary nominee is not elected, however, s/he will not be appointed as Party Secretary (SMBCA 2006). The document is unclear what should occur under these circumstances. It is possible that this lack of clarity is intentional rather than an unintended ambiguity: interviews at the local level certainly suggest that every effort is expected to be made to prevent such a circumstance arising, and this places interesting pressures on *shequ* residents/voters to contest such elections seriously.

In sum, as the announcement suggests, the recommendation of concurrent office holding must not follow a "one-size-fits-all" formula, but rather it must respect the voters' will (*xuanmin de yiyuan*) and respect the rules and procedures of democratic election. Party participation in *shequ* self-governance right from the beginning in the form of democratic election of committee offices is intended to build an organic relationship between the Party and *shequ*. But unlike civil society in the West, civil society in China does not enjoy autonomous space. Concurrent *shequ* and local Party office holding seems to follow the example of village elections in rural areas, in which concurrent office holding is favored by the central authorities (Guo and Bernstein 2004). As Guo and Bernstein point out in this parallel context, on the one hand, the Party does not allow any autonomous social force to emerge; on the other hand, Party secretaries must win popular support in regular elections (Guo and Bernstein 2004: 275).

Besides the Party's intimate involvement in the democratic election of *shequ* committee offices, its relationship with "homeowners' associations" (or, more precisely condominium committees) also poses a challenge to governance. Within increasingly heterogeneous *shequs*, homeowners' associations and property-management companies (*wuyeguanli gongsi*) are two new actors in local urban governance. The relationship between homeowners' associations, property-management companies and *shequ* committees is not always smooth. There is a trend for the homeowners' association to exercise wide-ranging self-governance in its contractual relationship with the property-management company for the condominium, thus making the *shequ* committee irrelevant in key areas of grass-roots urban governance. Unlike the *shequ* committee, neither of these local institutions is under Party guidance or leadership. Both Read and Tomba write about homeowners' associations' efforts at organizing fights for their rights against property management companies (Read 2003; Tomba 2005). Homeowners, as Read discovers, consider such organizing to be their right to democratic participation and self-governance. The Party Secretary of one *shequ* I interviewed in Shanghai told me how she fought with one homeowners' association in her *shequ*. "The association members told me blatantly they do not need the *shequ*," said the Party Secretary, "I was mad as hell. I told them the Communist Party is the governing Party. It is not an underground Party. As Party Secretary of this *shequ*, I have the right to attend the association's meetings. To deal with the association, you just need to stand firm and tough, otherwise, they win. Now we have a cordial relationship" (personal interview, June 22, 2006). In fact, the *shequ* office is housed in the association's building.

If the Party is concerned that community self-governance cannot be achieved at the price of weakening the Party, then why did the Party initiate *shequ* self-governance and encourage urban residents to participate in *shequ* affairs? The words of Deputy Director Li shed light on this question (personal interview, May 18, 2004). As he told me: "democratic election (*minzhu xuanju*) has several advantages in low-scale governance: elections publicize community/*shequ* so that residents develop a sense of community/*shequ*; directly-elected community/*shequ* officials can conduct community/*shequ* affairs more easily than government officials, because residents tend not to trust the latter; and finally, election can strengthen residents' 'democratic consciousness'" (again, democracy meant in the specific sense fixed in official Chinese discourse). Elections provide a platform (*pingtai*—a buzzword in China) to turn *shequ*/community from a state project for participation and Party revitalization into reality. In preparing and conducting elections, it is hoped that *shequ* residents start to see themselves as members of a *shequ* and to act as members in exercising their democratic rights. Every effort must be made to create an atmosphere (*zhizhao qifen*) that facilitates *shequ* building.

Whatever the final assessment should be about the democratic quality of these elections, it does seem clear that a great deal of attention is being paid to the electoral process and to the potential electoral outcomes. During my fieldwork in Shanghai in June and July 2006, the city was gearing up for its next round of elections (*huanjie xuanju*) for community/*shequ* committees. Every *shequ* I visited had banners, blackboards, and posters publicizing the upcoming election. Furthermore, *shequ* officials and members of the election committee visit every household to register voters. One day when I was conducting interviews in one street office, the Party Secretary had to rush off to one of the *shequs* to deal with an emergency. As it turned out, the emergency concerned the Director of one *shequ*, who, because of a misunderstanding of election rules and procedures, did not get the signatures of each and every ten endorsers (the required number) of a particular candidate. The Shanghai Municipal Residents Committee election notice also takes great care in outlining the proper procedures that elections must follow. The care given to following proper rules and procedures and the intimate involvement of the Party Secretary are notable features that deserve an explanation. A careful reading of the election notice suggests that following proper procedures is seen to guarantee that the election is legal and legitimate in the eyes of urban residents. In a time of social polarization, the Party considers it of utmost importance that people feel that they have a legal and legitimate channel of political participation so that they do not resort to collective actions outside the Party's control.

Self-governance is also considered an integral part of developing the modern subject. The Chinese state is now promoting the "full development of individual" (*ren de quanmian fazhan*) and overall national strength (*guojia de zonghe guoli*) (Sigley 2004). The two dimensions of this promotion are thought to be deeply interlinked. To the older, 1980s pairing of "material and spiritual civilization," is now added a campaign for *political* civilization. According to Lin (2004: Ch. 6) political civilization is about the "full development of individual," and one's political *suzhi* is measured in terms of the citizen's democratic consciousness, that is, their capacity to participate in politics and to discuss/deliberate in politics. To steer citizens towards being self-determined subjects, *shequ* building for self-governance has thus to be seen in the context of this new goal.

Material, spiritual, and political civilizations are now the three legs in the full development of the modern Chinese citizen. It is important not to mistake this for a purely humanistic goal, pursued for its own sake. Instead, it is valued primarily as a core component of national competitiveness in the new knowledge economy. "Knowledge economy" (*zhishi jingji*), as a new concept, started to circulate in newspapers, magazines, media, and leaders' speeches in 1998 after first appearing in the report on the fifteenth Party Congress. Han Qingxiang (2003), a senior scholar in the Central Party School, sees the focus on "the full development of individual" as inherent to the development of *zhishi jingji*. Using developmentalist logic, he divided human development through three stages of economic development from feudal, capitalist, and now knowledge economy. So to build the knowledge economy is necessary to promote the full development of individual, in a wider analysis that distinguishes the current period from capitalism.

How this goal is to be achieved is as important as the goal itself. As Han points out, China's preparation for the arrival of knowledge economy is really the *individual's* preparation. The individual has to improve his/her physical, mental, and psychological qualities to prepare for and act as an integral part of the new knowledge economy.

According to both Chinese officials and scholars, community building trains individuals' capacity to be self-determined subjects. It is also notable that many add that this also acts as a "dress rehearsal" for a democracy to come, albeit one that is of unspecified scope and character and should not be read outside of the Party's own understanding of the meaning of democracy. The latter follows because in participating in electing community leaders, community residents will have to learn the procedural matters of how to conduct an election (Lin 2003: 75, 83).

Moreoover, participation (*canyu*) in a much broader sense is considered key to democratic governance: electoral office holding is really but one technique among many others. Community/*shequ* residents are also encouraged to participate through volunteering and voluntary donations, so that services can be delivered without much government financing. The success of community/*shequ* relies on participation, and the government is especially interested in fostering the latter. Government at each level calls on social forces to "contribute with a loving heart" (*xian aixin*) to help those in need: the elderly; the unemployed; and the poor. Examples of volunteering are widely and favorably publicized. These may include: volunteering in neighborhood watch programs; helping police monitor traffic violations; helping with public hygiene; mediating conflicts; donating money to community/*shequ* projects such as repairing walls; helping the needy; caring for the elderly; and educating the young, and so on. That residents govern their own affairs not only delivers services without cost to government, but also is deemed to be more effective than direct government intervention, because self-governance gives to the *shequ* residents a sense of empowerment, bolsters self-esteem, and is self-directed.

Community/*shequ* as the space of self-governance: international context

What is emerging in the thinking and practice of governance in China more generally has strong parallels with global neo-liberal principles of governance: these qualities are represented in the slogan, "small government, big society" (*xiaozhengfu, dashehui*). In a Reader on *shequ* building and development prepared by the Ministry of Civil Affairs, the Ministry clearly situated China's *shequ* building in the international development of community building (Wang *et al.* 2001). In liberal democracies, the trend is away from welfare as citizenship rights. This is the so-called Third Way rights politics: no rights without responsibilities. In China, the trend is to move away from urban residents' reliance on *danwei* (and hence, ultimately, state) welfare provision, to the state handing such responsibilities off to society. While these turns occurred in different contexts, they have parallel political philosophies: government should not "row but only steer" (Osborne and Gaebler 1993), and citizens must take up more responsibilities for their own welfare, expressed as empowering citizens to solve their own problems.

We have explored briefly the kind of civil society that Chinese officials are eager to develop in the institutions and in the behavior of their citizens.

Critically, the Party initiated *shequ* building and the *shequ* now handles the delivery of social services and exercises social control over a much more heterogeneous urban population and a much more complex social landscape than the preceding Mao-era workplace units, or *danwei*. But in the community/*shequ* model of governance, central government plays only a supportive role in financing social-service programs. In social control, a community and its residents are called on to govern their own affairs.

Community in liberal democracies is not necessarily territorially bounded: it can include the gay community, the Chinese Canadian community, and so on. The discovery of community is also in specific response to the "crisis" of the welfare states (Schofield 2002; Rose 1999; 2000). At most, attempts have been made to "fix" communities geographically (Larner and Butler 2005: 84). In China, on the other hand, community/*shequ* is territorially bound and is decided by the government. Community building is in response to the "crisis" of the *danwei* system. Despite these differences, both share some common assumptions: community is the site for meaningful political actions, and it constitutes a moral/ethical space in which people take care of themselves, but at the same time are responsible to fellow community citizens.

The seductive positive connotations of community are apparently easy to understand. As Rose points out:

> the community of . . . the third way of governing is not primarily a geographical space, a social space, a sociological space or a space of services, although it may attach itself to any or all such spatializations. It is a moral field binding people into durable relations. It is a space of *emotional relationships* through which individual identities are constructed through their bonds to *micro-cultures* of values and meanings.
>
> (Rose 1999: 172)

But in contemporary China, there is no reason to believe that community/*shequ* residents, at least as currently constituted, share any organic relationship. Tönnies' concept of *Gemeinschaft* certainly implied such a relationship, in a pre-modern rather than a modern society. But the modern *Gesellschaft*, or society, is believed to be full of atomized individuals, sharing few if any organic social bonds. It is certainly *Gesellschaft* that more nearly approximates the meaning of community/*shequ* in many settings, if not most. "Community/*shequ* building" in China is understood to imply that a conscious effort has to be made to cultivate community/*shequ* consciousness so that individuals can *return to* a state of community/*shequ*.

Government considers community/*shequ* building to be a complex "social-system project" (*shehui xitong gongcheng*) that involves not only institutional change but also changes in people's behavior and identity: all this precisely to restore social cohesion (Tang 2004).[6] In China, those who worked in the *danwei* system relied on government to provide social benefits in return for their loyalty to government. With the smashing of the "iron rice bowl," people are asked to be responsible for their own affairs, though also to take up obligations to their fellow citizens in society/*shequ*. This move from taking care of oneself to taking care of oneself *and* others within one's community is presented as a sign of material social progress. In a report entitled "Steering Residents to Participate in Democratic Self-governance through Community Deliberative Mechanism" (*Yi Shequyishiyuan wei Zaiti, Yingdao Jumin Canyu Shequ Minzhu Zizhi*), the Gulou District Government (Nanjing) and Party Committee pointed out that more and more residents have moved from initially only caring about things concerning their own interests to caring about community building, moral/ethical development (*daode jianshe*)[7] and democratic participation.[8] Community/*shequ* building, seen in this light, involves what Rose calls an "etho-politics": it "concerns itself with the *self techniques necessary for responsible self-government* and the *relations between one's obligation to oneself and one's obligations to others*" (Rose 1999: 188).

The project of *shequ* building has been intended, in part, to set aside the economic and social costs of market reforms as "social problems" and have these tensions administered by local, non-state, non-economic institutions. The creation of *shequ* institutions occurs amidst a transition in Chinese urban landscape towards a thorough zoning of distinct social functions and social strata. The government officials and scholars aim to find common interests among community residents to ensure participation.

Some *shequ* are based on existing urban geography, consisting of old neighborhoods; some are newly-developed gated communities; some are based on neighborhoods of *danwei*-assigned apartments; some are almost shanty towns. Each type of community/*shequ* has a different history, which affects the degree of prior communal bonding and the residents' willingness to participate in community/*shequ* activities (Xu *et al.* 2002: 36–40).

During my field research in the summers of 2004 and 2006, I discovered that communities that were considered model communities amongst my informants—both frontline community workers and ordinary residents reflecting on community organization—are those composed of more or less homogeneous resident populations, such as residents of apartment blocks formerly assigned by government.

Communities considered less "good"—less liable to develop *shequ* organizations and thus less liable to show the etho-political development just described above—are composed of heterogeneous residents (*za*), such as a mix of local and migrant residents or a mix of rich and poor residents. Within some communities, homeowners' associations, property manage-ment companies, and community organizations co-exist, but in ways already alluded to, the relationship is not always friendly. Both from offi-cials and from casual observers, the suggestion seemed to be that social simplification of *shequ* (for instance, through western-style zoning or gradual self-segregation) would facilitate *shequ* development. For example, the Party Secretary in one such mixed *shequ* of luxurious apartment dwellers and shack-dwellers (*penghuqu*) told me happily that her work in this *shequ* will greatly be made easier when all residents from the *penghu* district are relocated to suburban Shanghai. (The *penghu* district is being torn down to prepare for road construction.) But she also told me that *shequ* workers in suburban Shanghai are concerned that their workload will be drastically increased because of the influx of residents from low social status.

If the functional purpose of this new system is to have social tensions resolved or administered at a local level, the internal simplification of *shequ* would run counter to the original reasons for having them as autonomous entities. Simplification ensures that social tensions will increasingly operate between *shequ* (and their administrative bodies) rather than within them. The resolution of social tensions and what might be called social contradictions will still tend to devolve back up to higher levels of organization and to state political bodies.

Conclusion

To conclude, there are therefore two transitions at work in the emergence of *shequ* as priorities in urban governance. In the first place, we see in the transition from *danwei* to *shequ* a significant *functional* shift in the social systems and subordinate institutions charged with social welfare provision. From welfare provision by institutions that are also intimately tied to productive work, we see the relentless separation of economic functions of the workplace from virtually all others, and in the process, the transfer of welfare functions from the workplace to community institutions.

In the second place, we see in the transition from neighborhood committees to *shequ* a significant shift in the *modes of governance*. This also involves a functional transition from state to community institutions, but all still under ever-vigilant party supervision. But what is more striking about this transition is the emergence of ordinary Chinese, not merely as policy instruments at the implementation stage, as they were before, but increasingly also as participants, in a mode of governance still being steered by the Party but now operating in carefully demarcated areas of social rather than state life. The question for the Party is how to walk a fine line between cultivating *shequ* self-governance and maintaining the Party's dominant presence in *shequ*. To say the least, this is proving to be a challenge.

Notes

1   For government policy documents and political leaders' speeches on building "harmonious *shequ*," see the Ministry of Civil Affairs official website. Available online: www.mca.gove.cn.

2   No effort is made to differentiate these models, as they all must follow the 1989 Organization Law.

3   "Work Program on Conducting Nation-wide Hundred-City Community Building Survey" [*Quangguo Baicheng Shequ Qingkuang Diaocha*]. Available online: www.mca.gov.cn/redian/shqgz/shequjs4.html.

4   See, for example, "State Council's Opinion on Strengthening and Improving Shequ Service Delivery," in State Council 2006.
5   Of course, local self-governance (*difang zizhi*) is no stranger to the Chinese. For example, in *Qing* China, county magistrates relied heavily on the local gentry to govern local affairs. This approach can be viewed as imperial "benign neglect." During the late *Qing* and the early Republican period, the state was weak and thus the public realm was open for political activism of various descriptions. Local self-governance was also attempted, in the form of elite civic participation. See, for example, Rankin 1986. Some scholars compare the crisis in governance faced by late Qing with the situation the post-Mao leadership faces. See, for example, Zhang 1998.
6   System control theory (*xitong kongzhi lilun*), the Chinese translation of cybernetics, is popular in China because it is the science of control and communication for complex machine systems. See, for example, Greenhalgh 2005.
7   In Chinese, *daode* means both morality and ethics.
8   www.mca.gov.cn/redian/shqgz/fayan9.htm.

Bibliography

Dean, Mitchell (1999) *Governmentality: Power and Rule in Modern Society*, London: Sage Publications.
Foucault, Michel (1991) "Governmentality," in Burchell, Graham, Gordon, Colin, and Miller, Peter (eds.), *The Foucault Effect: Studies in Governmentality, with Two Lectures by and an Interview with Michel Foucault*, Chicago, IL: University of Chicago Press, pp. 87–104.
Greenhalgh, Susan (2005) "Missile Science, Population Science: The Origins of China's One-Child Policy," *The China Quarterly*, 182(1): 253–76.
Guo Zhenglin and Bernstein, Thomas (2004) "The Impact of Election on the Village Structure of Power: The Relationship between Village Committee and the Party Branch," *Journal of Contemporary China*, 13(39): 257–75.
Han Qingxiang (2003) *Construct Capacity Society: Development Prospect for Chinese People of the 21st Century* [*Jiangou Nengli Shehui: Ershiyi Shiji Zhongguoren de Fazhan Yujing*], Guangzhou: Guangdong Education Press.
Hu Angang (ed.) (2003) *Xray SARS: Health and Development* [*Toushi SARS: Jiankang yu Fazhan*], Beijing: Tsinhua University Press.
Larner, Wendy and Butler, Maira (2005) "Governmentalities of Local Partnership," *Studies in Political Economy*, 75.
Lei Jieqiong (ed.) (2001) *Urban Grassroots Community Building in the Period of Transition: Research on Beijing Municipality Grassroots Community Organization and Development* [*Zhuanxingzhong de Chenshi Jicen Shequzhuzhi: Beijingshi Jicenshequzhuzhi yu Shequ Fazhan Yanjiu*], Beijing: Beijing University Press.
Lin Shangli (ed.) (2003) *Research on Cases of Community Democratic Governance* [*Shequ Minzu yu zili: Anli Yanjiu*], Beijing: Social Sciences Documentation Press.
—— (ed.) (2004) *On Shanghai Political Civilization Development Strategies* [*Shanghai Zhengzhi Wenmin Zhanglui Yanjiu*], Shanghai: Shanghai People's Press.
McAllister, Mary Louise (2004) *Governing Ourselves?: The Politics of Canadian Communities*, Vancouver: University of British Columbia Press.
Osborne, David and Gaebler, Ted (1993) *Reinventing Government: How the Entrepreneurial Spirit is Transforming the Public Sector*, New York: Plume.
Pei Minxin (2000) "Rights and Resistance: The Changing Contexts of the Dissident Movement," in Perry, Elizabeth and Selden, Mark (eds.), *Chinese Society: Change, Conflict and Resistance*, London: Routledge, pp. 20–40.

Rankin, Mary Backus (1986) *Elite Activism and Political Transformation in China: Zhejiang Province, 1865–1911*, Stanford, CA: Stanford University Press.

Read, Benjamin (2003) "Democratizing the Neighborhood: New Private Housing and Home-Owner Self Organizing in Urban China," *China Journal*, 49: 31–60.

Rose, Nikolas (1999) *Powers of Freedom: Reforming Political Thought*, Cambridge: Cambridge University Press.

—— (2000) "Community, Citizenship, and the Third Way," *American Behavioral Scientist*, 43(9): 1395–1411.

Schofield, Barry (2002) "Partners in Power: Governing the Self-Sustaining Community," *Sociology*, 36(3), 663–83.

Shanghai Municipal Bureau of Civil Affairs (SMBCA) (2006) *Shanghai Municipal Residents Committee Election Handbook* [*Shanghaishi Juminweiyuanhui Xuanjugongzuo Shouce*], Shanghai: SMBCA.

State Council (2006) *Document 14*. Available online: www.mca.gov/redian/Design7-3/zcwji.htm (accessed August 11, 2006).

Sigley, Gary (2004) "Liberal Despotism: Population Planning, Subjectivity, and Government in Contemporary China," *Alternatives: Global, Local, Political*, 29: 5.

Tang Jingsu (2004) "Prospects of Community Building" [*Shequ Gongzuo Zhanwang*]. Available online: www.mca.gov.cn/article/content/200422392114/20041129142805.html.

Tomba, Luigi (2005) "Residential Space and Collective Interest Formation in Beijing's Housing Disputes," *China Quarterly*, December: 934–51.

Tönnies, Ferdinand (2001) *Community and Civil Society*, Cambridge Series Text in the History of Political Thought, edited by Jose Harris, translated by Margaret Hollis, Cambridge University Press.

Wang Jinyao (2006) *Participatory Governance: A Positive Study on Urban Community Building in China*, Beijing: China Social Sciences Press.

Wang Qingshan, Cheng Haijun and Yan Jiaming (eds.) (2001) *Shequ Building and Development: A Reader* [*Shequ Jiaanshe yu Fazhan Tuben*] Beijing: Central Party School Press.

Wang Zhenghai, Dou Zexiu, Wang Zukang, Wang Zhiying and Ren Yishun (2003) *On Community Politics: The Quiet Social Reform (Shequ Zhengzhi: Renmen Shengbian Qiaoqiao Jingxin de Shehui Biange)*, Taiyuan: Shangxi People's Press.

Walder, Andrew (1986) *Communist Neo-Traditionalism: Work and Authority in Chinese Industry*, Berkeley: University of California Press.

Xu Yong and Chen Weidong (eds.) (2002) *China's Urban Community Self-Governance* [*Zhongguo Shequ Zizhi*], Wuhan: Wuhan Publishing House.

Zhang Shiping (1998) "Local Administration and Crisis Management: A Comparative Perspective from Post-1949 China," in Antony, Robert J and Leonard, Jane Kate (eds.) *Dragons, Tigers, and Dogs: Qing Crisis Management and the Boundaries of State Power in Late Imperial China*, Ithaca: Cornell University Press, pp. 303–21.

3 Chinese Labor Law in retrospect

Efficiency and flexibility legitimized

Hélène Piquet

Introduction

The development of China's legal system since the current reforms were launched by the late Deng Xiaoping in 1978, has generated an abundant legal scholarship in China as well as in Western countries. Just as important as the laws themselves, are the Chinese discourses about legal reforms since they shed light on the underlying motivations guiding the adoption of specific laws and regulations. This chapter will discuss the Chinese legal reforms in labor law, analyzing both the discourses and the legal texts. What, in essence, prompted the National People's Congress, China's legislative organ, to adopt, in 1994, the Labor Law of the People's Republic of China, promulgated in 1995? It will be argued that the new Labor Law was, in fact, conceived as a tool to bestow legitimacy on the new economic order envisioned by the Chinese leadership, namely, the "socialist market economy." At the time, the Chinese leadership decided to promote economic growth as a means to retain or regain legitimacy following the Tiananmen Square tragic events of 1989. This new project called for a revision of the existing labor laws and regulations, now deemed outdated and unfit for the upcoming economic changes.

The first part of this chapter will present the context of the labor law reform. First, the new importance of law in the Chinese discourse will be discussed, followed by a closer look at the political and economic context stemming from the implicit post-Tiananmen compact between the Chinese leadership and the Chinese population. The second part of the chapter will sketch some features of the new labor regime set by the Labor Law, with the aim of demonstrating that, using the argument of the "socialist market economy" warranting for renewal, the Chinese legislator brought about drastic changes which would have been unthinkable before and yet called for legitimization.

A new place and role for law since 1978

The limited rehabilitation of law

Deng Xiaoping launched the "Reform and Open Door Policy" in 1978; that is, two years after Mao Zedong's death and the end of the Cultural Revolution. The Reform program remains to this day limited to the economic sphere. Nonetheless, important changes have also been underway in these years in the legal area. Most notably, and in stark contrast with the preceding Maoist era, the very concept of law was rehabilitated, at least partially (Piquet 2005: 76). First and foremost there was a need to rebuild a legal system in order for China to attract foreign direct investment (Wang 2002: 13). However, accompanying this highly pragmatic motivation was a deeper one, namely, to use law as a tool to prevent a repetition of the abuses and arbitrariness of the Maoist era (Wang 2002: 12). The latter, most notably the Cultural Revolution, was labeled the "Rule by man" (*renzhi*) and it was deemed necessary by the new leadership to revert to "Rule by law" (*fazhi*). Both of these two terms generated important discussions as theories of government from the fifth century BC onwards. Rule by man (*renzhi*) was advocated by Confucianism while Rule by law (*fazhi*) was promoted by the Legalists.[1] This old debate surfaced again very early after 1978 (Bi 2006: 87–8), because, among other reasons, Deng Xiaoping himself, with other members of the new leadership, had been persecuted during the Maoist era and there was a genuine desire to prevent a repetition of the same events (Jones 2003: 38). However, a distinction needs to be made from the outset: the new role of law promoted by the CCP could by no means be equated with the notion of "Rule of Law" or with that of État de droit (Cabestan 1996: 650).[2] This vision of the legal reform was aptly characterized by Cabestan (1996: 650) as being "Rule by law" rather than "Rule of law."

This moderate legal rehabilitation of the concept of law spread, with time, to the Chinese population who began to use the legal system in order to vindicate its rights (Peerenboom 2002: 90), While this trend was not very significant during the 1980s, the number of lawsuits before the courts has steadily increased, particularly in the area of labor law (Fu and Choy 2004: 19). An impressive number of laws and regulations were enacted; a full legal system was recreated with courts, judges, procuratorate and, more recently, lawyers (Liechtenstein 2003: 288). Starting from 1978, priority was given to the development of commercial law as China opened itself to foreign investors. The regime then devoted efforts to developing legislation in areas such as administrative law, criminal law, procedure law, environmental law, Women's Rights, family law, etc. The Constitution was amended several times between 1988 and 2004. More recently, a Civil Code project was submitted to the National People's Congress (NPC) in December 2002. While China's legal system remains plagued with various problems,[3] and in spite of the bad reputation it gained,[4] it is fair to say that there have been constant efforts, since 1978, to rebuild and improve it. The CCP's interference in the decision process is a recurring problem well documented by legal scholars in China and in the West.[5] In addition to the judiciary's lack of independence, corruption is a widespread problem undermining the credibility of the Chinese legal system (Cai 1999: 148). Judicial competence is a pressing issue that the current regime has started to address. Starting from the late 1990s, Canada and several European countries developed extensive training programs for Chinese judges. The Chinese Law School's curriculum includes several courses on foreign legal systems. Studies abroad are now very popular among Chinese students and as of today, many Chinese lawyers working in Beijing, Shanghai, Guangzhou, hold a foreign degree in law. Therefore, while the technical competence of the judiciary and the Bar are still plagued with shortcomings, the situation is likely to improve during the next decade. When China emerged from the Cultural Revolution, also labeled as a period of legal nihilism (Lo 1997: 476), the Chinese leadership was confronted with a dire situation: not only were many of China's legal scholars and personnel decimated during the various preceding political campaigns (Zheng 1997: 72–3), but also, the few existing laws and regulations were ill-suited to the needs of the economic reforms. In order to remedy this situation, China opted officially to use legal transplants as a means to create new legislation (Wang 2002: 13).

Legal transplants have a very long history, as they can be traced back to antiquity (Gaudemet 2000: 93). The exemplary case of legal transplants, from the point of view of Western legal history, is that of Roman law to Europe between the twelfth and eighteenth centuries AD (Gaudemet 2000: 98). China, for its part, was first a source of legal transplants before becoming a borrowing country[6] in the early twentieth century. China's encounter with the West and its subsequent military defeats, in the nineteenth century, generated intense reflection on modernization and the place of law within this process. The famous legal scholar, Shen Jiaben, in very last years of the Qing dynasty, was mandated to carry on legal reform, in the hope of rescuing the dynasty. At that time, Shen Jiaben studied carefully the options for China: whether to import either common law or civil law. He favored civil law over common law for a host of reasons, one of them being the influence of Japan. Japan had, from China's viewpoint, successfully achieved its modernization because it had imported civil law (Shi 2006: 59; see also Fan 2001: 301–2). While China suffered from continuous encroachments upon her sovereignty, with the regime of extra-territoriality being put into place by Western powers, Japan, conversely, was winning the respect of the international community. One of Shen Jiaben's secret hopes was to achieve the same result and bring China's humiliating position to an end. His proposed reforms were partially blocked by the conservative faction at the Qing court, which deemed him too progressive in the field of criminal law (Ding 1997: 241) and in 1911, the dynastic era came to an end in China. Shen Jiaben passed away in 1913.

The new Republican government (1911–49) decided to pursue the legal reform, drawing heavily on Shen Jiaben's work. Hence, while there were some discussions about comparative law and the common law legal tradition, most notably at the Suzhou Law Faculty (Conner 2003: 213), the civil law model remained dominant until the Communist takeover of 1949. The Republican legal reforms are difficult to assess because of China's troubled history between 1911 and 1949, which included the Japanese invasion of 1937 and the civil war which raged between 1945 and 1949. They were depicted in highly negative terms during the Maoist period, for ideological reasons (Chen, J. 1999: 30). The legal reforms of the Republican era, nevertheless, consolidated the civil law model's influence on Chinese law and presented an interesting case of legal transplants. The legal texts from this period were totally abrogated, alongside imperial law, by the new Chinese leadership in 1949. The Chinese legal scholars could only rely on what was then called the Soviet legal model as a source of inspiration for the new legal order and system to be built (Chen, J 1999: 38). Therefore, the socialist conception of law became the dominant credo and remained so for several decades. Until this day, its influence can still be traced in various laws and regulations.

Between 1949 and 1957, China's first Constitution was enacted and a Ministry of Justice was created alongside a complete legal system. Those legislative efforts were rather abruptly interrupted by the Anti-Rightist campaign of 1957, which targeted China's legal scholars along with other so called "bad elements," for persecution. The amount of legislative work diminished after 1957 and was brought to an almost complete halt during the Cultural Revolution (1966–76) where "justice of the masses" prevailed. To this day, the scars and traumas left by this chaotic period are very deep (Chen, Y 2002: 265).

In 1978, Deng Xiaoping launched China on a new project, the economic reforms. Chinese legal scholars were then expressly instructed to borrow from all legal models, irrespective of their former labels ("bourgeois," "reactionary," "feudal") in order to develop new legislation (Piques 2001: 122). They enthusiastically followed this instruction and an impressive amount of legislative work has been done since, with common law and civil law as the main source of the borrowings. Gradually, however, internal discussions concerning the reliance on foreign legal models as opposed to the use of local paradigms (*bentuhua*) gave rise to a debate and this issue continues to generate much scholarship within Chinese legal circles since 1992.[7] However, discussions about the Labor Law focused on other issues, very delicate for a political regime owing its legitimacy, at least partly, to the workers' class it had literally created since 1949 (Rocca 2006: 83).[8]

The necessary reforms of the labor market

The Tiananmen movement of 1989 scared the Chinese leadership[9] and led, afterwards, to the setting aside of the reformist faction until 1992 and Deng

Xiaoping's famous southern tour (*nanxun*). This trip, with the subsequent adoption of the "socialist market economy" formula, marked the renewal of the economic reforms launched in 1978. Deng was in fact convinced of the absolute necessity to carry on the economic reforms in order to assure political stability in China and to wipe out (he hoped) the resentment which had given rise to the 1989 movement (Schell 1994: 360–1). He was also aware of the decreasing support (Schell 1994: 361) for "Marxism, Leninism, and Mao Zedong Thought," hence the need to find a project for rallying the Chinese population. He resorted to what Domenach (2002: 75) calls the "productivist compromise." He proved largely correct in his belief that Chinese people would forego political contestation in order to work at their own private enrichment, now allowed (Schell 1994: 406; Rocca 2006: 106). Orville Schell (1994: 401) depicts the atmosphere a year after Deng's southern trip: "China was now as drugged on business as it had once been on politics." Following the trend, foreign investors appeared to be possessed by a "China fever" (Schell 1994: 402) and intensified their presence in China to the point that, in 2000, the amounts of foreign direct investment reached unprecedented figures (Domenach 2002: 50). Issues of outsourcing and workers' rights, both linked to the presence of foreign investors and to the growth of a Chinese private sector, became important topics of discussion in academic and human rights circles (see Asia Monitor Resource Centre 1996; Gallagher 1997; Chan 1996). In fact, the foreign companies in China, as well as the Chinese private companies, contributed to the shape of the labor market along different standards.

The flexibility paradigm applied to the labor force became a new requirement for the Chinese workers (Rocca 2006: 110). New discourses also emerged, advocating individual responsibility in the search for jobs, emphasizing the need to skillfully market one's skills (Rocca 2006: 111) in accordance with the basic tenets of other market economies.[10] Jean-Louis Rocca (2006: 111) sees in these developments a clear sign of the commodification of labor, officially banned under the previous leadership as it was ideologically incompatible with the regime's credo that "workers are the masters of the state" (Gipouloux 1986: 7).

Economic growth became the new source of legitimacy for the CCP who gave it a high priority (Rocca 2006: 108) as it was perceived to be the source of political stability. The issue of restructuring unprofitable SOEs had been on the government's mind for a few years and became increasingly pressing. It complemented the objective of economic growth as well as the need for Chinese businesses to be competitive on the world's markets (Rocca 2006: 108–9). Competition, as a new paradigm, provided some justification for the dismantling of the work unit (*danwei*) system, characterized until then, by a system of social protection for the benefit of urban workers. The costs of this system were now deemed an obstacle to economic growth, especially the debts incurred by the SOEs (Kernen 2006: 32; Rocca 2006: 109; Gipouloux 2005: 114).

Other measures indicated a gradual shift in orientation with respect to labor issues, as compared with the Maoist period. Contract employment had been introduced in China in special economic zones in the mid-1980s. It was not well received by the workers, as it was associated with temporary employment (Josephs 2003: 30–1). While China's economic performance was booming after 1992, part of the Chinese population entertained fears about the new developments. Many workers were very well aware that they were at risk of losing their jobs, as there had been massive layoffs and plant closures in 1992–3 (Schell 1994: 418). They were met with anger and a sense of betrayal from the urban workers (Schell 1994: 420) who were apprehensive about the dismantling of the lifelong employment system. The new Trade Union Law of 1992 did not reassure the Chinese workers, as it was in tune with the emerging ideology according to which workers can not always behave as "masters" (Morin and Pairault 1997: 39).

Therefore, it can be seen from this context that the enactment of the Labor Law in the making was a highly sensitive affair. How could a regime, which had presented the working class as the "master of the state" (Morin and Pairault 1997: 10) reconcile the requirements of competition with the protection of workers' rights? Would the regime even attempt this conciliation or would it opt for more drastic measures in the name of economic development? How far could it go without threatening that very stability deemed so necessary? Such were the issues confronting the Chinese Communist Party during the drafting process of the Labor Law.

A new Labor Law regime suited to the "socialist market economy"

While the concept of "socialist market economy" remains an elusive one in terms of definition, it has played an extremely significant and liberating role in the development of Chinese legal doctrine (Chen, J. 1995: 55),[11] now freed from many ideological constraints. However, it also became the key concept legitimizing almost any new law, hence the numerous references made to it by the Chinese legal scholars.

The drafting process of the Labor Law was both long and arduous, taking more than forty years to complete. While the political turmoil in China between 1957 and 1976[12] accounts partially for the length of the drafting process, the highly sensitive nature of labor issues in a socialist state claiming to represent the "vanguard of the proletariat" also explains why the Labor Law took so long to be enacted (Josephs 2003: 42). It is divided into thirteen sections, comprises one hundred and seven articles and is followed by seventeen administrative regulations.[13] The Labor Law, by its structure and organization, is close to the continental legal tradition (or civil law tradition) marked by a strong preference for "codes" (Josephs 2003: 42). Once it was promulgated, Chinese legal scholars took great pain to present this new law under the most favorable light possible. Their arguments have rarely been presented and discussed in studies on Labor Law in China.

Chinese Perspectives on the Labor Law of 1994

The constant trend in the Chinese doctrine of the years 1994–8 is to insist on the spectacular progress represented by the Labor Law in comparison with the former era of the "planned economy" (Gao and Li 1996: 16; Wang and Gong 1994: 21–3). Several arguments along this official line are formulated by Chinese scholars. One claims that a definite improvement lies in the introduction of a legal regime to regulate labor relations (Liang *et al.* 1997: 14–15; Wang and Gong 1994: 22). Before the coming into force of the Labor Law, labor relations were regulated mainly through administrative procedures; Chinese workers had no legal recourse in cases where their rights had been violated and could only complain to their immediate superior. Now, they can rely on a more objective norm in order to vindicate their rights (Liang *et al.* 1997: 14–15). Other scholars justified the new law by clear references to abuses of workers' rights occurring in foreign enterprises and in privately-owned Chinese businesses (Guan 1994: 43; Wang and Gong 1994: 21). Viewed in this light, the new Labor Law is presented as a much-needed legal instrument to curb abuses and bring them to an end. Others promote the new law by arguing that it gives Chinese workers the right to freely chose their employers and, conversely, it gives the right to employers to recruit the workers they deem fit (Wang and Gong 1994: 28).[14]

For the first time, Chinese scholars openly admit that the workers' interest might conflict with the interest of the employer. This marks a decisive ideological and conceptual departure from the previous gospel on labor relations in China, namely that the state's interest and the worker's interest coincide. In other words, according to the previous political line on the subject, there could not be any conflict in labor relations because of the nature of the Chinese state defining itself as a socialist state where, by definition, no exploitation of labor can exist.[15] Under the socialist market economy, however, many changes have taken place in labor relations leading the Chinese legislator to recognize the need to provide for legal protection of the workers' rights (Liang *et al.* 1997: 15; Wang and Gong 1994: 21)[16] and the existence of a subordinate relationship between the worker and the employer. Another argument relates to the Chinese legal system. While many workers' rights are stipulated in the Chinese Constitution, one cannot directly invoke the Constitution as a basis for a legal recourse because "the Constitution only provides an abstract standard and its provisions lack the ability for enforcement. The protections for the constitutional rights of citizens in connection with labor issues lies directly in concrete laws and regulations" (Chen, K. 1997: 40). It follows that in order to acquire the status of "right," a constitutional norm must be enacted in a specific law which in turn will provide legal foundations for future legal recourses (Chen, K. 1997: 40; Gao and Li 1996: 15). That role is to be filled by the Labor Law.

Chinese scholars' treatment of the labor contract is noteworthy by the persuasive tone they revert to in order to present this institution as unprecedented and as a landmark progress for both workers and employers. Their major arguments can be summarized as follows. First, the labor contract is the instrument of the realization of the workers' right to work (Liang *et al.* 1997: 221; Wang and Gong 1994: 120), as well as the tool allowing for clear specifications of each party's rights and duties (Wang, Q. X. 1997: 146). By contrast, under the planned economy, it is said, workers' right to work lacked a clear legal channel for its realization and as the workers' tasks were not clearly defined, this led to a situation of general dissatisfaction, and damaged the productivity (Liang *et al.* 1997: 221). One would have expected legal scholars to defend the labor contract as the paragon tool for workers' rights protection. While this feature of the labor contract is clearly affirmed (Liang *et al.* 1997: 221; Wang and Gong 1994: 120), it does not always come first in the scholars' presentation of the institution. For Guan Huai, the major reform accompanying the labor contract is that it brings a welcome end to the "iron rice bowl" system, portrayed as a source of hindrances for both workers and employers (Guan 1994: 1990).[17] The "iron rice bowl" system consisted of the following elements for Chinese urban workers in the state sector: "cradle to grave welfare, permanent job tenure, housing provision, life-long medical and pension benefits, and guaranteed superior wages" (Ching 2000: 42–3).

Guan Huai's critical depiction of the "iron rice bowl" is indicative of a new trend with respect to the concept of workers' entitlements. Until then, China had taken great pride in this system, intimately linked to the SOEs and presented as a model for socialist countries. When the Labor Law was enacted, a new discourse on the SOEs was emerging, portraying them as a burden on the Chinese state (Wong 1998: 68). In September 1997, the CCP held its fifteenth Congress where the redefinition of public ownership and the reform of state enterprises were the dominant topics (*China Daily*, September 18, 1997).[18] Hence, Guan Huai's direct attack on the "iron rice bowl" is perfectly in tune with one feature of the Labor Law discussed in the next section, namely a general trend toward flexibility.

Workers' rights between flexibility and protection

The Labor Law was drafted at a time of transition in China, where some ideals and models of the past were no longer deemed suitable in the context of "socialist market economy." This shift in orientation can be related to the adherence of the CCP to the flexibility and efficiency paradigms. The latter became dominant after 1995 and replaced the previous emphasis on the equality paradigm (He 1998: 351). However, these ideological changes were well under way during the last phase of the Labor Law's drafting process, as can be seen with a close reading of Article 1 of the law. This provision articulates several goals of the Labor Law, and the question that arises is whether they are mutually compatible or contradictory. Article 1 reads as follows:

This Law has been formulated according to the Constitution with a view to protecting the lawful rights and interests of laborers, regulating labor relationship, establishing and safeguarding a labor system that is adaptable to a socialist market economy, and promoting economic development and social progress.

(Labor Law 1994: Art. 1)

A summary textual analysis of this provision highlights important language issues: it is only those rights and interests deemed "lawful," according to Chinese law, which are guaranteed. This issue is of significance, as the right to free and independent unions is not recognized in Chinese law, nor is the right to strike. Equally significant are the references to the establishment of a labor system *suited to the socialist market economy,* and to the promotion of "economic development." Article 1's significance must not be taken lightly. Important issues are referred to in this provision, and their contents must be elucidated in order to grasp the real orientation of the Labor Law.

One such notion is "development." China, along with other developing countries, has strongly defended the notion of a "right to development," whose contents and legal status remain controversial (Potter 1996: 28–31).[19] This being said, China's vision of development sheds an important light on the position of labor rights and places the issue within the broader context of China's position on human rights.[20] Briefly summed up, the Chinese Government promotes an outdated vision of development that is almost limited to economic growth at the expense of other rights. Such an opinion is expressed in the *People's Daily* which advocates a switch to a more inclusive vision of development:

> In the process of practice, the one-sided understanding of development as the growth of GDP is the root cause of unbalanced economic and social development. In view of this [. . .] we should advocate "balanced economic and social development which is the most absolute principle." [. . .] In the accelerated restructuring period, we should switch from the 'material'—centered development strategy to the "people oriented" development strategy.

(*People's Daily Online*, June 25, 2004)

The importance of economic development for China can be seen from this quote of then paramount leader, Jiang Zemin:

> The fundamental task of socialism is to develop the productive forces. During the primary stage, it is all the more necessary to give first priority to concentrating on their development. [. . .] *Hence we are destined to make economic development the central task of the entire Party and the whole country, and make sure that all other work is subordinated to and serves this task* [. . .] *Development is the absolute principle.* The key to the solution of all China's problems lies in our own development.

(Jiang, Z. 1997: S-3 [emphasis in original])

From this position, it can then be argued that the goal of promoting economic development stipulated in Article One of the Labor Law will take precedence over the protection of labor rights. While economic development and respect for labor rights are not intrinsically mutually exclusive, they can sometimes entertain a conflicting relationship. The wording in the Labor Law opens the door to such a conflict in practice, once China's notion of development is properly understood. The primacy given to the right to development and the right to subsistence, a specific Chinese construction (Chen, Z. 1997),[21] is reiterated in another article of the very official *People's Daily* (March 9, 2004): "For the Chinese people in the current development stage, rights to subsistence and development are the fundamental and therefore most important human rights to pursue, the Chinese government has repeatedly said."[22] Besides, as He Qinglian mentions, the new paradigm of efficiency justifies the Chinese Government prioritizing economic growth (He 1998: 351).

The Chinese legislator has, with the introduction of the labor contract, brought lifelong employment to an end. In retrospect, there is room for the argument that the Chinese legal scholar's efforts to present the labor contract in a highly positive fashion was meant to counter the perception that beneath the language lay a "trap" for the Chinese workers. Indeed, scholars' commentaries on the labor contract, such Guan Huai's, could well give ground to this fear. Chinese workers did not welcome the labor contract, as they understood very well that this meant the end of a permanent job (Morin and Pairault 1998: 33). The issue here is not the legitimacy of the labor contract *per se*, but its perception by the group most affected by this institution, the workers.

Article 26(3) introduces the possibility for an enterprise to reduce personnel, based on the doctrine of "change of circumstances"[23]:

> In one of the following cases, an employer may dissolve a labour contract but shall serve a written notice to the worker in person 30 days in advance: [. . .]
>
> 3. A labour contract can no longer be executed due to major changes in the objective conditions and a revision cannot be reached through consultation by both parties.
>
> (Labor Law 1994: Art. 26(3))

This legal doctrine means that a contract can be legitimately re-negotiated, with important changes to its original contents, if the circumstances under which it was concluded and signed have significantly changed. At worst, the "change of circumstances" doctrine can also lead to the termination of the contract,[24] the case set forth in Article 26(3). The issue is, of course, what amounts to a "major change" sufficient to trigger this doctrine. According to Liang Shuwen, this provision is applied in the context of business restructuring and *force majeure*. The latter is another legal doctrine referring to unpredictable events beyond control of the parties, which can lead to a complete unilateral termination of the contract while providing for exoneration of legal liability of the creditor (Cornu 2002: 403)—in this case, the employer. Liang Shuwen acknowledges potential for abuse on the part of the employer (Liang *et al.* 1997: 362). This provision opens the door to massive lay-offs, as "change of circumstances" between the time the contract was signed and the time of lay-off "can be interpreted broadly, with few legal safeguards."

Another provision in the Labor Law is perfectly adapted to the needs of a competitive business environment and to the flexibility and efficiency paradigms, namely, Article 27. It allows for enterprises to lay off workers under certain circumstances. Article 27 reads as follows:

> When an employer needs to cut employment due to the conditions of near bankruptcy and in a period of legal rectification or due to difficulties in its production or business operation, the trade union or all the workers should be informed of the true situation with their opinions heard and conveyed by the employer to the labor administration department. If an employer who has cut the employment according to the provisions of this article recruits workers again within six months, priority shall be given to the employees being formerly cut.
>
> (Labor Law 1994: Art. 27)

This provision also allows for drastic reduction of personnel by the enterprise if the latter is close to bankruptcy or meets with production difficulties. Hilary Josephs argues that these provisions establish important and serious safeguards of the workers' rights in the context of massive lay-offs (Josephs 2003: 47–8). But arguments to the contrary can be made. For one, the union's role in the context of Article 27 is merely consultative. In practice, it manages lay-offs instead of defending workers against them. Second, the only mention in favor of the workers is that laid-off workers will be hired first in the event that the enterprise overcomes its difficulties. The reality is that, once closed, an enterprise rarely reopens; this provision is, therefore, of little help to laid-off workers. Moreover, there are no set criteria for the appreciation of the enterprise's financial situation, or for production difficulties. Thus, this absence of clear legal criteria gives wide latitude to employers. Liang Shuwen *et al.* (1997: 366) affirm, in a discreet comment, that the implementation of Article 27 can lead to instability,[25] and this is revealing in itself. Today, the fate of laid-off workers (*xiagang*), is well documented and confirms that Articles 26 and 27 are widely used in the context of restructuring of state-owned enterprises.[26] Rocca (2006: 296) points out the difficulties of assessing the real numbers of unemployed people in China today as the government has developed a complex terminology to apply to them while avoiding the word "unemployed."

Laid-off workers entertain many grievances with respect to this new economic order. Not only have they lost income, but they have also lost status and are imbued with a deep sense of insecurity (Rocca 2006: 115). Their living conditions have seriously deteriorated as many of them do not possess the skills they need to find a new job (Rocca 2006: 113). Sometimes, they are able to secure a meager income stemming from atypical work (temporary, part-time or seasonal), with no social protection benefits (Rocca 2006: 113). Thus, in the current labor market in China, people can earn an income without actually having a job.

While these elements reveal an undeniable trend towards flexibility and insecurity of the Chinese work-force, the *Labor Law* also contains provisions aimed clearly at the protection of workers' rights. Article 3 sets forth the various rights enjoyed by the Chinese workers under the Labor Law:

> Workers enjoy rights to equal opportunities of employment and choice of jobs, the right to labor remuneration, the right to rest and vacation, the right to labor safety and health protection, the right to vocational training, the right to social insurance protection and welfare, the right to settlements of labor disputes and other rights as provided by law.
>
> (Labor Law 1994: Art. 3)

Discrimination on the grounds of nationality, race, sex and religious beliefs is forbidden (Art. 12). A more specific article expressly reiterates the prohibition of discrimination against women, but its formulation leaves open the possibility of discrimination if the job or work post is deemed not suitable for women, the latter determination to be made by the state (Art. 13). The issue of child labor is dealt with in Article 15, which makes it illegal to employ persons under the age of sixteen. Chapter Four is devoted to working hours, rest and vacation; Chapter Five deals with wages; Chapter Six contains provisions in relation to occupational safety and health; Chapter Seven provides for special protection for women workers and underage workers; Chapter Eight contains general rules relating to job training; Chapter Nine consists of six articles relating to social insurance and welfare; Chapter Ten provides mechanisms for dispute resolution; Chapter Eleven establishes general guidelines for supervision and examination of the law's implementation by employers. Only a few elements will be presented here.

The Labor Law sets limits to the amount of working time required from workers. A normal week consists of forty four hours (Art. 36), with working days of eight hours (Art. 36). The Law provides for one weekly day of rest (Art. 38). Workers are entitled to paid annual vacation during various Chinese festivals like Chinese New Year, Spring Festival, International Labor day, etc. (Art. 40). If overtime is necessary, it cannot exceed one hour a day, or three hours a day in special circumstances. All in all, overtime cannot go beyond thirty-six hours a month (Art. 41). Article 44 provides for the payment of overtime, according to various schemes.

Remuneration is based on the following principles: "equal pay for equal work" and "to each according to his work" (Art. 46). Most notably, the Law introduces a minimum wage, to be determined by each province, autonomous region and centrally administered municipality in accordance with its local conditions (Art. 48). However, the minimum wage paid by an employer cannot be lower than the local minimum wage (Art. 48). The wage is determined by taking into account various factors enumerated in Article 49, including the differences in economic development between regions. Thus, minimum wage can vary greatly within China. Article 50 stipulates that: "Wages shall be paid to the workers themselves in cash and on a monthly basis. In no circumstances is it allowed to deduct or delay the payment."

Many other articles in the Labor Law are to the benefit of workers. They provide a counterbalance to the elements of flexibility cited earlier that are found in the same law. The issue, as with much of the other Chinese laws and regulations, is not an "absence of law" but rather, one of enforcement of the existing texts (Wang, Y. 2002: 181).

Conclusion

China's Labor Law is very much in tune with broader trends identified in other parts of the world: it is partially based on the flexibility and efficiency paradigms, but this trend is counterbalanced by important developments with respect to the protection of workers' rights. In retrospect, the labor reforms, including the enactment of Labor Law, were substantially motivated by the desire to restructure the SOEs and to render Chinese economy more flexible and competitive (ILO 2001: 3). From 1997 onward, guidelines were issued encouraging mergers and acquisitions, the standardization of the bankruptcy process, laying-off "'redundant' workers, and improving profitability" (MLSS 2004: 14). The radical reforms of the SOEs were conceived in the early 1990s, but implemented from 1996. "Flexibility" is very favorably perceived by the Chinese Government, presented as a remedy to the "rigidity" of the former era characterized by planned economy (MLSS 2004: 27). It was obvious that some provisions of the Labor Law would be detrimental to workers, especially Articles 26 and 27. The insistence of many Chinese scholars to give a positive image to the then new Labor Law has to be understood against this background.

The Chinese Government places high hopes on private enterprises, small and medium-sized, to create new jobs and absorb part of the "surplus labor" (MLSS 2004: 21). If this is to be part of the solution, many reforms are needed. Private entrepreneurs need a better access to capital, for sure, but stronger supervision mechanisms of the Labor Law are also required as workers' rights violations are a recurring problem in these enterprises.[27]

Chinese workers are thus caught between conflicting paradigms, reflected in the Labor Law. Their hopes lie in an improved legal system, and in a shift of paradigms giving space to quality employment and real protection. In this perspective, China's collaboration with the ILO is welcomed, as the latter promotes more humane paradigms for workers around the world. The Labor

Law itself should be partially reformed, *inter alia*, in the following areas: the elimination of the time limitation provision to submit grievances to the arbitration committee; the provision of better supervision mechanisms for infringements of workers' rights; and the provision of protection of workers' rights with respect to the assets of an enterprise going bankrupt. The Chinese authorities, to be fair, are developing, at the local level, various measures to alleviate the effects of the lay-offs brought about by the reforms. These efforts are serious and deserve credit. However, they are far from sufficient to solve the problems (Rocca 2006: 294; Roux 2006: 169). Lastly, China should allow for the creation of independent trade unions and freedom of association. In the long run, China's objectives of social stability and scientific development will be better served by decent treatment of their workers rather than by letting them suffer abuses without effective organizations to defend them.

Overall, the Chinese people are becoming more aware of their rights, and are exhibiting a growing willingness to use the legal system to vindicate their rights. The Chinese Labor Law is being relied on as the legal basis for workers' claims in courts (Chan 2004: 28), and this is both important and positive in its assessment. The fact that Chinese workers rely on this law and win some of their claims also refutes arguments to the effect that "there is no law in China," or that this country has no "legal system." Thus, the Labor Law, first conceived as a tool of legitimacy of the new economic order following Deng Xiaoping's Southern Tour in 1992, is now becoming a tool legitimizing contestation of the abuses stemming from this very new order.

Notes

1 For a discussion contrasting both schools' positions, see Vandermeersch (1965: 209). See also Chen, J. (1999: 7–14) for a discussion of Confucianism and Legalism.

2 The Chinese Constitution was amended in 1999 to incorporate a reference to the "*shehuizhuyi fazhi guojia*" that is, China has adopted the "socialist rule of law" concept. This amendement took place after the enactment of the Chinese Labor Law and will not be discussed here.

3 Most notably, the problem of enforcement of judgments by the courts affects all areas of law. See Jiang, Q.-y. (2006: 200).

4 Randall Peerenboom (2003) studied in detail the images of the Chinese legal system. Teemu Ruskola (2002) made a similar study, focusing on the notion of "orientalism." Both authors point out that the current legal reforms have been met with skepticism in Western countries, and Peerenboom notes at p. 4 that the notion that China lacks a "legal system" is still widespread.

5 Chinese scholars Cai Dingjian and He Weifang have published several articles on this problem. In the West, Stanley Lubman , Randall Peerenboom and Jean-Pierre Cabestan have also researched this specific problem

6 The notorious Tang Code of the Tang dynasty exerted an important influence on Japanese law from the seventh century AD, while the Ming Code was a major source of inspiration in Vietnam.

7 For a forceful argument in favor of "local paradigms," see Zhu (1996: 217). Professor Zhu Suli is the leading scholar in the debate about *bentuhua* and teaches at the Law Faculty of Beijing University.

8 Before 1949, the urban workers were three million; in 1952 that number jumped to fifteen million. It reached seventy million in 1978. Rocca specifies that the CCP bestowed several important privileges on the workers' class.

9 That fear was reinforced by the political changes that took place in Eastern Europe in 1989. According to Orville Schell (1994: 181), the party elders were infused with a spirit of paranoia.

10 The transition, up to this day, remains by no means easy, as young graduates are facing a shortage of jobs.

11 The Chinese Constitution was amended to include this new concept in 1992.

12 1957 was the year of the Anti-Rightist Campaign, which took a heavy toll among intellectuals, particularly among legal scholars, and 1976 marks the year Mao Zedong died, after ten years of the "Cultural Revolution," a very troubled period for China during which many intellectuals were again persecuted. The legislative activity was almost brought to a complete end during between 1957 and 1976.

13 For a complete list of the regulations, see Chen, K. (1997: 32–3).

14 This remark warrants some contextual explanations. Until the early 1990s, Chinese urban workers were assigned jobs by the local authorities, according to the needs defined by the latter. Under such a system, the workers could not chose their jobs, nor their employer, and remained with the enterprise (the "work unit" or "*danwei*") on a lifelong basis.

15 This argument was even stronger after the Chinese state completed the wave of nationalizations of virtually all enterprises. Once the public ownership regime was in place, the workers were, in theory, the "masters of the state" (Morin and Pairault 1997: 11). In fact, practice contradicts this representation, as there were important workers' uprisings in China, especially in 1956–7, less than ten years after the founding of the PRC. For details on these uprising, see Gipouloux (1986: 189–211).

16 One must also add that new forms of businesses were slowly developing, for which there was no legal regulation of labor relations. Such was the case, for example, with private enterprises, viewed with suspicion in the early days of the reforms.

17 In fact, early in the 1990s, the decision had been taken by the Chinese Government to break the "iron rice bowl." That meant bringing to an abrupt end employment security for urban workers (ILO (International Labor Office) 2001). The end result of the labor reforms in China is, to borrow from Ian Gough (2004: 39), that "the idea of livelihoods replaces that of wages and salaries. Individuals and families use diverse strategies to make a living, involving various types of labor." It is now common in China for couples to have one member working in the state sector, in order to secure certain advantages, while the other works in the private sector, with higher salaries but fewer benefits.

18 This article is one of a series covering the fifteenth Congress, on file with the author. This issue was a source of dilemmas for the Chinese Government, as summed up by Mr. Xiong Zhijun, Director General of Enterprise Remuneration, Bureau of State-Owned Assets Supervision and Administration Commission: "how to combine restructuring of state-owned enterprises, to improve their economic efficiency and the re-employment of laid-off workers. The policy of low income and high employment under a centrally planned economy had led to decreased efficiency in many state-owned enterprises, as had become apparent when China gradually opened up is [sic] economy to foreign investors" (MLSS (Ministry of Labor and Social Security) 2004: 27).

19 In this article, Potter (1996: 31) affirms that at the time, China's vision of development was characterized by "an overemphasis on economic growth with lack of attention to social, cultural and political elements."

20 It is beyond the scope of this chapter to discuss the general human rights situation in China. However, a brief reference to wider debates is inescapable as labor rights bear a close relation to economic development.

21 At p. 169, Chen Zishang affirms that in China, the right to subsistence is the most basic human right. At p. 170, he explains the hybrid nature of the right to subsistence, which is both an individual right and a collective right.
22 One legal scholar advocates that the right to development should be the new foundation of the Chinese legal system (Wang, X. 2005: 107). At p. 108, Wang stresses that the conflict between fairness and efficiency in Chinese society is very acute. Therefore, the findings of He Qinglian (1998) with respect to the primacy of efficiency as new paradigm in Chinese society are still valid.
23 The English translation of this provision uses the expression "major changes in the objective conditions." However, the terminology used by Chinese legal scholars when they comment on this provision refers to the civil law doctrine of "change of circumstances."
24 A functional equivalent of "change of circumstances" in common law terminology is "hardship clause" (Cornu 2002: 156).
25 This vision is also endorsed by a Chinese official, almost a decade later; see MLSS (2004:21); Mr. Xiong Zhijun affirms that massive lay-offs can lead to social instability.
26 According to Chinese sources, between 1998 and 2003, the state-owned enterprises laid-off 28.18 million of workers (Information Office of the State Council 2004).
27 The case is especially acute in foreign labor-intensive companies (Chan 2004: 32).

Bibliography

Asia Monitor Resource Centre (1996) "How Hong Kong Makes Toys in China," *Asian Labour Update* (April–July): 19–23.
Bi Xiaoqing (2006) "Basic Contradiction between Rule of Law and Rule of Man" in Li, Buyun (ed.), *Constitutionalism and China [Xianzheng yu Zhongguo]*, Beijing: Law Press, pp. 69–91.
Cabestan, Jean-Pierre (1996) "Chine: Un État de lois sans État de droit" [China: Rule by Law Without the Rule of Law], in Aubert, Claude, Cabestan, Jean-Pierre and Lemoine, Françoise (eds.), *La Chine après Deng [China After Deng]* (July–September), *Revue Tiers-Monde*, 147: 649–68.
Cai Dingjian (1999) "Development of the Chinese Legal System since 1979 and Its Current Crisis and Transformation," *Cultural Dynamics*, 11(2): 135–65.
Chan, Anita (2004) "Condition ouvrière: les signes d'une évolution" [Labor's Condition: Signs of an Evolution], *Perspectives Chinoises*, 86: 25–34.
—— (1996) "A Factory-Boot Camp in Guangdong: Martial Discipline in a Guangdong Shoe Factory," *Perspectives Chinoises*, 38 (November–December): 12–17.
Chen Jianfu (1999) *Chinese Law. Towards an Understanding of Chinese Law, Its Nature and Development*, The Hague: Kluwer Law International.
—— (1995) *From Administrative Authorization to Private Law*, Dordrecht: Martinus Nijhoff Publishers.
Chen Ke (1997) "Peoples' Republic of China," in Blanpain, Roger (ed.), *International Encyclopedia for Labour Law and Industrial Relations,* Supplement 185 (November), The Hague: Kluwer Law International.
Chen Yan (2002) *L'éveil de la Chine. Les bouleversements intellectuels après Mao 1976–2002 [China's Awakening : Intellectual Upheavals After Mao]*, Paris: Éditions de l'Aube.

Chen Zishang (1997) "Philosophical Foundations of Human Rights in China," in Mendes, Errol P. and Traeholt, Anne-Marie (eds.), *Human Rights: Chinese and Canadian Perspectives*, Ottawa: Human Rights Research and Education Centre, University of Ottawa, pp. 161–82.

"Chinese Society in an Accelerated Restructuring Period," *People's Daily Online*, June 25, 2004. Available online: http://english.people.com.cn/200404/27/eng20040427_141620.shtml (accessed July 13, 2005).

Ching Kwan Lee (2000) "Pathway of Labor Insurgency," in Perry, Elizabeth J. and Selden, Mark (eds.), *Chinese Society. Change, Conflict and Resistance*, London: Routledge, pp. 41–61.

"Congress Redefines Public Ownership," *China Daily*, September 18, 1997: 4.

Conner, Alison W. (2003) "The Comparative Law School of China," in Hsu Stephen C. (ed.), *Understanding China's Legal System. Essays in Honor of Jerome A. Cohen*, New York: New York University Press, pp. 210–73.

Cornu, Gérard (2002) *Vocabulaire juridique* [*Legal Dictionnary*], Paris: PUF.

Ding Linghua (1997) *Zhongguo falü sixiang shi* [*History of Chinese Legal Thought*], Beijing: Zhongguo Zhengfa Daxue chubanshe [Zhengfa University Press].

Domenach, Jean-Luc (2002) *Où va la Chine?* [*Where is China Going?*], Paris: Fayard.

Fan Zhongxin (2001) *Zhongyi fawenhua de anhe yu chayi* [*Convergence and Divergence in Chinese and Westerm Legal Cultures*], Beijing: Zhongguo Zhengfa Daxue chubanshe [Zhengfa University Press].

Fu Hualing and Choy, D. W. (2004) "From Mediation to Adjudication: Settling Labour Disputes in China," *China Rights Forum*, 3: 17–22.

Gallagher, Mary (1997) "An Unequal Battle: Why Labor Law Fails to Protect Workers," *China Rights Forum* (Summer): 12–15.

Gao Xin and Li Jun (eds.) (1996) *Laodong falü jieshi yong yu anlie pinxi* [*Introduction to Labor Legislation*], Beijing: Renmin Fayuan Chubanshe [People's Legal Press].

Gaudemet, Jean (2000) *Sociologie historique du droit* [*Historical Sociology of Law*] Coll. "doctrine juridique" [Legal Doctrine], Paris: PUF.

Gipouloux, François (2005) *La Chine du XXIe siècle. Une nouvelle superpuissance?* [*China in the Twenty-First Century: A New Superpower?*], Paris: Armand Colin.

—— (1986) *Les cents Fleurs à l'usine. Agitation ouvrière et crise du modèle soviétique en Chine 1956–1957* [*One Hundred Flowers at the Factory. Labour Unrest and the Crisis of the Soviet Model*], Paris : Éditions de l'École des Hautes Études en Sciences Sociales.

Gough, Ian (2004) "Welfare Regimes in Development Contexts: A Global and Regional Analysis," in Gough, Ian and Wood, Geoff (eds.), *Insecurity and Welfare Regimes in Asia, Africa and Latin America*, Cambridge: Cambridge University Press, pp. 15–47.

Guan Huai (ed.) (1994) *Zhonghua renmin Gongheguo Laodongfa dao du*, Beijing: Falü Chubanshe [Publishing House of Law].

He Qinglian (1998) *Zhongguo de Xianjing* [*China's Pitfall*], Beijing: Jinri Zhongguo Chubanshe.

"Human Rights to be enshrined in Constitution," *People's Daily Online*, March 9, 2004. Available online: http://english.people.com.cn/200403/09/print2004030 9_136924. html (accessed on July 14, 2006).

Information Office of the State Council (2004) "China's Employment Situation and Policies," (released to the media on April 26, 2004). Available online: http://english. people.com.cn/200404/26/print20040426_141553.shtml (accessed July 14, 2006).

ILO (International Labour Oganization) (2001) "China: Labour Market and Income Insecurity" (July 15). Available online: www.ilo.org/public/english/protection/ses/info/database/china.htm (accessed July 20, 2006).

Jiang Qing-yun (2006) *Court Delay and Law Enforcement in China. Civil Process and Economic Perspective*, Wiesbaden: Deutscher Universitäts-Verlag/GWG Fachverlage GmbH.

Jiang Zemin (1997) "Hold High the Great Banner of Deng Xiaoping Theory for an All Around Advancement of the Cause of Building Socialism with Chinese Characteristics to the 21st Century" (Historical Party Congress/Full text of Jiang Zemin's report delivered at the 15th National Congress of the Communist Party of China on September 12, 1997), *China Daily, 15th Party Congress Supplement* (September 23): 5 pages.

Jones, William C. (2003) "Trying to Understand the Current Chinese Legal System," in Hsu, Stephen C. (ed.), *Understanding China's Legal System. Essays in Honor of Jerome A. Cohen*, New York: New York University Press, pp. 7–45.

Josephs, Hilary K. (2003) *Labour Law in China* (2nd ed.), Huntington, NY: Juris Publishing.

Kernen, Antoine (2006) "L'impact sur l'emploi de la restructuration des entreprises d'État en Chine" [The Impact of State-Owned Entreprises' Reform on Employment], in Lasserre, Frédéric (ed.), *L'éveil du dragon. Les défis du développement de la Chine au XXIe siècle [The Dragon's Awakening: The Challenges of Development in the Twenty-First Century]*, Montreal: Presses de l'Université du Québec à Montréal: pp. 31–51.

Labor Law of the People's Republic of China (1994) (adopted by the Eighth Session of the Standing Committee of the Eight National People's Congress on July 5, 1994, promulgated by Order no. 28 of the President of the People's Republic of China and effective as of January 1, 1995). Available online: http://english1.peopledaily.com.cn/data/laws/details.php?id=52 (accessed January 16, 2007).

Li Zhao (1996) "L'évolution récente de la Constitution chinoise" [The Recent Evolution of China], *Les Cahiers de droit*, 37: 643–52.

Liang Shuwen, Ming Hui Hi and Jun Jian (eds.) (1997) *Laodong fa ji peitao guiding xinshe xinjie [New Explanations on the Labor Law and Related Texts]*, Beijing: Renmin Fayuan Chubanshe [People's Court Press].

Liechtenstein, Natalie G. (2003) "Law in China's Economic Development," in Hsu, Stephen C. (ed.), *Understanding China's Legal System. Essays in Honor of Jerome A. Cohen*, New York: New York University Press, pp. 274–94.

Lo, Carlos Wing-Hung (1997) "Socialist Legal Theory in Deng Xiaoping's China," *Columbia Journal of Asian Law*, 11: 469–87.

MLSS (Ministry of Labour and Social Security), People's Republic of China—International Labour Office (2004) *Summary Proceedings. China Employment Forum, Beijing, China, April 28–30, 2004*. Available online: www.ilo.org/public/english/chinaforum/download/proceedings.pdf (accessed July 20, 2005).

Morin, Alexandre and Pairault, Thierry (1998) *La Chine au travail (II). Les contrats de travail et les conventions collectives [China at Work II: Labour Contracts and Collective Agreements]*, Paris: Gestion de l'entreprise en Chine [Business Management in China].

—— (1997) *La Chine au travail (I). Les sources du droit du travail [China at Work I: The Sources of Labour Law]*, Paris: Gestion de l'entreprise en Chine [Business Management in China].

Peerenboom, Randall (2003) "The X-Files: Past and Present Portrayals of China's Alien 'Legal System'," University of California: Los Angeles School of Law Research Paper Series, Research Paper no. 03–2.

—— (2002) *China's Long March Toward Rule of Law*, Cambridge: Cambridge University Press.

Piques, Marie-Chantal (2001) *Les miroirs de la négociation en Chine. Voyage dans l'univers mental et social chinois* [*Bargaining in China. A Journey in the Chinese Mental and Social World*], Paris: Éditions Philippe Picquier, Librairie le Phénix.

Piquet, Hélène (2005) *La Chine au carrefour des traditions juridiques* [*China at the Crossroads of Legal Traditions*], Bruxelles: Bruylant.

Potter, Pitman B. (1996) "The Right to Development. Philosophical Differences and Their Political Implications," *China Rights Forum*, 28–31.

Rocca, Jean-Louis (2006) *La condition chinoise. La mise au travail capitaliste à l'âge des réformes* [*The Chinese Condition: Capitalism's Set-up of Labour During the Reform Era*], Paris: Coll. Recherches internationales du CERI, Karthala.

Roux, Alain (2006) *La Chine au XXe siècle* [*China in the Twentieth Century*], Paris: Armand Colin.

Ruskola, Teemu (2002) "Legal Orientalism," *Michigan Law Review*, 101: 179–234.

Schell, Orville (1994) *Mandate of Heaven. The Legacy of Tiananmen Square and the Next Generation of China's Leaders*, New York: Simon and Schuster.

Shi Jiayou (2006) *La codification du droit civil chinois au regard de l'expérience française* [*The Codifying of Chinese Civil Law in Light of the French Experience*], Paris: LGDJ.

Vandermeersch, Léon (1965) *La formation du légisme* [*The Formation of Legalism*], Paris: École Française d'Extrême-Orient.

Wang Quan Xing (1997) *Laodong fa* [*Labour Law*], Beijing: Falu Chubanshe [Publishing House of Law].

Wang Xigen (2005) "Lun Dangdai Zhongguo falü tixi de zhongxin dingwei" [On Focus of Legal System in Modern China], *Faxuejia*, 3: 104–10.

Wang Yan (2002) *Chinese Legal Reform. The Case of Foreign Investment Law*, London: Routledge.

Wang Yiying and Gong Jianli (eds.) (1994) *Zhongguo laodongfa shiwu* [*History of Labor Law*), Beijing: Jinri Chubanshe [Today's Press].

Wong, Linda (1998) *Marginalization and Social Welfare in China*, London: Routledge.

Zheng Shiping (1997) *Party vs. State in Post 1949 China. The Institutional Dilemma*, Cambridge: Cambridge University Press.

Zhu Suli (1996) "Faxue yanjiu de guifanhua, faxue chuantong yu bentuhua" [Normalization in Legal Research, the Legal Studies Tradition, and Indigenization], in Zhu, Suli (ed.), *Fazhi qi bentu ziliao* [*Rule of Law and Local Resources*], Beijing: Zhongguo Zhengfa Daxue chubanshe [Zhengfa University Press], pp. 211–19.

4   Shifting power relations

State–ENGO relations in China

Jonathan Schwartz

Introduction

Faced with the realization that it can no longer ignore the environmental fallout resulting from unfettered economic growth, the Chinese state has sought solutions to the challenges of balancing economic growth with environmental degradation.[1] Indeed, the state recognizes that environmental degradation, both directly and via its impact on economic development and public satisfaction, constitutes a growing challenge to its legitimacy to rule. As a result, the state has developed a broad array of environmental protection laws and policies and enhanced the powers of those institutions charged with environmental protection in order to control and mitigate the environmental impacts of rapid economic growth. Despite these efforts, environmental degradation continues apace. The state has responded, in part, by looking to civil society organization in the form of environmental non-governmental organizations (ENGOs) for assistance. This response raises an important question regarding possible challenges to the traditional role of the state in China. Do ENGOs offer a solution to the environment challenges facing the leadership, or a challenge to the leadership itself?

To address this question, I begin by evaluating the need for action on the environment in China, and the reasons why the state cannot, on its own, successfully address these challenges. I then turn to examples of the cooperative, but increasingly confrontational role played by Chinese civil society organizations as reflecting the uneasy relationship between ENGOs and the state. Finally, I draw on the civil society literature on the structure and potential direction of state–civil society relations to conclude that China shares many similarities with former Eastern European communist regimes, and may move along a similar trajectory.

Environmental conditions in China

China's leading government environmental protection organ, the State Environmental Protection Agency (SEPA), draws on a number of categories to assess pollution levels.[2] For the sake of illustrating the severity of China's pollution problems and by extension the need for action on environmental protection, it is sufficient to draw on a limited sampling of these categories. In this section I consider only the water and atmospheric environments.[3]

Water

According to Chinese standards, surface water is classified into five categories based on intended use. Category I mainly applies to water sources and nature reserves; category II applies to areas protected as centralized drinking water sources, sanctuaries for rare species of fish and spawning grounds for fish and shrimps (etc.); category III applies to drinking water of lower quality, sanctuaries for common species of fish, and swimming zones; categories IV and V apply to water intended for industrial (IV) and agricultural (V) activities. Water quality is measured at 741 key sections along China's seven main river basins.[4]

Data from 2002 indicate that 29.1 percent of water tested met water quality categories I–III, 30 percent met categories IV or V, while a significant 40.9 percent exceeded category V.[5] Pollution was especially severe in the Liao and Hai River basins, where category V was exceeded in over 60 percent of cases. Conditions were even worse in the tributaries to these major rivers and along the border regions between provinces.[6] The Yellow River suffered from heavy pollution with water quality ranging mostly between categories III–IV. Yellow River tributaries were even more polluted.[7] The least polluted of the major river basins was the Yangtze, with water quality dominated by category II (SEPA 2002a).[8]

These results compare poorly with data from the year 2000. In that year, 57.7 percent of the sections of the mainstream of the main river basins achieved category III water quality, while 21.6 percent achieved category IV and 6.9 percent achieved category V. At that time, only 13.8 percent exceeded category V (SEPA 2000).

Atmosphere

China's air quality standards are also divided into categories. Air quality standards are measured based on three categories. A category I region is defined as a nature conservation area, scenic spot and/or historic site, as well as any region requiring special protection. A category II region is defined as a residential area, a mixed region of commercial traffic and residences, a cultural area, industrial area and/or rural area. A category III region is defined as a special industrial area. Pollutants tested for include particulate concentrations (TSP), particulate concentrations at PM_{10} or less, and SO_2 concentrations.[9]

Results for 2002 in 343 monitored cities and counties found that only 34 percent of cities achieved the goal of category II air quality. Approximately 35 percent of cities achieved only level III air quality, while 30 percent exceeded category III. In terms of population, almost 75 percent of the urban population was concentrated in regions exceeding the category II target level (SEPA 2002a).

These results contrast with year 2000 results where 37 percent of cities enjoyed category II or lower air quality, 35 percent reached category III and 33 percent exceeded category III air quality. This reflects a slight decline in the number of cities exceeding category III air quality and a slight rise in the number of cities achieving category II or less (SEPA 2000).

Faced with these and other serious environmental challenges, the state has steadily increased investment in environmental protection. In 2002, the total investment in pollution treatment in the country was 136.34 billion Yuan, accounting for 1.33 percent of GDP. This compares favorably with 2000 investment levels of 106.07 billion Yuan, or 1.1 percent of GDP.[10] While these figures represent encouraging growth in environment-related investment, they pale beside the estimated cost of environmental degradation to the country. According to recent World Bank estimates, pollution is costing China 8–12 percent of its $1.4 trillion GDP on an annual basis (*The Economist*, August 21, 2004: 55–7). Other studies calculate that the cost of environmental degradation and pollution to China's economy essentially nullifies GDP growth over the past 20 years, with China's economy producing little new net national wealth (US Embassy Beijing 2000a; see also Mao 1998). Indeed, according to Samuel Kim, though estimates put China's annual GDP growth at 8–9 percent, by including ecological debt, China's GDP is growing at about zero percent each year (Kim 2000: 20).

Constraints on protecting the environment

Investment in the environment is clearly proving insufficient to mitigate environmental degradation. Two key developments contribute to this reality. First, as noted in the introductory chapter of this volume, China's leadership has chosen to base its ongoing legitimacy to rule upon its ability to provide consistent and expanding economic growth. By providing the conditions for economic prosperity, the Party hopes to preserve social stability and public support. As a result, the Party invests heavily in activities that contribute to economic growth, often at the expense of other activities, including social service provision, and importantly, environmental protection. Second, further aggravating the Party's inability to address environmental degradation is its ongoing policy of devolving responsibility for policy development and enforcement to provincial and sub-provincial authorities.

With the initiation of Deng Xiaoping's economic reforms in the late 1970s, China entered a new era. The impetus for the reforms was the Party leadership's failure under Mao to meet the expectations of the population in terms of improved living standards. Indeed, following the death of Mao and the end of the Cultural Revolution, China found itself well behind its neighbours in terms of development. This was a difficult reversal for the once uncontested leader of Asia. Not only had the promise of a steadily improving quality of life under the Communist Party not been fulfilled, but dissatisfaction and disillusionment grew rife as the public became aware of the abuses and failures of the Great Leap Forward and Cultural Revolution.[11] In order to regain public support and secure legitimacy for continued Party rule, Deng Xiaoping chose to reform the economy. Under Deng Xiaoping's leadership, the economy was released from previous constraints, with the result that the country entered a long and ongoing period of explosive growth. Thus, between 1985 and 2000, China's GDP growth rate averaged over 8 percent (Consulate General of the People's Republic of China in New York, n.d.).[12]

In an effort to sustain this robust growth, the Party initiated a process of withdrawal from its previous policy of micro-control over the Chinese system, focusing instead on macro-control (*People's Daily Online*, August 4, 2004). In practice, this meant that decision-making, enforcement powers and revenue collection largely devolved to the local level, while the centre focused on providing guidance and appointing top officials. For example, local officials gained responsibility for deciding which industries to allow in their jurisdictions and in which industries to invest. As a consequence, industries became increasingly dependent on local officials for support in obtaining required permits, land access, water allocations, tax relief and so on. In turn, local officials grew increasingly dependent upon the tax revenue and jobs created by these industries.

In the new, productivity-driven economy, local Chinese officials often find themselves forced to choose between supporting increased production, and by extension, tax revenues and jobs, and cracking down on abuses of the environment that clearly contravene national standards. Thus, mutual dependence continues to grow and taking action against local industry becomes increasingly unattractive to local officials (Mok 2000: 156–9).[13] This further exacerbates the limitations on enforcement arising from local officials' recognition of the importance of good economic results in obtaining promotion, and retaining the support of local populations (see Cheung 1998:10–17).

The declining effectiveness of enforcement is starkly illustrated by the example of local Environmental Protection Bureaus (EPBs). Local EPBs are responsible to both the national level SEPA and to their local governments.[14] EPBs monitor the local environment and enforce centrally dictated environmental protection laws and regulations (Ma and Ortolano 2000: 122–4). However, they receive no funding from the central government and SEPA, and only partial funding from local governments. The majority of their funds derive from fees and fines levied against local factories. Thus, it is not in the interest of local EPBs to enforce environmental regulations to the extent that they lose local government funding and/or local factories are forced to close down or move to a different jurisdiction, thereby depriving the EPBs of their main funding source.

Specific examples of local government and EPB failures to adhere to national policy due to conflicting local interests are rife. Efforts to clean up Lake Tai—one of the largest bodies of fresh water in China—and the Huai River—one of China's seven key rivers—have largely failed, despite highly visible campaigns driven by the central government (for Tai lake, see Schwartz 2003: 50–3; for Huai river, see Economy 2004: 1–27). Faced with pressure from local businesses and employees of those businesses, local government and EPB officials have consistently skirted central government commitments to clean up these sites. As a result, the data reflects continued deterioration of environmental conditions in these sites despite public government commitments.[15]

This failure of enforcement contrasts with the fact that the actual laws, regulations and policies that inform environmental protection in China are highly developed (Schwartz 2003: 54–8). As Vaclav Smil (1998) points out, "the [Chinese] government pays more attention to the environment than was the norm in virtually all western countries at comparable stages of their economic development."[16]

Clearly a major challenge to advancing Chinese environmental protection is the inability to close the gap between central level initiatives and implementation of those initiatives by lower levels of government. This gap is a direct outcome of both decentralization and the intense focus on economic development as a source of Party legitimacy. An important effort to explain this decentralizing political system is provided by Michel Oksenberg. Oksenberg (2002: 193–5) divides the political system into three components: the core; intermediary institutions; and legal, semi-legal and illegal organizations and associations arising in the space made available by the state's withdrawal from its past extensive control.

The core fits within the context of the Fragmented Authoritarian model (Lieberthal and Oksenberg 1998). Enormous power is concentrated in the hands of 20–30 people—members of the Standing Committee of the Politburo of the Party Central Committee. The core controls the military, legal committees, the central law enforcement apparatus and a large (though shrinking) part of the means of production, via still powerful state-owned enterprises (SOEs). The core recognizes the importance of economic modernization, assuming that material progress will produce a happier, more stable and just society (and hence, legitimacy to rule).

The center has, nonetheless, become aware of the importance of environmental protection. In addition to the economic cost of environmental degradation noted earlier, factors driving this awareness include international pressure to clean up the environment, as well as growing domestic public awareness and activism (*The People's Daily*, April 22, 2002; See also *The Economist*, August 21, 2004).[17]

Responding to the more than 74,000 public protests recorded in 2004 (up from 58,000 in 2003), the Central Committee issued an October 2005 statement tying these protests to public dissatisfaction with the state of the environment. In its statement, the Central Committee identified pollution as one of the key contributors to public unrest (Nankivell 2006; Tremblay 2005: 21–8).[18] While no specific breakdown of causes for the protests is available, the government makes this assumption based on the numerous cases of pollution-related protests described in local and international media outlets. These include protests over the polluting of the Chaoshui and Qingshui rivers in the Guizhou-Sichuan-Hunan region; in Quanzhou a town in Fujian province; and in Dongyang city, Zhejiang province (Cody 2005; *AsiaNews*, April 12, 2006).[19]

Constrained by its growing inability to enforce policies in a decentralizing system, among the alternative approaches the state has chosen to tackle environment challenges has been a resort to ENGOs. A part of civil society, these organizations constitute the third component identified by Oksenberg legal and semi-legal organizations.[20] The state views these organizations as capable of taking on some of the responsibilities for environmental protection, once the sole province of the state.

The role of Chinese ENGOS in environmental protection

The state sees a number of distinct advantages to involving China's ENGO community in advancing pollution control. First, ENGOs are able to obtain funding from international organizations and governments otherwise reluctant to (or legally barred from) providing funds to Chinese Government agencies.[21] By supporting the existence of ENGOs, the Chinese Government increases the funding entering the country to address environmental challenges, thereby easing its own financial burden. Second, enabling local ENGOs to form and take action, reflects positively on China's often criticized human rights record. ENGO activism exemplifies the Chinese Government's openness to an active civil society. Third, ENGOs are viewed by the central government as relatively benign. Given their focus on environmental protection, they are viewed as working towards a shared goal under central government guidance.[22]

However, opening up political space for environmental non-state actors by no means suggests that the central government is providing carte blanche for Hundred Flowers-like criticism of the state. Thus, while then-General Secretary Jiang Zemin called for the need to cultivate and develop social intermediary organizations at the 1997, fifteenth CCP Congress, the message was also clear that these ENGOs were expected to cooperate closely with government institutions and agencies.[23] As one SEPA official opined, "Westerners view Chinese environmental NGOs as providing a path to greater public participation in a wide range of issues, a crack in the door of eventual democratization," the Chinese Government is well aware of this Western expectation and makes every effort to ensure that no such democratization develops.[24]

The number of ENGOs in China has increased dramatically since the first were established in 1994. While the numbers are disputed, in 1994 there existed approximately nine ENGOs, while in 2002 the number had increased to seventy-three with an additional 184 student ENGOs (ENGOs based on university campuses) (Yang 2005: 50–1).[25] Chinese ENGOs range from those closely affiliated with the state (government-organized NGOs) to those with relative autonomy ("traditional" NGOs). All NGO types focus largely on developing plans and recommendations for the state and increasing awareness and knowledge about the environment, while avoiding direct criticism of the state. Examples of these different types of NGOs include the Center for Environmental Education and Communications (CEEC)—a government-organized NGO, BEDI (Beijing Environment and Development Institute) a semi-autonomous ENGO, and Friends of Nature—a traditional NGO (see Wu 2002: 46; Knup 1998; Otsuka 2002: 229–30).

The goal of CEEC is building environmental awareness through training and education. The organization trains young children and society in general. It also occasionally works with EPB officials. Sometimes CEEC activities occur at the behest of the SEPA—for which a small sum of money is paid—sometimes they are independent of SEPA. The central role of CEEC is to assist SEPA in developing and advancing initiatives in the following spheres: enhancing environmental awareness by organizing major environmentally related commemoration days; organizing and publishing education materials relating to environmental protection; developing training programs for directors of local and provincial level EPBs from around China; establishing a network for institutions that provide on-the-job training for county level EPBs; training for ISO 14000 (environmental management) certification; and, developing international contacts for training and cooperation on publicizing, educating about, and training in, environmental protection. The CEEC director notes that SEPA provides her organization with no funding (all of which comes from international donors) however, SEPA does provide useful contacts and exposure that enables her organization to reach a wide audience. SEPA has turned to CEEC because its own staff was slashed in government reorganizations. SEPA has only three employees working on public education and "propaganda," whereas CEEC employs twenty-six full-time workers.[26] CEEC is based in a SEPA building. It has good access to government officials and provides studies and reports that are read by SEPA officials as well as government ministers.

In 1995, Professor Ma Zhong established BEDI under the auspices of Beijing People's University. BEDI's goal is to strengthen awareness among government officials about environmental protection. While this requires extensive training, given the size of the government bureaucracy and the focus on economic growth, BEDI also takes the approach that training alone is insufficient. Thus, BEDI members focus on identifying means to illustrate the economic benefits of environmentally sound economic development projects to local officials. BEDI identifies and develops opportunities by focusing on practical research projects that result in policy recommendations to the government in the spheres of development planning and protection.[27] In this vein, BEDI has developed numerous pilot projects that illustrate the economic benefits of environmentally sound production.[28] For example, BEDI identified an important economic niche in northern Heilongjiang province. This region is home to black bees that produce an unusually popular type of honey. However, in order to flourish, the bees require that the existing eco-system remain untouched. The eco-system is under considerable pressure from developers, including heavy logging. BEDI successfully illustrated to local officials that maintaining a healthy eco-system while investing heavily in the black bee honey would prove more economically beneficial than the one-time extraction of resources from the region. The result: local officials are taking advantage of Heilongjiang's comparative advantage in black bee honey to increase income and employment (growing exports to Europe) while maintaining a sound eco-system.

Friends of Nature, a "traditional" NGO, is far more limited in the scope of its activities and access (Jin 2001).[29] This Beijing-based environmental NGO employs six full-time staff and two part-time staff in addition to a large volunteer base. It has 1,500 members, but based on the level of public interest could have over 100,000 members and numerous regional branches.[30] As with CEEC, Friends of Nature depends on foreign organizations to cover costs. The NGO offers education programs in schools as well as organizing environment-related campaigns such as one to save the Tibetan Antelope. Despite these seemingly a-political activities, Friends of Nature must remain circumspect in its activities. As well as limiting the number of members it accepts,[31] Friends of Nature limits its activities and outspokenness, focusing on public education and clean-up campaigns while avoiding criticism of the state. Even given its sensitivity, Friends of Nature has faced threats to its continued existence. Thus, following the government crackdown on *Falun Gong* activities, legislators met with Liang Congjie, the head of Friends of Nature, to warn him to avoid public activism. However, despite the limited nature of NGO political space, there are growing signs of change.

While lobbying the state remains both difficult and illegal in a formal sense, this is a direction in which many members of Friends of Nature would like to move, over time. In fact, members of Friends of Nature increasingly feel that becoming politically active, while still difficult, has grown far easier over the years since the NGO was established. According to one member, NGOs in general have become very attractive to young people in China, especially among the well educated. These people view ENGOs as providing a new path for expressing opinions that were once highly controlled.[32] An additional sign of growing change in the state–ENGO relationship is the increasing willingness of officials in government-organized ENGOs to consider establishing independent NGOs. While in the past taking such a step would radically limit the opportunities available to NGOs and expose the NGOs to the risk of closure, these officials express confidence that this is increasingly not a problem.[33] Indeed, they argue that over time, ENGOs will become more powerful and influential, challenging the state to take action it might otherwise refuse to take.

This confidence is bolstered by state encouragement of ENGOs to draw on international funding from foundations, foreign governments and corporations (Economy 2004).[34] Furthermore, due to rising cynicism over corruption abuses in government, the public is increasingly turning to civil society organizations for support on, and information about, environmental protection (US Embassy Beijing 1997).

Indeed, examples of a more activist, and less pliant ENGO community are increasingly to be found. ENGOs have grown willing to resort to "boundary-spanning contention," meaning that they are engaging in activism that skirts the boundaries of that which is allowed and that which is viewed as extra-legal (O'Brien 2003: 53–5).[35] One example is the ENGO community's response to the 1999 Go West Campaign—an initiative advanced under Jiang Zemin to spread the economic benefits and successes of coastal China to the interior. While the initiative included requirements for ecologically sound development,[36] environmentalists expressed concern that the environment would ultimately be sacrificed in favor of stronger economic growth. As a result, ENGO activists such as Liang Congjie (Friends of Nature) and Liu Xiaoyi (Global Village Beijing) actively pressed the state to include the SEPA and environmental NGOs in overseeing the campaign. The results have been positive, with greater SEPA involvement and NGO pressure via the media.

Other examples include environmental NGOs in Yunnan province that are lobbying for clearer agro-chemical laws (Cooper 2003), as well as Beijing-based CLAPV (The Center for Legal Assistance to Pollution Victims). This non-governmental environmental organization was established by Wang Canfa in October 1998 at Beijing University of Law and Politics. Its goals include training practitioners of the law regarding the state's environmental laws and regulations; increasing public awareness of environmental laws and their rights under those laws; and providing assistance to citizens who have suffered from a breach of their rights under China's environmental law. To fulfil this role, CLAPV relies on numerous lawyers and law professors (normally unavailable to NGOs).[37] *Xinhuanet* on December 14, 2005 reported that CLAPV, essentially, seeks to pressure government officials to clarify and enforce existing laws (current enforcement of environmental laws is estimated by Wang Canfa, at only 10 percent).[38]

The state's growing willingness to allow ENGOs to come into existence and take active, sometimes boundary-spanning roles, reflects the state's recognition of the important role environmental NGOs can play in protecting the environment and ensuring that government officials fulfil their responsibilities vis-à-vis the environment. If, as a result of NGO collaboration and pressure, the state is seen as more effectively protecting the environment, this serves to strengthen the Party's legitimacy to rule. If, by contrast, ENGOs expand the political space available for non-state activism at the expense of the state, this may reflect a weakening of the state and a challenge to its legitimacy to rule in an ongoing negotiated relationship.

The growing numbers of ENGOs, and their expanding range of activism reflect the changing relationship between the Chinese state and ENGOs and the growth of a vanguard of civil society that is pressuring the Chinese state. These changes require a new conception of Chinese civil society as one that may challenge the state rather than simply working for it.

The conceptual development of Chinese civil society

Civil society is an amorphous term that has been defined in numerous ways (see McCormick *et al.* 1992: 187–8). Largely a Western concept, civil society is often categorized into sociological and political definitions. The sociological definition broadly identifies civil society as an intermediate associational realm situated between the state and the building blocks of society (individuals, families and firms), that is populated by organizations separate from the state, enjoying a level of autonomy from the state and formed voluntarily by people in order to protect or advance their interests and values (Gellner 1994; Misztal 2001; Shigetomi 2002: 10–13; White 1996: 197–8; Yu 2002:1–2;). Political definitions of civil society describe a more confrontational relationship between the state and social groups, resulting in, or by nature a part of, the democratization process. Democratization arises over time as a result of individuals combining their otherwise disparate grievances against the state, and learning norms of democratic interaction in the process.[39] These groups eventually create institutions capable of resisting the authoritarian state. Drawing on this definition and examples from Eastern Europe, some scholars identify civil society as a political weapon in the hands of a public intent on curbing the arbitrary powers of authoritarian regimes (White 1996; Wiktorowicz 2000: 43).

The Eastern European experience

In the 1980s, Eastern Europe saw the rise of intellectuals, the clergy and workers who began challenging their Communist governments over corruption and cruel treatment. In the early stages, civil society organizations did not aim to curb or replace existing communist governments but rather to work to achieve shared goals within parameters set by the government. However, forming a "self-limiting" civil society, one that remained under state control, proved difficult. Almost inevitably, civil society began to challenge the state. In the Polish case, civil society first worked with the state, and only after concluding that domestic politics were controlled by external and negative (Soviet) forces did Polish civil society become "anti-political" and begin challenging the state (Baker 1998: 31). Thus, the initial goal of these civil society organizations was non-confrontational. These organizations were intended to enable individuals to decide how they should live, while reconciling this greater individual autonomy with the regime ideology of socialist solidarity.

According to di Palma (1991: 61), East European Communist regimes enabled the shift from total state control and adherence to an ideology of party infallibility, offering instead assurances of protection from past state abuses and rising living standards. In return, the public was to forego its own civil and political rights. This "paternalistic" model in which the regime "knew best" and promised to offer quality of life equivalent to the West was, however, doomed to failure when the easily compared promised prosperity was not achieved. With ideology no longer the source of legitimacy to rule and living standards failing to achieve Western levels, the position of the East European Communist regimes became increasingly untenable.[40] Despite intense, though increasingly reluctant repression by the state, civil society organizations began to grow in both number and outspokenness.[41] In time, as demands for improvements in living standards were joined by demands for greater voice and representation, confrontation became almost inevitable.

The rise of civil society in Eastern Europe enables us to draw some tentative conclusions regarding our definition of civil society. While the political definition includes a democratic component, the Eastern European examples do not necessarily support its existence. The Eastern European transition from communist to post-communist regimes illustrates the power of civil society to confront and weaken authoritarian governments, yet the ultimate outcome is not necessarily democratization (Madsen 1993: 189). As in the Polish case, civil society can successfully remove an existing regime (the Polish Communist Government), but fail to bring about democratization (the birth of a consolidated Polish democracy).[42] Civil society challenged East European Communist regimes through formation of disparate groups that were in many cases extremely divisive, violent and invested in contradictory visions of the direction their country should take.

The political definition of civil society that includes a confrontational relationship between a once dominant authoritarian state and a rising civil society finds support in the East European example. The likelihood of democratic transition remains contested (Bryant and Bailey 1997: 25; 144–6; Frolic 1997; Lee and So 1999: 300). How do these cases contribute to our understanding of trends in China?

Chinese civil society as unique

Drawing on Philip Khun, some China scholars adopt the sociological definition of civil society, describing civil society as an ideal type where individuals make rational decisions about the common good as they link society and the state (Brook and Frolic 1997: 8; 12–13; Ding 2000).[43] Based on this perspective, Chinese civil society is viewed as non-confrontational, arising from recognition of shared goals. The relationship with the state is cooperative, resulting in good governance.[44] Scholars often support this definitional choice by drawing on factors such as China's long, independent history, its Confucian and Maoist traditions and a history of citizens' obedience to the state.

Unlike the participatory Greek *Polis*, China developed under a Confucian system where respect for authority played a central role. The state was not challenged. The Chinese public, educated and raised in Confucian and later Maoist traditions, expected and desired of the state that it provide the support and services often assumed by civil society in a Western setting. The Chinese state was expected to address the needs of its people while occupying the space between state and society (Figure 1).

As the state increasingly turns to NGOs to take on additional responsibilities, it withdraws from the political space it once dominated. This withdrawal is similar to that which occurred in Eastern Europe where Communist regimes negotiated a new balance of power with civil society organizations. The East European paternalistic model was replaced with a confrontational one. As Chinese NGOs expand their roles and increase their independence from the state, and as the state grows increasingly dependent on NGOs, the NGOs are unlikely to willingly return to past state domination. This mirrors the process in Eastern Europe where the state was unable to regain control over political space it had ceded, despite a resort to military might to suppress public activism.[45]

From the perspective of the state, while remaining Leninist in disposition, it recognizes that it cannot continue to control all aspects of state–society interaction and must allow increasing space for non-state actors if it is to resolve the challenges it faces (Shigetomi 2002: 25). The result is constant negotiation of political space between the state and non-state actors. However, the negotiations occur largely within a framework established by the state.[46] Even recognizing that there must necessarily be "slippage" in state control, the framework is largely accepted and adhered to by non-state organizations.[47] From this perspective, Chinese civil society is not a vehicle for overthrowing a totalitarian state, but rather a mediator between state and society in an increasingly complex socio-political environment. Chinese civil society organizations act largely as intermediaries conveying state policies, initiatives and expectations to society. Civil society is a mechanism to prevent disorder and maintain links between the state and society. Arising from the expectation that the state will provide for society, civil society is enabled at the discretion

Figure 1 Space occupied by the state and society

of the state in order to contribute to the state's effort to ensure order. This essentially top-down conception is described as corporatist, or state-led civil society (Frolic 1997: 49).

Chinese civil society as common

However, this conception of Chinese civil society is challenged elsewhere. Saich (2000: 125) argues that the state-led civil society argument ignores state weakness and the ability of non-state organizations to influence policy-making processes while pursuing the interests of their own members. In the early stages of state–civil society relations, non-state actors search for points of contact with the state, opportunities to embed themselves within, and influence the state, while drawing on the state's resources. The state–civil society relationship is a "negotiated," symbiotic one, with non-state actors and the state benefiting from the interactions. This bears similarities with early state–civil society relations in Eastern Europe. And yet, in Eastern Europe, state–civil society relations became confrontational. Might China follow the same path?

As noted, with decentralization, circumventing and diminishing the impact of administrative controls became easier in the economic, political and social spheres. Decentralization has therefore enabled the birth, or according to some scholars, the re-emergence of Chinese civil society (Figure 2).[48] Already in summer 1992, McCormick, Su and Xiao were arguing that while China had not developed autonomous organizations, a private economy or intellectual ferment to match those in pre-Communist collapse Eastern Europe, it had made "important progress" in that direction. Much has occurred since their assessment.

China's ENGO community has taken on a dual role. On the one hand it functions as a support to the state in the shared goal of environmental protection. However, on the other hand, ENGOs have become active in activities that are boundary spanning. These ENGOs may represent a vanguard of the Chinese NGO community because, as one member of Green River—an ENGO in Yunnan province—noted, "environmental NGOs definitely enjoy more [political] space than other kinds of NGOs" (quoted in Cooper 2003). Furthermore, these NGOs represent far more than

Figure 2 NGOs take over tasks in the public sphere that once were a state responsibility

what Saich describes as "disgruntled workers in the northeast, rebellious farmers in the southwest and an uppity intellectual in Beijing"—groups that lack a common, bonding vision and might more correctly be described as "uncivil society" (Saich 2002–3). ENGOs organize, inform, train and activate government officials and the public in an effort to protect environmental interests. This does not suggest that NGOs in general, or ENGOs in particular, represent civil society in China, but rather that they reflect an important aspect of a nascent civil society and the potential direction of other expressions of Chinese civil society.

Conclusion

China's environment faces continual serious deterioration. Recognizing the long-term threats to development and to the Party's legitimacy to rule, which arise from a deteriorating environment, the state has chosen to take action. However, with decentralization has come the realization that the state is unable to address China's environmental challenges alone. As a result, the state has increasingly turned to ENGOs—an advanced manifestation of Chinese civil society—for assistance. The result is growing political space for ENGOs and shifting state–civil society relations. The relationship between the state and society is not static, and political space once ceded, is very difficult to reclaim. Reclaiming this space is made all the more difficult when the capacity to do so is weakened through the steady process of decentralization.

The initial relationship between Chinese civil society and the state was one of state-led, cooperative efforts on behalf of common goals. This would aptly describe conditions in pre-collapse communist Eastern Europe as well. While Chinese civil society may indeed be viewed as arising from a very different —Confucian—tradition, the process currently underway bears numerous similarities to the Eastern European cases. In its earlier manifestations, Chinese civil society enjoyed a cooperative relationship with the state. However, with the failures of the state in the environment sphere and the growing capacity of Chinese ENGOs, we see examples of growing willingness to challenge the state. Chinese ENGOs have grown increasingly numerous and active. While China scholars often refer to China as being unique in the state-led nature of state–civil society relations, at least insofar as the relationship between the state and ENGOs, this assessment should be challenged. Although the process may still be in its infancy, Chinese civil society seems to be following a more confrontational path, expanding its role and moving in the direction of challenging the state. Thus, in its efforts to enhance its legitimacy by drawing on civil society organizations to contribute to achieving shared, environmental protection goals, the state finds itself confronted by an increasingly activist and growing ENGO movement that is developing the willingness and capacity to test, and press, the limits of Chinese political space.

Notes

1   For the purposes of this chapter I conflate the state and the Chinese Communist Party.
2   For a full listing refer online to the SEPA website at www.sepa.gov.cn/english/ SOE/soechina2002/water.htm.
3   In doing so, I draw on SEPA data. While these data are, arguably, skewed, they remain sufficient to illustrate the problems China faces. Even if biased, the results clearly indicate significant environmental problems requiring major pollution amelioration initiatives. A comparative study drawing on multiple years of data clearly illustrates pollution trends. A comparative study can be completed drawing on data from the above website (see note 1).
4   The major pollution indicators are petroleum, BOD (biological oxygen demand), ammonia nitrogen, permanganate index, volatile phenols and mercury.
5   The river basins are: Yangtze, Yellow, Pearl, Songhua, Huai, Hai, and Liao.
6   This represents a significant challenge of decentralized pollution control enforcement. Because there is little benefit to provinces in enforcing water pollution standards on waters departing the province, provinces are likely to ignore enforcement and allow a build up of polluting industries, passing the pollution on to the downstream province. Chinese government efforts to address this challenge are discussed in Wang and Ongley (2004).
7   The SEPA report describes Yellow River water as "relatively bad in general," with the tributaries commonly suffering from "severe pollution."
8   It is worthwhile to note that a major contributing factor to the relatively high quality Yangtze River water is the high volume of water passing through. The result is that pollutants are relatively diluted and flushed into the ocean. The impact of the Three Gorges Dam will likely include rising pollution levels as the "flushing" effect is negated.
9   Level II TSP > 0.20mg/m^3; PM$_{10}$ > 0.10 mg/m^3; SO$_2$ > 0.06 mg/m^3. PM-10 refers to respirable particles 10 microns or less in diameter—considered to be the size fraction that poses the greatest health risk.
10   The improvement is even more noticeable in comparison with the 1990s when China invested only 0.8 percent of GDP in environmental spending.
11   The rise of civil society is often linked to economic crises that result in authoritarian governments offering economic and political concessions to society. See for example, Wiktorowicz (2000: 47–8) in his discussion of authoritarian regimes in the Middle East, specifically Jordan.
12   According to the World Resources Institute (2003), between 1990–2000 the rate was over 10 percent. According to the *People's Daily Online* (August 4, 2004), China's GDP growth in 2003 was 9.1 percent.
13   Mok's focus can be viewed as on what Oksenberg (2002) describes as legal, semi-legal and illegal organizations and associations (see pp. 8–9).
14   This reflects horizontal (*kuai*) and vertical (*tiao*) linkages.
15   Interview with Yangxi (department of Environmental Sciences, Nanjing University) (November 1998); Interview with Zhou Ze-jiang, Senior Research Scientist, Director, Information Center, Nanjing institute of Environmental Science, SEPA. (January, 1999).
16   Confirmed in interview with Zhou Ze-jiang (1999).
17   For example, the governments of South Korea and Japan have registered official complaints with China. They have also organized a tri-national committee with Chinese lawmakers to devise a strategy to combat cross-border pollution (*People's Daily Online*, April 22, 2002). In a joint SEPA–Ministry of Education environmental awareness survey of 10,000 households throughout China, nearly 60 percent of respondents replied that they believe China's environmental problems

are "very serious" or "fairly serious" (US Embassy Beijing 2000b). In a separate survey of 3,000 Chinese in ten cities, the The *Yangcheng Evening News* (Guangzhou) reported that environmental protection became the top concern in 2000 Horizon (Lingdian) Market Research company survey. This news was later reported in *Beijing Environment, Science and Technology Update* (September 8, 2000).

18 According to Li Lianjiang, Hong Kong Baptist University (quoted in Tremblay 2005), whereas in the past excessive and arbitrary taxation were the main causes of peasant protests; illegal land seizures and pollution are now becoming the main sources of contention.

19 There are a tremendous number of relevant examples. For a detailed discussion, see Economy (2004).

20 The second identified component is not relevant to the current analysis. Additional actions include increased participation in international environmental initiatives, including Kyoto (1994); raising the status of SEPA; and, increasing investment in environmental protection (Vermeer 1998: 953; Tremayne and De Waal 1998: 1030; see also SEPA 2002b).

21 Interview 65 (July 2002) Jock Whittlesey, Environment, Science and Technology— US Embassy in Beijing. Also Interview 72 (July 2002) Research Fellow in a Beijing-based Government Organized NGO.

22 According to Elizabeth Economy (2004: 229), this view is one that was shared by East European counterparts. ENGOs were regarded as relatively safe outlets for expressions of general discontent.

23 In February 2006, Zhou Shengxian, the director of the State Environmental Protection Administration, noted that the State Council has increased its focus on the environment as part of China's evolving development model (see *China.org* February 2006)

24 Interview 72. Chinese government officials are well aware of the danger of a potential "slide towards democratization." Hence the strong efforts to tightly regulate all civil society organizations (see Economy 2004: 129–31).

25 According to SEPA, China had approximately 2,000 registered environmental NGOs by the year 2000. China based NGOs are listed at www.zhb.gov.cn/english/NGO/index.htm (accessed March 3, 2003). A more conservative estimate of forty such NGOs is offered by Turner and Wu (2001).

26 Interview with Niu Lingjuan, Director, CEEC (July 2002).

27 Interview 68.

28 Recall that economic criteria continue to dominate in evaluating government officials.

29 "Traditional" in the sense that it is largely independent of the state, with ties limited to the required relationship with a sponsoring organization (*danwei*) and registration with a government ministry (Ministry of Civil Affairs). This is in accordance with the 1998 regulations governing registration and management of social organizations.

30 Interview with Liang Congjie, FN head (1999). Interview 67, member of staff, Friends of Nature (July 2002). The cost of membership is not a constraint— 50 RMB/year. In 1999 FN had 600 members and only two full-time staff. Chinese NGO-related regulations ban establishment of branch offices.

31 According to one NGO member, they receive daily emails and calls requesting membership.

32 Interview 67.

33 Interview 64. Director of Environmental Economics Program (July 2002).

34 Also, interview 63, Director international foundation (July 2002) and interview 74—foreign director of a Chinese GONGO (July 2002). Both describe growing access to funding sources.

35 O'Brien discusses the activities taken on by non-state actors that are partly prescribed and partly not. These actions often enjoy the support of the state as it seeks to achieve particular policy goals.
36 The state identified environmentally sound development as one of five key tenets of the campaign.
37 Interview with the Director of CLAPV, Wang Canfa, June 2002.
38 CLAPV is describe in detail on its website www.clapv.org/new/.
39 Dittmer and Hurst (2002–3) suggest that civil society is typically defined in an unrealistic liberal fashion that is more relevant to US realities than to those of Asia; see also Di Palma (1991).
40 A similar dynamic can be observed in the Middle East, see Wiktorowicz (2000).
41 According to di Palma (1991: 61–4, especially 62) reluctance arose due to increased recognition by the Communist leadership itself that the basis for their continued rule was becoming unjustified; see also Feher (1982). Other examples include Hungary and Czechoslovakia (Ehrenberg 1999: 194–7; Dittmer and Hurst 2002–3: 23–4; Linz and Stephan 1996: 261–76).
42 According to Linz and Stepan, to be considered consolidated, a democracy requires the presence of four elements: the rule of law; institutions of civil society; free and fair elections; and governors who are held accountable. "Towards Consolidated Democracies" *Journal of Democracy* vol. 7 (2) (1996).
43 These authors tend to draw on the sociological definition.
44 Good governance is defined as effectively exercised management of a country's economic and social resources for development. The World Bank (1992) identifies four components: public sector management; accountability; a solid legal framework; and, information and transparency (*Governance and Development*, 1992).
45 The Tiananmen crackdown and later political and economic retrenchments illustrate the ability of the Chinese state to re-concentrate power in its hands. However, the rapid return to the reform agenda illustrates the limits of the state's ability to continue this effort.
46 Interviews 66, 67, 71, 74, July 2002.
47 Occasional crackdowns such as those against the *Falun Gong* and organizers of China's Democracy Party are examples of continued state willingness to act to preserve its dominance when feeling threatened.
48 For example, McCormick *et al.* (1992: 182–3; 199) view civil society as having arisen during the Qing dynasty, finding reflection in the May Fourth movement.

Bibliography

"A Great Wall of Waste," *The Economist*, August 21, 2004: 55–7.
Baker, G. (1998) "Civil Society and Democratization Theory: An Inter-regional Comparison," unpublished thesis, University of Leeds.
Brook, Timothy and Frolic, Michael B. (eds.) (1997) *Civil Society in China*, Armonk, NY: M. E. Sharpe.
Bryant, Raymond and Bailey, Sinead (1997) *Third World Political Ecology*, London: Routledge.
Cheung, Peter T. Y. (1998) "Introduction: Provincial Leadership and Economic Reform in Post-Mao China," in Cheung, Peter T. Y., Chung, Jae Ho and Lin, Zhimin (eds.), *Provincial Strategies of Economic Reform in Post-Mao China: Leadership, Politics and Implementation*, Armonk, NY: M. E. Sharpe, pp. 10–17.
"China Improves Enforcement of Environmental Laws," *Xinhuanet*, October 9, 2005. Available online: www.clapv.org/new/show_en.php?id=72&catename=MR (accessed April 21, 2006).

"China, S. Korea & Japan to Establish Network to Share China's Yellow Dust Storm Monitoring Information," *People's Daily*, April 22, 2002. Available online: http://english.people.com.cn/200204/22/eng20020422_94495.shtml (accessed May 23, 2007).

Cody, Edward (2005) "China's Rising Tide of Protest Sweeping Up Party Officials: Village Chiefs Share Anger Over Pollution," *Washington Post Foreign Service* (September 12).

Consulate General of the People's Republic of China in New York (n.d.) *China Says Good-bye to Blind Pursuit of GDP Growth*. Available online: www.nyconsulate. prchina.org/eng/xw/t84117.htm (accessed July 28, 2004).

Cooper, Caroline (2003) "Quietly Sowing the Seeds of Activism," *South China Morning Post* (April 10).

Ding Yijiang (2000) "The Conceptual Evolution of Democracy in Intellectual Circles' Rethinking of State and Society," in Zhao Suisheng (ed.), *China and Democracy*, New York: Routledge, pp. 115–29.

Di Palma, Guiseppe (1991) "Legitimation from the Top to Civil Society: Politico-Cultural Change in Eastern Europe," *World Politics*, 44(1) (October): 49–80.

Dittmer, Lowell and Hurst, William (2002–3) "Analysis in Limbo: Contemporary Chinese Politics Amid the Maturation of Reform," *Issues & Studies*, 38(4)–39(1): 11–48.

Economy, Elizabeth C. (2004) *The River Runs Black: The Environmental Challenge to China's Future*, Ithaca, NY: Cornell University Press.

Ehrenberg, John (1999) *Civil Society: The Critical History of an Idea*, New York: NYU Press.

Feher, Ferenc (1982) "Paternalism as a Mode of Legitimation in Soviet-type Societies," in Rigby, T. H. and Feher, Fernec (eds.), *Political Legitimation in Communist States*, New York: St. Martin's Press, pp. 64–81.

Frolic, Michael B. (1997) "State-Led Civil Society," in Brook, Timothy and Frolic, Michael B. (eds.), *Civil Society in China*, Armonk, NY: M. E. Sharpe.

Gellner, Ernest (1994) *Conditions of Liberty*, London: Hamish Hamilton.

Jin Jiaman (2001) "The Growing Importance of Public Participation in China's Environmental Movement," *Green NGO and Environmental Journalist Forum* (April), Washington, DC: Woodrow Wilson International Center for Scholars.

Kim, Samuel S. (2000) "East Asia and Globalization: Challenges and Responses," in Kim, Samuel S. (ed.), *East Asia and Globalization*, New York: Rowman & Littlefield.

Knop, Elizabeth (1998) "Environmental NGOs in China: An Overview," *China Environment Series*, Washington, DC: Woodrow Wilson Center, the Environmental Change and Security Project.

Lee Yok-shiu and So, Alvin Y. (1999) "Conclusion," in Lee, Yok-shiu and So, Alvin Y. (eds.), *Asia's Environmental Movements*, London: M. E. Sharpe.

Lieberthal, Kenneth and Oksenberg, Michel (1998) *Policy Making in China: Leaders, Structures and Processes*, Princeton, NJ: Princeton University Press.

Linz, Juan J. and Stepan, Alfred (1996) *Problems of Democratic Transition and Consolidation*, Baltimore, MD: Johns Hopkins University Press, pp. 261–76.

Ma Xiaoying and Ortolano, Leonard (2000) *Environmental Regulation in China*, Lanham, MD: Rowman & Littlefield.

McCormick, Barret L., Su Shaozhi and Xiao Xiaoming (1992) "The 1989 Democracy Movement: A Review of the Prospects for Civil Society in China," *Pacific Affairs*, 65(2): 182–202.

"Macro Control Proved to be Timely and Effective," *People's Daily Online*, August 4, 2004. Available online: http://english.peopledaily.com.cn/ (accessed August 4, 2004).

Madsen, Richard (1993) "The Public Sphere, Civil Society and Moral Community: A Research Agenda for Contemporary China Studies," *Modern China*, 9(2) (April).

Mao Yushi (1998) "The Economic Costs of China's Environmental Degradation: Summary," in Smil, Vaclav and Mao, Yushi (eds.), *The Economic Costs of China's Environmental Degradation*, Cambridge, MA: American Academy of Arts and Sciences.

Misztal, B. A. (2001) "Civil Society: A Signifier of Plurality and Sense of Wholeness," in *The Blackwell Companion to Social Theory*, Oxford: Blackwell.

Mok Ka Ho (2000) *Social and Political Development in Post-Reform China*, Basingstoke: Macmillan.

Nankivell, Nathan (2006), "China's Pollution and the Threat to Domestic and Regional Stability," *Japan Focus* (January 3).

O'Brien, Kevin (2003) "Neither Transgressive Nor Contained: Boundary-Spanning Contention in China," *Mobilization*, 8(1).

Oksenberg, Michel (2002) "China's Political System: Challenges of the 21st Century," in Unger, Jonathan (ed.), *The Nature of Chinese Politics: From Mao to Jiang*, Armonk, NY: M. E. Sharpe.

Otsuka, Kenji (2002) "China: Social Restructuring and the Emergence of NGOs," in Shigetomi, Shinichi (ed.), *The State and NGOs: Perspective from Asia*, Singapore: Institute of Southeast Asian Studies.

"Pollution Control Top Priority," *China.org*, February 2006. Available online: www.china.org.cn/english/2006/Feb/158007.htm (accessed April 23, 2006).

Saich, Tony (2002–3) "The Essential Bookshelf," [interview with Nick Young] in *China Development Brief* (Winter). Available online: www.chinadevelopmentbrief.com/article.asp?sec=19&sub=1&toc=1&art=1040187853 (accessed August 11, 2004).

—— (2000) "Negotiating the State: The Development of Social Organizations in China," *The China Quarterly*, 161 (March): 124–41.

Schwartz, Jonathan (2003) "The Impact of State Capacity on Enforcement of Environmental Policies: The Case of China," *Journal of Environment and Development*, 12(1) (March): 50–81.

SEPA (2002a) *Report on the State of the Environment*. Available online: www.sepa.gov.cn/english/SOE/soechina2002/water.htm (accessed July 28, 2004).

—— (2002b) *China's National Tenth Five-Year Plan for Environmental Protection*. Available online: www.zhb.gov.cn/english/plan/Tenth.htm (accessed July 30, 2004).

—— (2000) *Report on the State of the Environment*. Available online: www.sepa.gov.cn/english/SOE/soechina2000/english/water/water_e.htm (accessed July 28, 2004).

Shigetomi, Shinichi (2002) "The State and NGOs: Issues and Analytical Framework," in Shigetomi, Shinichi (ed.), *The State and NGOs: Perspective from Asia*, Singapore: Institute of Southeast Asian Studies.

Smil, Vaclav (1998) "The Environmental Outlook for China," unpublished manuscript.

Tremayne, Bruce and De Waal, Penny (1998) "Business Opportunities for Foreign Firms Related to China's Environment," *The China Quarterly*, 156 (December).

Tremblay, Jean-François (2005) "Tempers Flare in China," *Chemical and Engineering News*, 83(39) (September 26): 21–8.

Turner, Jennifer and Wu Fengshi (2001) "Development of Environmental NGOs in Mainland China, Taiwan and Hong Kong," *Green NGO and Environmental Journalist Forum*, Washington, DC: Woodrow Wilson International Center for Scholars.

US Embassy Beijing (2000a) *The Cost of Environmental Degradation in China*. Available online: www.usembassy-china.org.cn/sandt/CostofPollution-web.html (accessed August 11, 2004).

—— (2000b) *Beijing Environment, Science and Technology Update* (September 8). Available online: www.usembassy-china.org.cn/sandt/estnews0908.htm (accessed May 23, 2007).

—— (1997) *Environmental NGOs in China: Green is Good, But Don't Openly Oppose the Party* (December). Available online: www.usembassy-china.org.cn/sandt/ sandtbak-hp.html#Environment--target (accessed August 6, 2004).

Vermeer, Eduard B. (1998) "Industrial Pollution in China and Remedial Policies," *The China Quarterly*, 156 (December).

"Violent Protests Against Polluting Factories," *AsiaNews*, April 12, 2006. Available online: www.asianews.it/view.php?l=en&art=5897 (accessed April 21, 2006).

Wang Canfa and Ongley, Edwin (2004) "Transjurisdictional Water Pollution Management: The Huai River Example," *Water International*, 29(3) (September).

White, Gordon (1996) "The Dynamics of Civil Society in Post-Mao China," in Hook, Brian (ed.), *The Individual and the State in China*, Oxford: Clarendon Press.

Wiktorowicz, Quintan (2000) "Civil Society and Social Control: State Power in Jordan," *Comparative Politics*, 33(1) (October): 43–61.

World Resources Institute (2003) *Earth Trends Data Tables: Economic, Business and the Environment*. Available online: http://earthtrends.wri.org/pdf_library/data_tables/ ecn1_2003.pdf (accessed July 28, 2004).

Wu Fengshi (2002) "New Partners or Old Brothers? GONGOs in Transnational Environmental Advocacy in China," *China Environment Series* 5, Washington, DC: Woodrow Wilson Center, the Environmental Change and Security Project.

Yang Guobin (2005) "Environmental NGOs and Institutional Dynamics in China," *The China Quarterly*, 181.

Yu Keping (2002) "The Emerging of Chinese Civil Society and its Significance to Governance in Rural China." Available online: www.ids.ac.uk/ids/civsoc/final/china/ chi1.html (accessed February 20, 2004).

5 "Harmonious society," "peaceful re-unification," and the dilemmas raised by Taiwanese philanthropy[1]

André Laliberté

Introduction

The claims that the Chinese Communist Party (CCP) can provide people with an improvement in their welfare and that it can enforce national unity represent two major pillars of its legitimacy. The assertion that the Chinese party-state can offer quasi-universal access to social services has been increasingly challenged as the reforms launched by Deng Xiaoping and implemented by his successor Jiang Zemin have gradually eroded the affordability of services in education, health care, and pensions. Concerned that this situation could lead to social instability, Jiang, and his successor Hu Jintao, decided to respond to this challenge by giving the private sector greater importance in the delivery of social services, and by calling upon the philanthropic sector for help. One can assume from these premises that the offer by a Taiwanese charity to provide disaster relief in the People's Republic of China (PRC) should be well received, because it can help meet the two central priorities of "harmonious society"—which Hu Jintao links to a greater emphasis on social development, and "peaceful re-unification" with Taiwan.[2] Yet, as this chapter documents, since 1991 the activities in the PRC of Taiwan's largest charity, the Tzu Chi Foundation (hereafter Tzu Chi),[3] have elicited a wide variety of responses at local levels, ranging from some cases of genuine cooperation to cases of outright rejection and mistrust—despite their impeccable credentials as non-political compatriots. Is this diversity of responses to a policy determined at the center an illustration of fragmented authoritarianism, of conflicts between central and local governments, or of competition between local governments? This chapter takes a different approach and argues instead that these diverse responses display the capacity of the Chinese state to adapt to change.

The argument unfolds as follows: by including provisions for the inclusion of Tzu Chi volunteers in the implementation of some of its policies, but simultaneously giving local government considerable leeway in accepting or refusing them in the territory they administer, the Chinese central government tries to strike a balance between a variety of objectives and interests from different tiers of governments as well as across different regions. Welcoming major actors of a Taiwanese civil society like Tzu Chi represents a political gesture of symbolic importance by the central government that can reinforce the CCP's claim to enforce national unity. In addition, by letting Tzu Chi's volunteers provide relief in regions that are impoverished, this initiative can reinforce its claim that it cares for the poor. The evidence provided below, however, will show that many local cadres do not agree with that perspective and do not believe that it buttresses their legitimacy. Although some pessimistic accounts of Chinese politics may look at this diversity of views as an indication of incoherence and fragmentation in the governance of the CCP, the argument presented here proposes a different view, premised on the state capability to adapt to a wide variety of circumstances.

The chapter is based on fieldwork in six counties in Hubei and Hebei during the spring of 2004 and 2006, where interviews were conducted with local government officials, and representatives of various charities located in these two provinces. The activities of Tzu Chi in Hubei and Hebei are typical of most activities it has undertaken in China since 1991 in provinces as prosperous as Jiangsu and as poor as Guizhou. The chapter also relies on interviews conducted in Taiwan and in Canada over a period of seven years with Tzu Chi volunteers, staff in its TV network, and members of the organization's board of directors involved in cross-strait relief operations. The information gathered from these interviews has been supplemented and cross-checked with government publications, research reports, newspapers articles and studies by academics, as well as an extensive survey of Tzu Chi archives. This chapter does not claim that the response of local governments to the activities of that charity organization is representative of their response to all other charities, philanthropic societies or NGOs, but it does shed light on how local governments relate to an organization with a background that is seen as politically problematic. In addition, the sensitivity of this issue can hardly be overestimated: during periods of tensions in cross-strait relations, the operations of Tzu Chi in the PRC were criticized by many Taiwanese, and as a result, its volunteers are hesitant to disclose too much detail about their activities on the Mainland. For similar reasons, as will be made clear later, local Chinese officials have, for various reasons, often been reluctant to discuss the presence of Tzu Chi in areas under their jurisdiction. These constraints on both sides have imposed limitations in the course of the fieldwork, and therefore results presented here cannot claim to be exhaustive. Nevertheless, the central point of local government's diverse response to Tzu Chi can be substantiated.

The chapter is organized as follows: it first presents the theoretical framework used to analyze the varied responses of the state to the presence of Tzu Chi in the PRC. Then, it provides context by presenting the revival of charities in China, and points to the contribution of organizations from Taiwan, whose presence in the PRC embodies the CCP claims that it works for national unification. A third section summarizes the rationale for the inclusion of charities in the implementation of social policies, thereby emphasizing their relevance to another dimension of state legitimacy. Then, a fourth section describes the contribution of Tzu Chi to disaster relief and the provision of social services. The final section documents the state's role in facilitating or hindering this work, by presenting examples from the central government and three lower tiers of governments in Hubei and Hebei, at the provincial (*sheng* 省), prefectural (*shi* 市), and county (*xian* 县) level.

Theorizing the dilemmas raised by charities for State legitimacy

Political sensitivities in the central government

The ability to provide welfare and to enforce national unity represents a foundation of regime legitimacy in the PRC, but in some cases, it also presents the government with some thorny dilemmas. For example, should the CCP accept the involvement of religious organizations in the provision of social services, at the risk of undermining its legitimacy as a provider of social services? In particular, should the Chinese Government accept the valuable connections of religious organizations coming from abroad, whether Western, Asian, or overseas Chinese, or reject it on the ground of ideological purity, lest it undercut its claim that under its guidance, China is self-reliant? The evidence presented below will show that in the last few years the CCP has accepted change to long-held policies and has decided to face these dilemmas head on by leaning on the side of greater openness.[4] Hence, the regime has opted to let Chinese grass-roots religious organizations provide social services,[5] and has accepted help from foreign aid organizations, regardless of whether they are faith-based or not.

Religious organizations from Taiwan, however, put CCP officials in an additional quandary. Taiwanese residents are officially not considered "foreigners" by the PRC authorities, and should, therefore, theoretically abide by the regulations followed by other Chinese religious organizations when in the PRC. These organizations, therefore, should not proselytize and, obviously, should not get involved in politics. As this chapter will elaborate later, Tzu Chi could meet these constraints because in Taiwan it has presented itself as a charity rather than as a religious organization in order to perform its activities during the period of martial law in the island.[6] Within these very narrow parameters, the CCP can expect to reap some substantial benefits from the visit of Taiwanese religious organizations in the PRC: authorizing such a presence could demonstrate to the Chinese and to outsiders the CCP's commitment to exchanges across the strait, and underwrites the PRC's pledge to protect freedom of religion. In sum, the PRC central government has reasons to accept provision of relief by Taiwanese religious organizations on its territory, and it has acted accordingly by letting them into China, and ensuring their presence conforms to legislation. Yet, the activities of Tzu Chi in China do not receive much publicity.[7] This could suggest that not everyone in the central government believes in the expected benefits for state legitimacy that could be brought by welcoming a charity from Taiwan.

Access to central leaders to discuss this issue is impossible because relations between China and Taiwan are considered too sensitive.[8] This chapter will not attempt to speculate on possible disagreements between various agencies in the central government to explain its lukewarm response to the activities of Tzu Chi in China. But that still leaves us with the issue of regional variations in the response to its activities. Are these variations responding to a plan designed by the central government—however reluctantly it may want to publicize it—or do they reflect local realities? Assuming that the central government has such a plan, one may expect that Tzu Chi has been directed in the Western regions and in the poor areas. The available evidence discussed later in this chapter about the presence of Tzu Chi in China does not show a clear fit between the regions where Tzu Chi has been and the regions that face greater need. Which elements account for this situation? In other words, while authorization for charities' activities, especially for those that come from outside the PRC, depends on decisions made by the central government agencies, implementation of these decisions is left to provincial governments and authorities at lower levels. To what extent do the latter comply with decisions made in the center?

The latitude of provincial and prefecture governments

Recent research on the political economy of China's provinces has underlined the increase in provinces' power and influence in determining their own future, and therefore the likelihood that they will pursue economic policies different from each other (Hendrischke 1999). But this provincial leeway does not mean that the central government is losing control. Chung Jae Ho (2001: 66) has argued that the center can relinquish its prerogatives for policies local governments can manage for the benefit of the whole country, but maintain its prerogatives for issues it deems more sensitive. Hence, successive cycles of decentralization since the beginning of the post-Mao era have led to growing autonomy in the area of economic policy for local governments, and as a result, uniform compliance in that domain has been increasingly difficult to enforce. Yet, on controversial issues such as political reform, the center's authority has remained decisive. This ability of provinces to determine their own economic policies, in other words, could provide explanations for the diverse approaches provincial governments adopt for their social policy, including their reliance on charities. The widening disparity of social and economic conditions between provinces matches the diversity of priorities and the variety of calculations among provinces about the best trade-offs between self-reliance, and cooperation with outside charities and NGOs for the provision of social services. Yet, the cleavage between the wealthy coastal provinces and the poor interior does not help predict where charities are going to be active.[9] This suggests that different provinces with similar social and economic conditions may have different views on the most appropriate way to handle potentially sensitive issues.

This chapter argues that this variation observed among provinces in their relations with organizations like Tzu Chi, should not be taken as an indication that the central government is losing control. Alarmist statements have been made in the past about increasing regional inequalities and the stress this imposes on governance. Some have argued that the state is losing the capacity to hold the country together because of fiscal imbalances.[10] Yet, despite widespread stress in Chinese society coming from workers' unrest and peasants' protests, and challenges raised by environmental disasters and epidemics, the regime has proven resilient. More recent scholarship has taken a different view and sees in the Chinese state an impressive ability to withstand important challenges despite in-depth economic changes. The greater leeway granted to provinces in decision-making for policy areas that are deemed less important, goes hand in hand with a steady control by the CCP over issues the party consider critical to legitimacy (Naughton and Yang 2004: 7). This leaves the question of explaining why there are variations at lower levels of government, once provincial authorities have decided that the presence of charities in the areas under their control does not threaten their legitimacy.

Prudent calculations from county leaders

Dissimilarities in the approaches adopted by neighbouring prefectures may result from dynamics that are similar to those of provinces. If this level of government was mandated after 1949 to merely supervise county governments on behalf of provincial authorities, research by Yang Zhong has shown an expansion of prefecture governments' powers in the 1990s, and therefore, their ability to adopt policies that may differ with those of neighbouring prefectures in similar conditions (Yang 2003: 68). Differences between neighbouring county level governments, however, cannot be explained by greater scope in decision-making or policy implementation: counties have seen their power decline while the prefecture government's has increased. Yang Zhong attributes differences in policy implementation between neighbouring counties' governments to cadre's material and career interests, and the use they make of the institutional constraints of the political system. In particular, he suggests that some cadres implement policies determined at the center more faithfully than others according to varying degrees of scrutiny from authorities above them.[11]

Another factor likely to influence variance in policy implementation is the structure of incentives for cadres, which vary according to whether they are "promotable" or "terminal." The former are younger and more educated and because they are more likely to be promoted, they are more likely to implement governments' policies, while the latter, who cannot expect promotion because of their age and educational shortcoming, are more likely to adopt rent-seeking behavior (Yang 2003: 188–9). Differences between local governments in policy implementation, finally, should be greater for policies that are judged less important: failure to meet objectives such as providing local stability, developing the local economy and managing population growth threatens any chance of promotion and is likely to receive more attention from cadres, especially when they are "promotable," but consequences are not serious for policies that are considered less critical (Yang 2003: 189). The next sections will introduce two sets of policies that bear on the acceptance of Taiwanese charities, and then will turn to the responses of local governments to the guidelines put in place by the center.

Opening China for development

China under Mao looked at self-reliance and autarky as a means to ensure regime legitimacy. This approach was taken to a deadly extreme in 1976 when the CCP, then under the influence of the Gang of Four, rejected the offer of international assistance after the Tangshan earthquake killed over 255,000 people. Upon assuming power in 1978, Deng Xiaoping chose to adopt a different approach and prioritized economic growth. Two policies were proclaimed to help achieve this central goal: the policy of reform and opening, to attract foreign investments; and the policy of "one country, two systems," ostensibly to achieve national unity and assume control over Hong Kong, Macau, and Taiwan, but also to benefit from the support of ethnic Chinese business networks. At the beginning of the twenty-first century, the goal of national unification remains unachieved because of the *de facto* independence of the Republic of China (ROC) in Taiwan. Meanwhile, the success of the reform and opening policy has come at the cost of increasing social inequalities and mounting unrest. In that new context, the development of a social safety net has emerged as a priority to ensure regime legitimacy, and the targeting of the most destitute in the Western regions and in designated poor counties, is a symbolically important component of that policy. Transnational organizations were considered an important instrument to help achieve these two policies.

The first charities that the government promoted were domestic. In 1982, the CCP encouraged the creation of the Soong Ching Ling Foundation [*Song Qingling Jijinhui* 宋庆龄基金会] (SCLF). The organization was supporting CCP United Front work within China and among overseas communities, helping the government attract investments from abroad. The China Youth Development Foundation (CYDF) [*Zhongguo qingshaonian fazhan jijinhui* 中国青少年发展基金会][12] and the China Welfare Institute (CWI) [*Zhongguo fulihui* 中国福利会],[13] were set up with similar goals in mind. However, these appeared insufficient to meet the growing needs of Chinese society. In welcoming overseas-based NGOs, including trans-national philanthropic societies and religious charities, the PRC could find the international cooperation, as well as the financial and technical support, for the resolution of socio-economic problems that the state was ill equipped to deal with in the early 1980s.

In contrast to the response to the Tangshan earthquake of 1976, in 1991 the Chinese Ministry of Foreign Economic Relations and Trade (MOFERT) launched an appeal to the international community for help in disaster relief after devastating floods affected over 120 million residents of Central China. Among these organizations, not only were there humanitarian and development organizations linked to the UN system such as UNICEF and the WHO, but also philanthropic societies, including various national branches of the Red Cross, Care, and *Médecins sans frontières*, as well as religious charities such as World Vision and the Amity Foundation (UN Department of Humanitarian Affairs 1991). The presence of international organizations affiliated to the UN did not represent a dramatic change: UNICEF had opened a branch office in China in 1979. The presence of wealthy organizations with strong technical and scientific expertise was not a major innovation either: the Asia Foundation and the Ford Foundation had been active in China since 1979. The acceptance of trans-national religious charities, however, represented an unprecedented development in the PRC.

The authorities had realized that they should not close the door to trans-national religious charities[14] if they wanted to benefit from international resources. Therefore, the Adventist Development Agency, the Young Men's Christian Association (YMCA), the Mennonite Committee, and the Salvation Army, were all welcome alongside secular organizations, such as Care International, Oxfam, and the Red Cross, to assist the government during the 1980s with programs in education, relief provision, and poverty alleviation.[15] The late 1990s saw a deepening of those trends. Throughout the decade, a greater number of Chinese NGOs were created to assist the government with poverty alleviation in impoverished and remote rural counties, and many more overseas organizations were welcomed to provide expertise, training and technical support. The Hong Kong AIDS Foundation (since 1996), *Médecins sans frontières* (since 1995), and the Mercy Corps (since 2000) have opened branches in China during that decade (see Hong Kong AIDS Foundation 2007, Médecins sans frontières 2007, and Mercy Corps 2007).

The decision to rely on foreign, Western or Chinese religious charities for the provision of social services for the last decade has received scant attention from media outside China. Yet, this trend not only represents a marked departure from the CCP approaches to social welfare between 1949 and 1978, but it also reveals some remarkable continuity with traditional Chinese practices established before 1949. In China's long history, organizations that were autonomous from the state have been offering relief to the poor and taking care of some social services. Gernet (1995: 217–23) has documented the role of Buddhist institutions in the provision of welfare between the sixth century and the eleventh century. Liang (1997: 37–40) has described the spread of the "benevolence hall" (*shantang* 善堂), from the late Ming to the end of the Qing, which provided relief to some of the poor and to orphanages across China. Because they embodied traditional structures of power, however, these institutions were rejected outright after 1949 and reliance on religious-inspired philanthropy became unconceivable during the Maoist era on ideological grounds: any suggestion that the CCP was unable to look after the needs of the masses was unacceptable, and any thought that these "feudal" institutions could act positively was considered anathema. The Chinese Government has moved a long way since then: trans-national religious organizations are now seen as part of an economic development strategy, not only because they can provide some relief to the poor, but also because they can foster a boom in tourism.

Improving social policy

This reliance on NGOs suggests that the government has adopted an approach to social policy that does not rely exclusively on the state. This choice, in turn, results from a continuing reflection within Chinese epistemic communities, on the different welfare regimes available around the world, and on the best option for China (see Tang 2004; Shi 2005; Guan 2005; 2000). Chinese scholars have their own approach to the comparative study of social policies, in light of China's own national conditions (*guoqing* 国情), but one can identify their preferences among the three welfare regimes identified in the classical literature on the subject (Gough and Wood 2004; Lin 2000; Merrien 2000; Esping-Andersen 1990). A consensus had already emerged about the inapplicability of the universalist or social-democratic welfare regime being implemented in Scandinavia, which was seen as too onerous and unaffordable (Chou 2003; Wang, M. 2001; Ka 2001; Chen, Y. 2000; Lei and Wang, S. 1999; Xu, D. *et al.* 1999; Zhang and Chen, H. 1999) and the government considered a mix between the two other types of welfare regimes. The corporatist welfare regime, used to define the approach developed initially in Germany and France, was adopted by Japan and Taiwan at earlier stages of their social welfare development, and is implemented in other developing Asian states (Ramesh 2000). The residual welfare regime, which is market-based, emphasizes minimal state intervention, and has been developed most steadfastly in the United States. Decision-makers in the PRC believe that China's own characteristics warrant an approach that mixes together elements of the corporatist welfare regime, which provides for comprehensive social security to state-owned Enterprises (SOEs), employees and civil servants, and elements of the residual approach, which stresses self-help and individual responsibility but also reinforces the commodification of labour (Phillion 1998: 533). Because workers in SOEs are concentrated in urban centers, these policy choices leave the rural population, working the land or in non-state firms, with a more limited number of services, which cannot always be provided by local governments (Zhao, M. 2003). Since the Hu Jintao and

Wen Jiabao team has assumed power, the central government has proposed to improve the livelihood of peasants, but the measures envisioned have one perverse consequence: deprived of revenue, local governments claim that they lack resources for social services provision.[16]

The contrast between the relative social security experienced by urban residents and the limited access to social services for rural residents represents the major difference between China and industrial countries that have adopted a market-based social policy. The principles of a residual welfare regime guide local governments in rural China: health care and education are offered on a fee-for-service basis, and pensions are simply non-existent—many believe that land usage qualifies as wealth.[17] This approach, in China as elsewhere, tends to stigmatize the poor as unable, or unwilling, to find employment, and therefore, as unworthy of public support (Esping-Andersen 1990; Tittmuss 1958). When personal circumstances and misfortunes prevent someone from gaining access to resources for their welfare, proponents of this market-based approach to social policy expect that the family, the community, or private networks—whether they are NGOs, philanthropic societies, charities or religious institutions—should provide help, and believe that the state represents only a last resort (Song *et al.* 2005). Recent research suggests that when the state cannot, or does not want to, intervene in the provision of social services, the family and the community are not always reliable, and therefore the NGOs represent one of the only sources of help that is left.

Hence, the reliance on family does not always deliver the social services expected by the promoters of a residual welfare regime. Although recent research has underlined the redistributive mechanism created by the remittances that workers sent back to their hometown, many of them are compelled to return because of ill fortune and present new challenges for rural welfare policies (Murphy 2002). Brandt and Rozelle (2000) found in their 1995 household survey that extended families play a smaller redistributive role than in the period before 1949. Their findings, which did not find a major discrepancy between urban and rural settings with respect to the role expected of the family, noted that the urban elderly benefit from more generous state-funded pensions, and concluded that it would be wrong to assume that the traditional virtue of filial piety can guarantee better living standards for the elderly in rural areas. On the same issue, Xu Y. (2001: 318) concludes that "while China currently maintains filial laws demanding that children provide for their old parents," the finding in his fieldwork leads him to conclude that to insist on family care for the elderly may put both at great disadvantage and, potentially, at great risk. More recent studies sponsored by CASS on specifics such as health care confirm this finding and question the viability of schemes that rely solely on self-help and the family (Lin 2003).

When the decision-makers in the central government seek an alternative to the SOEs in the provision of social services, and when traditional sources of support in the countryside have failed, reliance on NGOs, whether domestic or international, fulfil a real need. NGOs do not replace the state for the provision of social services but their presence can serve a number of political objectives: easing the pain of transition, and thereby providing an indirect measure of legitimacy to the regime (Wang, Ming 2004; Zhao L. 1999). One particular kind of overseas NGO should represent an especially valued partner for the PRC government in that respect: ethnic Chinese, Hong Kong-, Macau- and Taiwan-based charities. These organizations have the advantage over foreign-based NGOs of a shared Chinese cultural heritage. Taiwan-based charities can also help the Chinese Government achieve another political goal: cooperation with them could demonstrate a good disposition vis-à-vis the Taiwanese compatriots and therefore help the cause of reunification.

Tzu Chi in China

Tzu Chi represents only one actor among the multitude of grass-root Chinese NGOs and the great number of foreign-based ones, but its presence in the PRC is significant because it is a Taiwanese organization active in China despite tensions between the PRC and the ROC. Moreover, Tzu Chi is by far the largest of its kind in Taiwan: with endowments worth 12 billion NT$, it has twice as much in resources as the second largest foundation in Taiwan, the National Arts and Culture Foundation (see Himalaya Foundation 2002). Tzu Chi is the largest of the only seventy-eight organizations, out of the 300 largest Taiwanese foundations that the Himalaya Foundation documents, that are devoted to charity and social welfare. Most of the other foundations finance projects in culture, education and the arts, twenty-seven for medicine and health; twelve for economic development; and three for environment protection. Among the Taiwanese foundations that are involved in charity and social welfare, Tzu Chi has a budget twelve times larger than the Chang Yung-fa Foundation (*Chang Rongfa Jijinhui* 張榮發基金會), the second largest in Taiwan in this particular category (Himalaya Foundation 2002). The foundation does not disclose its budget for activities in the PRC, but it was included in the data bank of the China Development Brief (1999) among the 300 most important NGOs based in Hong Kong, Macao and outside the PRC.[18]

Before moving to the activities of Tzu Chi in China, some more context is in order. Even if one accepts the claim that Tzu Chi is a NGO involved in humanitarian work and charities, this represents a drop in the ocean: in 2001, it was only one among more than 165,000 registered by the (MCA) Ministry of Civil Affairs's NGOs Administrative Bureau, a figure provided by Chen Guangyao (2001), Deputy Bureau Director. Li Yong (2002: 24), head of the MCA's NGO Administrative Bureau, used a different methodology to his subordinate Chen Guangyao; in an article for *Caijing* 財经 he suggested that NGOs could number as many as 830,000 (Bentley 2003: 13; 19). To be sure, NGOs [*feizhengfu zuzhi* 非政府组织] is a label used for many different kinds of organizations: non-profit organizations [*feiyingli* 非营利

zuzhi], community-run non-commercial work units [*minban feiqiye danwei* 民办非企业单位], social groupings [*shehui tuanti* 社会团体] (Ogden 2002; Pei 1998; Saich 2000), and this figure may overestimate the number of NGOs. If one excludes associations related to industry, trade, business and advocacy, and those that are related to academia, this leaves one-third of the above number. This number can be reduced further if, to be defined as NGOs, an organization has to be truly independent. In many cases, as examples in the next section will illustrate, it is often difficult to ascertain when specific organizations are truly independent from government and when they are just government-organized NGOs (GONGOs). On the other hand, many autonomous organizations that are not registered officially are not counted as NGOs (Bentley 2003: 13;19).

Shih and Young (2003) have looked at a possible relationship between the presence of international NGOs in China and the growth of grass-roots NGOs in the PRC. The economic impact of remittances from overseas Chinese, they noted, was significant from the end of the nineteenth century to the 1940s, and after 1978 there has been a remarkable renewal in the donations to health care, education and other projects that philanthropy from overseas Chinese communities has established. Their investigation, however, has found that wealthy people from Hong Kong, Macau and Taiwan have contributed significantly to the endowments of major universities, but have yet to make a big difference to Chinese charities. Their study also shows that international charities such as World Vision have targeted overseas Chinese communities in North America to finance their projects in the PRC.

A major study by David Zweig (2002: 253–4) also reveals that often local governments took the initiative in attracting this wealth. After Deng Xiaping's Southern Tour in 1992, and especially after the 1994 taxation reform affected local governments' revenues, he demonstrates that international NGOs were welcomed by authorities at the prefecture and county levels that wanted help for many welfare projects but could not afford to finance them. It is in this rather favourable set of combined circumstances that the board of directors of Tzu Chi, through the kinship connection existing between people across the Taiwan strait, could respond positively to the demands for help from victims of a flood in Jiangsu in 1991 (Tzu Chi Foundation 2001a: 23).

The presence in the PRC of volunteers from Tzu Chi has been accepted by the relevant authorities at the highest level since the beginning. The agency responsible for coordinating relief work with Tzu Chi and all other NGOs based outside the PRC is the MCA. Its Minister between 1991 and 1994, Yan Mingfu 阎明复 , was a prominent liberal in the previous Zhao Ziyang adminis-tration, and an advocate of greater NGO participation, whether they were Chinese or foreign, secular or religious (Carnes 2003: 34). Acceptance of Tzu Chi in China, in the climate of improving cross-strait relations, was natural. In 1994, Yan resigned from the Ministry to head a new organization set up to encourage cooperation between local and international NGOs, the China Charity Foundation (CCF) [*Zhonghua cishan zonghui* 中华慈善总会]. As

CCF head until 2000, he continued to support the presence of Tzu Chi in the PRC and in 2005, his successor appeared willing to continue this policy of cooperation. One indicator of Tzu Chi's importance to the CCF was the presence among the CCF's honorary advisors [*rongyu guwen* 荣誉顾问] of Wang Duanzheng 王端正, Tzu Chi's vice-director [副执行长] (Zhonghua cishan zonghui 2003). This cooperation, however, does not mean coordination between Tzu Chi and the CCF. In 2005, the CCF counted fifty-nine affiliated organizations within the PRC, but a survey of these branches' location did not match the location of the counties visited by volunteers from Tzu Chi.

The operations of volunteers from Tzu Chi in China are limited to the provision of social services, and exclude proselytizing: in that particular respect, they differ from the activities undertaken in Taiwan and in other countries where the Foundation has established branches. The activities of Tzu Chi in Taiwan cover eight different categories: charity; medical help; education; cultural services; bone marrow donation; international relief; environmental protection; and community work. The activities in mainland China do not fall within the category of international relief, as inhabitants of the People's Republic are considered "compatriots" in the literature available at Tzu Chi cultural center. They cover all the other seven categories but to a varying extent, relief representing the most important contribution, followed by medical services, education, and the development of the bone-marrow data bank. Volunteers have distributed diverse forms of emergency relief in areas affected by flood, drought, or harsh winters. The relief delivered included food, clothes, quilts, and sometimes cash, coal, fertilizers and seeds to help people recover from natural disasters. The medical help included free clinics and financial support for the rehabilitation of children's hospitals. The education component of Tzu Chi activities included helping to rebuild primary and junior high schools, as well as the grant of scholarships to pupils in impoverished areas.[19]

Volunteers from Tzu Chi have been present in fourteen provinces and two autonomous regions since 1991, mainly in the coastal and central parts of the country. In 2005, they had not yet gone to most provinces and autonomous regions of the Western area, except for relief operations for national minority people in Guizhou and brief operations in Gansu, Qinghai, and Inner Mongolia.[20] With only a few exceptions, a majority of the sites visited by Tzu Chi were located in impoverished counties affected by flood, droughts, typhoons, and other natural disasters. The activities of Tzu Chi have focused primarily on emergency relief, and have sometimes included medical care and free clinics. But the organization has also sought to leave a more permanent mark in China. In 1997, the board of directors approved the building of schools, from kindergarten to junior high, in twenty-four counties scattered through seven provinces. In 1991 and 2000, it also helped in the construction of nursing homes, primarily in Quanjiao 全椒 (Anhui), and in Xinghua 興化 (Jiangsu). Since 2000, the board of directors of Tzu Chi has approved the grant of scholarships to students in Jiangxi, Fujian and Guizhou, as well as technical assistance for water conservation in Gansu (Tzu Chi Foundation 2005).

All these activities had to follow a rigorous protocol determined by the directors of Tzu Chi and the MCA. Demands for help by local authorities in areas in need are transmitted to local civil affairs bureaus, which then communicate requests to the central government. The MCA informs the CCF, which, in its capacity as a charity, can deal directly with local and international NGOs and relevant agencies and then select the organizations that will be invited to provide relief. If they have received an invitation from the CCF to that effect, a delegation sent by Tzu Chi can investigate (*kanzai* 勘灾) the situation in disaster areas within less than a week and report back to the headquarters in Hualien, where relief projects are designed and approved by its founder herself.[21] The projects approved are classified as disaster relief (*zhenzai* 赈灾), or distribution of food (*fafang* 发放). Volunteers who go to China are recruited primarily in Taiwan, but occasionally, overseas Chinese also join the operations.[22]

The activities of volunteers from Tzu Chi in China are guided by the same five principles that they must respect in Taiwan or elsewhere. The first of these principles is directness (*zhijie* 直接). It means that aid must directly reach the hands of the natural disaster victims, without the intervention of a third party. The application of this principle cannot, obviously, mean bypassing the authorities in the People's Republic: volunteers for Tzu Chi fulfill this part of their pledge by ensuring they are present alongside local party and government officials in public meetings in which hundreds of people from the affected communities are assembled to receive relief. The second principle, priority (*zhongdian* 重点), emphasizes the necessity to offer relief to the areas that face the worst situation.[23] The three other principles advocated by volunteers for Tzu Chi do not present a particular problem for the Chinese authorities at any level: respect for local lifestyle, customs, cultures, and traditions (*zunzhong* 尊重); timeliness of the relief provision (*jishi* 章华); and parsimonious use of resources (*wushi* 务实).[24] Finally, during the distribution of relief, volunteers for Tzu Chi must respect an additional principle with special relevance for the People's Republic, the Three No's: no politics, no religion, and no propaganda (Tzu Chi Foundation 2001b). Volunteers have always been scrupulous in respecting this requirement, realizing that to violate this principle would compromise their future in China.

These activities, inoffensive politically and helpful from the perspectives of impoverished county leaders, have been emulated by others in the late nineties. Hence, the *Hebei fojiao cishan gongdehui* 河北佛教慈善基金会 claim to have adopted the same methods and approach of Tzu Chi, which are derived from the theological innovation of a prominent monk of the early twentieth century, Taixu 太虚 .[25] Similar developments have been observed in Hubei province, where the Wuzu 五祖 temple in Eastern Hubei[26] and the Zhanhua 章华 temple in Jingzhou[27] provide some relief to the poor. Other groups from Hong Kong, such as the *Cihui fojiao jijnhui* 慈辉佛教基金会 , have adopted an approach that bears striking similarities with the method used by Tzu Chi. In sum, this process of imitation (or mutual borrowing, it is too early to say) suggests that the government policy was a success for both the CCF and Tzu Chi. The central government, and the MCA in particular, have unambiguously welcomed the activities of Tzu Chi in the PRC since 1991, despite the ups and downs of cross-strait relations and changes in the administrations, because they serve immediate humanitarian concerns as well as long-term objectives such as national unification; for Tzu Chi, it fosters the spiritual goals of its volunteers and thereby gives a boost to the organization. The relations between volunteers from the Foundation and local officials, however, presents a more complex picture, as the next section on the interaction between these volunteers and local authorities in Hubei and Hebei shows.

Analysis

The CCP seeks to present to the outside world the image of a unified direction, but as the response, documented below, to the presence of Tzu Chi in China since 1991 illustrates, lower levels of governments have understood the guidelines from above in different ways and as a result have not implemented them uniformly. This variety of outcomes is found between different local governments, and it is indicative of a diversity of views about the most effective ways to meet the challenge of poverty alleviation. These disagreements over policies, however, are not indicative of a fundamental and widespread cleavage between all local governments and the center: some local governments have approved the decision of the central government to let in trans-national religious charities, while others have refused to comply. With the exception of the MCA, and later, the CCF, no other ministry, commission or institution of importance is known to have been involved in the negotiations to let volunteers from Tzu Chi move to China; and until CCP departments are willing to disclose publicly their views on the acceptance of a charity with a religious identity from the "rebel province," this article cannot reach conclusions about the degree of consensus about this policy in Beijing. Yet, the evidence below will point to some of the factors likely to explain the diversity of outcomes observed before: unease in the central government over potentially sensitive issues; increasing latitude in provincial governments' ability to determine their priorities; and local cadres' calculus about the consequences for their careers if they implement the policies.

Political sensitivities in central government

Domestic charities in China must first secure approval from the MCA for their operation: they must comply with regulations and rules relevant for charities, foundations and NGOs. If they are religious organizations, they must also be approved by the bureau for religious affairs. Similar rules apply to trans-national organizations, whose affairs are handled by bureaux for foreign affairs (*waishi*) at various levels of government, even if they are invited by a local partner organization. However, Tzu Chi raises a particular conundrum: the organization has established branches in all continents, and some of its members are American, Canadian, and European citizens, which should be enough to qualify as a trans-national organization. However, the headquarters of Tzu Chi is in Taiwan, which is officially considered "Chinese territory." If the religious nature of Tzu Chi does not represent an insurmountable difficulty, its "Taiwanese-ness" could have been problematic because relations between the PRC and the ROC have gone through a series of tensions in 1995–6, 1999 and 2000. Yet, the CCP has demonstrated a remarkable resilience and continuity with respect to Tzu Chi since 1992, because every year Tzu Chi volunteers have been allowed to perform disaster relief at various locations in the PRC.[28]

Different signs suggest that even while the leadership of the CCP has accepted the presence of Tzu Chi in China throughout that period, some unease has remained. Even though the MCA has been instrumental in bringing volunteers of Tzu Chi to China since 1991, no mention of this activity is available in its data bank on Hong Kong, Macau, and Taiwan affairs (Minzhengbu 2005). A similar lack of interest is expressed by the Bureau for Taiwan Affairs. Its section on cross-strait exchanges since 2003, does not make any reference to Tzu Chi either (*Taiwan shiwu bangongshi* 2005), despite the existence of relief activities in Guizhou and Anhui sponsored by the Foundation in 2004. This shortcoming appears all the more surprising since the activities of Tzu Chi should, in theory, appeal to the Chinese government as a demonstration of patriotism from Taiwanese. The same indifference towards the activities of Tzu Chi exists in the media: surveys of the *Renmin Ribao* between 2000 and 2005 yields forty eight stories about the presence of the organization in the PRC, the majority of them relating to the bone marrow operations that the Tzu Chi hospital is known for, while a search with Sohu, which also reports stories from Hong Kong, Taiwan, and overseas Chinese communities, yields over 6,000 stories on the charity in China. At lower levels of governments, in the provinces, prefectures, and counties where volunteers from Tzu Chi were present, interviews with local officials would reveal a similar reluctance to mention the existence of such activities.

Once volunteers from Tzu Chi were authorized by the MCA to visit China and provide relief, cooperation from the other branches of central government was necessary. For example, volunteers who provided relief to victims of the 1993 flood in Hunan used clothes made in Anhui and had to rely on the PLA for the distribution of these goods. The MCA had to send instructions to three provincial governments and coordinate efforts with the Ministry of National Defense (Tzu Chi Foundation 2000a: 33). Even when the volunteers from Tzu Chi received such support from the MCA, the PLA and other institutions such as the CCF, they could not always assume that they could reach the population they wanted to help. This was especially true when the organization wanted to establish a more lasting presence and contribute to the expansion of existing institutions, the reconstruction of old ones, or the creation of new others. Direct observations from two provinces and evidence from the organization itself are enough to demonstrate this disparity of approaches from local governments. Even when provincial governments afflicted by natural disasters welcomed the presence of such charities, authorities below at the level of the prefecture or the county could oppose it. The next section attempts to understand why that is the case.

The latitude of provincial and local governments

The governments of fourteen provinces and the two autonomous regions of Inner Mongolia and Guangxi, and the three special municipalities of Beijing, Shanghai and Tianjin, have authorized, at some point or another, volunteers from Tzu Chi within the territory under their control to offer some social services. For the eight provinces, the three autonomous regions and the special municipality of Chongqing where volunteers were not invited to provide relief, it is not clear whether this was because their presence was not allowed, because the central government refused to let them in, or because the board of directors of Tzu Chi, for whatever reasons, did not want to go there. It is certainly not because these territories did not need support from the outside: seven of them are included in the central government's plan for the Western region development. The rural counties where volunteers from Tzu Chi went were impoverished, but they were not always among the poorest within the lists of designated counties drawn up by central agencies to help the government plan its strategies for poverty alleviation. Conversely, many of these poor counties were not visited by volunteers from the Taiwanese charity (Zhongguo fupin xinxi 2005). Despite its many resources, Tzu Chi could not afford to go to all counties affected by poverty. Yet, many of those counties where it did go, were not necessarily those where the needs were the greatest. This suggest that if some local governments were willing to have relief provided by Taiwanese or other outside NGOs, others did not want such form of help.[29]

The provincial governments that have admitted volunteers from Tzu Chi have cooperated with varying degrees of enthusiasm. On the one hand, provincial governments of Anhui, Jiangsu, Hebei, Jiangxi, Hunan, and Fujian have accepted assistance from the Taiwanese charity to finance the building of schools and even clinics for rural residents. Anhui provincial authorities went the furthest: they let volunteers establish nursing homes and rebuild villages destroyed by flood in Quanjiao 全椒 county in 1991. On the other hand, other provinces that have received emergency relief support from Tzu Chi have not let it contribute to the establishment of a more lasting presence. The provincial authorities of Hubei, for instance, welcomed emergency relief for over 10,000 rural residents from Tzu Chi's volunteers after the deadly floods of 1998 and 1999, but would not invite them in to establish more permanent institutions in the countryside, as the authorities of Anhui did in the 1991 and 1992 floods (Tzu Chi Foundation 2000b; 2000c). This disparity of approaches reflects the fact that provincial governments have adopted different policies in their response to the threats posed by natural disasters and in their poverty alleviation strategies. Dissimilarities in the administrative structure of local governments reflect these differences over policies.

The governments of Hubei and Hebei appear to have adopted similar mechanisms to address the welfare needs of the population, replicating the structure found in the central government. Both provinces' Departments (*ting* 厅) of Labour and Social Security look after the welfare of urban workers, and both provincial governments' Departments of Civil Affairs (DCA) manage the welfare of the rural population and relations with NGOs. The provinces, however, have adopted different approaches in the implementation of their social policy targeted at the poorest. The Hubei government's DCA has encouraged the creation of a Hubei Charity Federation (*Hubei cishan zonghui* 湖北慈善总会), an organization that provides social services to children in impoverished counties, and whose links with the provincial DCA are quite close: the office space is located in the DCA building and its staff comprises former DCA officials.[30] The Hebei government has adopted a different approach: it has not established a province-wide charity organization. Instead, the authorities have supported the creation of a charity affiliated to the provincial Buddhist organization, the *Hebei fojiao cishan gongdehui* 河北佛教慈善功德会, or they have allowed the creation of their own charities by prefecture (in Xingtai 邢台, Shijiazhuang 石家庄 and Zhangjiakou 张家口), or county (Qianxi 迁西 and Luan 滦) governments.

Prefecture governments can implement differently the policies adopted by the provinces. In the primarily rural prefectures of Jingzhou 荆州 Ezhou 鄂州 and Huangshi 黄石, in Hubei, local governments have welcomed the presence of volunteers from Tzu Chi in their midst but have not let them establish any lasting presence. In the urban prefecture of Wuhan, the Taiwanese charity was successful in helping to reopen a children's welfare institute in Wuchang, the *Ciji Ertong Fuliyuan*. These differences reflect the diversity of approaches prefecture governments have adopted to deal with quasi-governmental local charities affiliated to the CCF (*Zhongguo cishan zongshi* 2005). The prefectures of Wuhan and Xiaogan 孝感 have established their own charities, and the Yichang 宜昌 and the Enshi 恩施 autonomous prefecture (*cizhizhou* 自治州) have set up preparatory committees (cishan xiehui 慈善协会), but the other prefectures in Hubei have not. The rationale for these differences remains to be investigated: social and economic indicators suggest for 2000 that the prefecture initiatives are not related to their respective wealth or poverty. Wuhan is the wealthiest of the province's prefectures (the value of its production was three times that of the second wealthiest prefecture in 2000), but Enshi ranks among the lowest tier (*Hubei sheng tongji* 2001: 22). Some of the prefecture governments that have experienced important natural disasters and may have had reasons to wish for the establishment of charities preferred not to set up one and rely instead on other sources of support, from the private sector or the community.

This was the case in the Jingzhou prefecture, which oversees Jianli 监利 , a rural county known during the 90s for the desperate situation of its people (Li, C. 2001).[31] Jingzhou officials did not see the necessity for setting up a prefecture-wide charity: they believed that economic development would suffice to help them assess the needs of the poor.[32] Reconstruction initiatives in the prefecture were achieved without the intervention of a quasi-official charity nor the provincial charity federation. For example, schools that were damaged by the flood in the county of Gong'an 公安 have been rebuilt with the support of major firms, such as the Chinese carmaker Liaoyuan 燎原 .[33] Rural residents of Gong'an had received relief from the rural branches of the Zhanhua 章华 temple in Jingzhou city.[34] A similar approach to charity was found in Huanggang 黄冈 prefecture, in the eastern part of Hubei. The government of this prefecture did not set up a charity either but the community of the Wuzu 五祖 temple, a popular tourist destination, offered relief to the local people and rural emigrants in Wuhan.[35]

In sum, significant variations in policies toward NGOs have been seen between two provinces, as well as between prefectures and between counties with similar characteristics. The contrasts between provinces can be explained by their respective political preferences: Hubei has inherited from a more conservative political culture that prefers to focus on a macro-economic strategy of "rising abruptly" (Zhao L.Y. 2001) rather than bold social experiments. The diversity among prefectures remains to be explained since they are, in theory, supposed to merely represent the provincial authority and coordinate counties under their jurisdiction. Yang Zhong, however, has noted that in the 1990s, the bureaucracy of the prefectures has increased, and their power has grown significantly at the expense of the counties (Yang 2003: 69). Disparities in the implementation by counties of policies adopted above them represent a different matter.

Calculations from local leaders

Finally, even when a prefecture government agrees on a policy determined at a higher level, county authorities can trump what has been decided above them. The fate of the school projects supported by Tzu Chi in the prefecture of Shijiazhuang illustrates this situation. Impoverished peasants living in the arid foothills in the prefecture's Western region had been affected by a sudden flood, caused by the Herb Typhoon in 1996. Volunteers from Tzu Chi had cooperated with provincial and prefecture governments to provide relief. One year later, after negotiations with the provincial Civil Affairs department, Tzu Chi had planned to establish four schools in the three adjacent counties of Pingshan, Jingxing 井陉 and Zanhuang 赞皇 and memoranda of understanding were obtained to rebuild schools in these regions.[36] By 2004, only the Junior High School of Jieshan 皆山 , in Jingxing, was running: the projects for the other schools had been abandoned. This was not because Jingxing County was more impoverished than its neighbors: rural household per capita net income for the county residents ranked higher than for residents of Pingshan and Zanhuang, the two poorest counties in the prefecture (HSRZ 2003: 447). Not only did Jingxing welcomed Tzu Chi to help build a school, it also accepted support from another Taiwanese charity, the *Cixin Cishan Shiye Jijinhui* 慈心慈善事业基金会 .

In Pingshan county, negotiations for the building of a school with the help of volunteers from Tzu Chi floundered after local county authorities and representatives of Tzu Chi refused to agree on the issue of acknowledgment for the latter's contribution. Donators from Tzu Chi wanted an advertisement recognizing their contribution in front of the school they planned to help rebuild, as is the case with other donators, like the carmaker in the Gong'an county school, for instance, and as was the case with the school Tzu Chi helped build in the neighbouring county. This was not the first time the charity from Taiwan had to face this issue: in Wuhan, for example, staff responsible for the child rehabilitation center ignored—or were reluctant to acknowledge—the contribution of Tzu Chi, although a modest commemorative plaque, or *gongdepai* 公德碑 , giving details about the identity of the donor organization, was established in a courtyard within the center. In Pingshan, however, acknowledging the identity of an organization from Taiwan had proven to be too sensitive a political issue.

Pingshan ranks high in the CCP list of sites with an historical significance: this is where Xibaipo 西柏坡 is located, the CCP headquarter between 1947 and 1949. In this case, national historical memories cast a long shadow on local considerations and the prospect of welcoming an organization with ties to the "renegade province" have appeared unbearable to the local government. Although the local People's Political Consultative Conference's members could demonstrate the need for relief for orphans and children from poor families, relief from such an organization was considered totally unacceptable.[37] That is, despite agreement with governments in the center, the province and the prefecture above the county, the project was rejected even though a neighbouring county with analogous social and economic conditions had accepted a similar plan.

It is too early to tell whether the provision of social services in impoverished rural areas by Chinese faith-based charities is going to expand significantly in the near future. The activities of Tzu Chi in counties scattered throughout the PRC, albeit limited in the duration of each "mission," certainly demonstrates the interest of the MCA for this approach to emergency relief. The adoption by the official Hebei Province Buddhist Relief Foundation of Tzu Chi's method also indicates that some provincial authorities approve of this type of philanthropy: its lower profile in Hubei, where the Wuzu and the Zhanhua temples operate similar charities, indicates at best acceptance by the provincial government, but not official sponsorship. The contrasted response of the two contiguous counties of Pingshan and Jinxing, however, shows that even if the provincial and prefecture-level authorities approve of philanthropic societies' activities for education and welfare relief, lower tiers of governments can turn down an offer of such services.

Differences between local governments in their implementation of a policy encouraging the participation of charities in the provision of social welfare could be explained if access were granted or some information was made available. It is difficult to assess the respective impact "promotable" or "terminal" cadres can have on a specific policy issue when access to data on the personnel of county governments is not possible. Likewise, surveys about the material and career interests of all Party and government cadres in specific counties and township face even more important methodological challenges: even data about the basic socio-economic indicators of the area they administer have proven difficult to obtain.[38] Finally, testing the hypothesis that a greater or lesser degree of scrutiny from above can help us understand why local Party and government cadres are more or less likely to carry on policies and directives from higher levels of government faces a formidable method-ological challenge: information on local governments' issues of discipline are even more sensitive than data on a county's socio-economic situation.

The relationship between the PRC and the ROC is bound to be perceived differently across the PRC: some localities, such as Shanghai, are welcoming Taiwanese investors to develop their economy and are therefore more likely to accept their presence. In many other cases, close relations with Taiwanese compatriots may be problematic for "promotable" local officials: they don't want to appear too close to people whose loyalty to Chinese unification can be dubious. For example, officials in Pingshan County, an area with a very important place in the CCP historiography, were upset by the prospect that a school would be built with capital coming from Taiwan, which was governed until 2000 by the KMT, the CCP's historical adversary. Even if Taiwanese are considered compatriots, in the end, local governments still consider they don't fit policies of localization (*bentuhua* 本土化)—or reliance on local actors—and look at them as outsiders, not really foreigners, but not entirely Chinese either.[39]

Officials from Jingxing County, on the other hand, were indifferent to the Taiwanese origins of the capital and the volunteers who came to help build a school in the countryside: on the contrary, they were sincerely happy to receive support from people whom they consider their compatriots rather than their adversaries.[40] Volunteers from Tzu Chi have themselves confirmed that local cadres vary considerably in their opinion about the Tzu Chi relief activities and although they could not identify any specific reason explaining this variation, they asserted that one factor was clearly *not* helping: cultural affinity. The ability to communicate with the local population of Fujian in *minnanhua*, where Tzu Chi undertook many operations, proved to represent a formidable obstacle to surmount: some provincial cadres who could only communicate in Mandarin were especially suspicious of Tzu Chi volunteers who spoke the same language as the local population.[41]

Cooperation with a Taiwanese religious-based charity like Tzu Chi, in the end, represents a remarkable development when one considers the variety of obstacles that stand in the way; besides the remaining prejudice against religion held by CCP cadres and the political sensitivity of dealing with Taiwan, there are other ways to reinforce national unity and encourage poverty alleviation. Hence, local leaders may rely on actors other than the state or religious organizations when they seek help for their development projects. Corporate philanthropy is often pressured by local governments to provide "help" in exchange for a right to operate in a given county. While private entrepreneurs are sometimes compelled to give, others simply pre-empt jealousies and take the initiative of giving voluntarily. This corporate philanthropy, although still modest, represents an interesting alternative that is far less politically problematic than Taiwanese and/or religious charities. Yet, despite this possibility, the Chinese government lets Tzu Chi volunteers return to PRC for relief work, and even encourages the development of other Buddhist charities that have adopted approaches similar to Tzu Chi, from the PRC itself,[42] Hong Kong[43] or Taiwan.[44]

Conclusion

Because of limited means, poverty alleviation in the Chinese countryside cannot rely only on state resources; the central government thus welcomes the provision of disaster relief and social services in impoverished areas by domestic and overseas charities as a useful complement to its welfare policy. A Taiwanese charity such as Tzu Chi should, *prima facie*, be especially welcomed in the interior of China because of a shared cultural heritage, the possibility to attract more investments from Taiwan, and the nurture of a climate of mutual trust that could help the CCP cause of unification. Yet, despite some notable successes, this chapter has provided evidence from Hubei and Hebei that Tzu Chi volunteers have not been welcomed everywhere they go. The varying degrees of receptiveness to the institutions Tzu Chi has left or tried to leave in the counties its volunteers have visited in these provinces shows a wide variety of perceptions between central and local governments, and also, more interestingly, between neighbouring local governments. Some of the evidence discussed has demonstrated that the specific concerns of county governments can nullify decisions made at higher levels of government even when they are approved by the provincial level.

Central authorities may see some benefits for united front work and for their policies targeting the poor by letting volunteers from Tzu Chi provide disaster relief, but the limited coverage they give to this activity suggests an awareness that many local cadres are uncomfortable with the realization that success from Taiwanese compatriots could potentially undermine CCP claims to legitimacy in the area of national unity and poverty alleviation. Interviews with local cadres have confirmed these worries that their legitimacy is undercut when organizations like Tzu Chi appears too successful and better organized than themselves in the provision of relief. Some of them therefore prefer to work with grass-root philanthropic associations with local knowledge, others prefer to use the resources of wealthy private entrepreneurs, and finally some prefer to rely on more traditional forms of state support. The central authorities are aware of these local concerns and accordingly give prefecture and county-level governments the latitude to determine which policy towards Tzu Chi they should adopt. The finding strongly suggests that whether or not there is coordination between the central government and Tzu Chi, the views of local governments matter. The policy divergences between local governments have been facilitated by a set of factors: greater autonomy in decision-making power than before, especially at the provincial and prefecture levels; differences in local political culture and interests that are related to specific social and historical conditions; and different calculations from local cadres, depending on their status. This diversity of responses should not be interpreted as a sign of incoherence from the state, but rather as the indication of greater flexibility and willingness from the central government to let local authorities determine what is more adapted to their conditions.

Notes

1   I would like to express my heartfelt gratitude to the following individuals: my assistants Wang Xiaochuan, Zhu Guohan, Zheng Keyi, Marijo Demers, and Wu Pengfei for their help in the research leading to this article; colleagues at the Hebei Academy of social sciences and the Zhongnan University of Economic and Law (Wuhan), for their cooperation; volunteers and employees from the Tzu Chi Foundation in Taiwan for generously giving access to their archives and arranging many interviews; local governments, NGOs and charities in Hubei and Hebei who have kindly given their time; Linda Wong, from the City University of Hong Kong, Helene Piquet, from the Universite du Quebec a Montreal, for their helpful comments, and three anonymous reviewers for their useful remarks on previous versions of this paper. The individuals mentioned above are not responsible for any shortcomings that may remain. Finally, I would like to thank the Social Science and Humanities Research Council of Canada, which has generously supported this project financially.
2   The Republic of China (ROC) recovered Taiwan from Japan in 1945 and established its government there after 1949. The People's Republic of China has never ruled Taiwan so "*re*-unification" is inappropriate.
3   This is the script for which it is known in Taiwan and abroad. Translations for *Ciji Gongdehui* 慈济功德会 are unsatisfactory: *Ci* 慈 (*tzu* in Wade Giles transliteration) refers to "compassion," as in the coumpound *cibei* 慈悲, but also constitutes the first character for *cishan* 慈善, or "charity"; *Ji* 济 (or *chi*), "to succour" is used for *jipin* 济贫, as in "helping the poor." *Gongdehui* can be translated as "Merit society."
4   New rules have been adopted to that effect in 2001 and 2004. In 2001, the National People's Congress (NPC) passed legislation on charitable trusts, and in 2004, adopted regulations for the management of foundations. See State Council, *Xintuofa* 信托法, effective October 1, 2001; State Council, *Jijinhui guanli tiaoli* 基金会管理条例, effective June 1, 2004.

5 The regulation on religious affairs voted by the NPC and approved by Wen Jiabao in November 2004 states in Article 34 that religious organizations and venues can run social welfare services.

6 Tzu Chi was founded in 1966, and in that year, the Buddhist Association of the Republic of China was the only authorized organization.

7 In fact, modern search engines make it possible to assert quite confidently that the Chinese major media have not publicized the activities of Tzu Chi in China, even while the organization itself has provided tangible proof of its presence in China in its documentation center and fieldwork in Hubei and Hebei has confirmed the veracity of these claims.

8 Especially when they are raised by a foreigner.

9 The evidence discussed below about Tzu Chi shows that this charity was absent in poor provinces such as Shanxi and Sichuan, but present in poor ones such as Guizhou and Anhui. Meanwhile, it was also present in wealthy Jiangsu.

10 Representative of that trend was a text published in 1993, and translated in 2001: Wang Shaoguang and Hu Angang (2001) *The Chinese Economy in Crisis: State Capacity and Tax Reform*. Armonk: M.E. Sharpe.

11 Yang (2003: 156–7) also makes the argument for townships, the lowest level of government.

12 Established in 1989.

13 Established in 1991.

14 The qualification "religious" relates to the identity of these organizations, not to the nature of their activities. Available online: www.chinadevelopmentbrief.org.cn/ (accessed August 24, 2007).

15 The list is culled from China Development Brief, *Guoji* NGO [International NGOs].

16 Premier Wen unveiled a plan in March 2004 to release the burden of farmers by diminishing or even scrapping taxes and proposed increases in targeted subsidies to grain farmers. Although this measure helped improve peasants' revenues, it also increased risks of bankruptcies for township governments. See "Farm Taxes Scrapped in 22 Chinese Provinces," *Xinhua/Shenzhen Daily*, January 18, 2005.

17 Interviews 22 and 23, Jingzhou, with prefecture government officials (April 20); 53, Jingxing county, with director of the county education bureau (May 17); 54, with Jingxing county director of the social welfare bureau (May 17); 55, Pingshan county, with director of the civil affairs bureau (May 19); and 56, with Jingxing county director of the health bureau (May 19).

18 See *Zhongguo fazhan jianbao* [China Development Brief] "Guoji NGO [International NGOs]," 2007. Available online: www.chinadevelopmentbrief.org.cn/ml/ml-1.jsp?jb=B (accessed August 24, 2007).

19 From the archives of the Tzu Chi Foundation in Taipei, from 1991–2004.

20 This is gathered from several documents produced by the Tzu Chi Foundation (2005; 2000a; 2000c; 1999).

21 Interview 1, with Tzu Chi board of directors' member, Taipei Tzu Chi Cultural Center, (June 24, 2000); 7, with volunteer, Tzu Chi headquarters in Hualian (February 25, 2004); 8, with public relations staff, Tzu Chi headquarters (February 25, 2004); 9, with monastic, Tzu Chi headquarters (February 25, 2004).

22 Interview 2, with foreign language publications staff, Taipei Tzu Chi Cultural Center (June 24, 2002); 16, with Da Ai TV journalist in Kuandu (February 27, 2004); 17, with Da Ai TV staff in Kuandu (February 27, 2004); 18, with physician volunteering for the Chia-i branch (February 27, 2004); 19, with businessman volunteering for the Chia-i branch (February 29, 2004).

23 It is impossible to tell whether Tzu Chi volunteers have access to the information that could allow them to make such decisions, and even if they could access it, this does not imply that Tzu Chi would have enough resources to go there, or that the

governments of the most affected areas would call upon volunteers for Tzu Chi to help them. Hence, not all areas which have been affected by various natural disasters since 1991 could receive help from Tzu Chi.

24 Tzu Chi Foundation, *Bu hui da ai liang'an qing* 不悔大愛两岸情 (Taipei: Ciji wenhua zhiye zhongxin, 2000), p. 11.

25 Interview 61, with a member of the Hebei provincial Buddhist association in Zhengding, Hebei (May 20, 2004).

26 Interview 39, with administrative personnel of the Wuzu temple (May 7, 2004), 40, with monk of the Wuzu temple (May 7, 2004).

27 Interview 25, with temple abbott, Jingzhou (April 22, 2004).

28 Disagreements over the best way to handle the issue of cross-strait relations have existed since 1992, and these have been exemplified by important shifts in the CCP's Taiwan policy. Under the helm of Jiang Zemin, the CCP had failed to sell to Taiwanese its policy of "One country, two systems," and briefly adopted a more confrontational approach in the mid-1990s. Under his successor Hu Jintao, the party has returned to a more flexible approach.

29 Evidence presented below about Pingshan 平山 county will point to some of the reasons for this refusal.

30 Interview 31, with official of the Hubei province charity federation, Wuhan (April 29, 2004), 32, with staff of the Hubei province charity federation, Wuhan (May 4, 2004).

31 Li Changping 李昌平, *Wo xiang Zongli shuoshi hua* 我向總理說實話 (Beijing: Guangming ribao shubanshe, 2001).

32 Interview 24, interview with the public procurator, Jingzhou (April 20, 2004).

33 Interview 26, interview with teacher in primary school, Gong'an (April 21, 2004), 27, interview with school director, Gong'an (April 21, 2004).

34 Interview 25, with temple abbott, Jingzhou (April 22, 2004).

35 Interview 39, with temple abbott, Wuzu (May 4, 2004), 40, with temple personnel, Wuzu (May 4, 2004).

36 From the archives of the Tzu Chi Foundation, Taipei, year 1997, 1998 and 2000.

37 Interview 51, with county elementary school director, Pingshan (May 15, 2004), 52, with people's political consultative conference committee member, Pingshan (May 15, 2004).

38 The Jingzhou county yearbook—and a host of others—were available in Hong Kong, but not in Jingzhou city itself. It was also impossible to obtain a recent copy of the Shijiazhuang prefecture, despite the best efforts of my colleagues at the Hebei Academy of Social Sciences.

39 I am grateful to Hélène Piquet for that insight.

40 Interview 54, with school director and local cadres, Jingxing (May 18, 2004); interview 55, with people's government official, Jingxing (May 18, 2004).

41 Interview 19, with head of volunteers' mission to Fujian and head of central section of Tzu Chi, Taizhong (February 29, 2004).

42 E.g. the Hebei Fojiao Cishan Gongdehui.

43 E.g. the Cihui Fojiao Jijinhui.

44 E.g. the Cixin Cishan Shiye Jijinhui.

Bibliography

Bentley, Julia G (2003) "The Role of International Support for Civil Society Organizations in China," *Harvard Asia Quarterly* (Winter): 11–20.

Brandt, Loren, and Rozelle, Scott (2000) "Aging, Well-being, and Social Security in Rural North China," *Population and Development Review*, 26: 89–116.

Carnes, Tony (2003) "About-Face on Charities: Communist leaders invite even Christians to help the poor," *Christianity Today*, 47(10) (November): 34. Available online: www.christianitytoday.com/ct/2003/011/13.34.html (accessed May 28, 2007).

Chen Guangyao (2001) "China's Nongovernmental Organizations: Status, Government Policies, and Prospects for Further Development," *International Journal For Not-For-Profit Law*, 3(3) (March).

Chen Yin'e 陈银娥 (2000) *Xiandai Shehui de Fuli Zhidu* 现代社会的福利制度. Beijing: Jingxi kexue chubanshe.

China Development Brief (2007) "Directory of International NGOs." Available online: www.chinadevelopmentbrief.org.cn/ml/ml-l.jsp?jb=B (accessed August 24, 2007).

Chou Yulin 仇雨临 (2003) *Jianada shehui baozhang zhidu de xuanze jiqi dui zhongguo de qishi* 加拿大社会保障制度的选择及其对中国的启示. Beijing: Jingji guanli chubanshe.

Chung Jae Ho (2001) "Reappraising Central–Local Relations in Deng's China: Decentralization, Dilemmas of Controls and Diluted Effects of Reform," in Chao, Chein-min and Dickson, Bruce J. (eds.), *Remaking the Chinese State: Strategies, Society, and Security*, London: Routledge, pp. 46–75.

Esping-Andersen, Gösta (1990) *The Three Worlds of Welfare Capitalism*, Cambridge: Polity Press.

"Farm Taxes Scrapped in 22 Chinese Provinces," *Xinhua/Shenzhen Daily*, January 18, 2005.

Gernet, Jacques (1995) *Buddhism in Chinese Society: An Economic History from the Fifth to the Tenth Century*, trans. Franciscus Verellen, New York: Columbia University Press.

Gough, Ian and Wood, Geoff (eds.) (2004) *Insecurity and Welfare Regimes in Asia, Africa and Latin America: Social Policy in Development Contexts*, Cambridge University Press.

Guan Xinping 关信平 (2005) "Dangdai Ouzhou Pinkun Wenti ji Oumeng de Fan Pinkun Zhengce Yanjiu 当代欧洲贫困问题及欧盟的反贫困政策研究" [The Issue of Poverty in Contemporary Europe and Research on EU Poverty Alleviation Policies], *Zhongguo Zhengfu Menhu Wangzhan* 中国政府门户网站 [Chinese Government's Internet Portal] (December 31). Available online: www.gov.cn/ztzl////////200512/31/content_143773_3.htm (accessed May 29, 2007).

—— (2000) "Ouzhou Lianmeng shehui zhengce de lishi fazhan 欧洲联盟社会政策的历史发展" [The Historical Development of EU's Social Policy and its Objecitves, Nature, and Principles], *Nankai Xuebao: Zhexue Shehui Kexue Ban* 南开学报：哲学社会科学版 [*Nankai University Journal: Philosophy and Social Sciences Edition*], 2 (March–April): 78–85.

Guo Sui Noi (2004) "Natural Disasters Push More Chinese Below Poverty Line," *Straits Times* (July 22).

Hendrischke, Hans (1999) "Provinces in Competition," in Hendrischke, Hans and Feng Chongyi (eds.), *The Political Economy of China's Provinces: Comparative and Competitive Advantage*, London: Routledge, pp. 1–25.

Himalaya Foundation (2002) "Directory of 300 Major Foundations in Taiwan." Available online: www.foundations.org.tw/English/docs/index.asp (accessed May 28, 2007).

Hong Kong AIDS Foundation (2007) Online: www.aids.org.hk/gb/index.html/ (accessed May 29, 2007)

HSRZ (Hebei sheng renmin zhengfu) (2003) *Hebei jingji nianjian* 年鉴 *2003*, Beijing: Zhongguo tongji chubanshi.

Hubei sheng tongji 统计 (2001) *Hubei sheng tongji nianjian 2000* (Wuhan): 22.

Ka Lin (2001) "Chinese Perceptions of the Scandinavian Social Policy Model," *Social Policy and Administration*, 35(3) (July): 321–40.

Lei Jieqiong 雷洁琼 and Wang Sibin 王思斌 (1999) *Zhongguo shehui boazhang tixi de jiangou* 中国社会保障体系的建构, Taiyuan: Shanxi renmin chubanshe.

Li Changping 李昌平 (2001) *Wo xiang Zongli shuoshi hua* 我向總理說實話, Beijing: Guangming ribao shubanshe.

Li Yong (2002) "Chinese NGOs Struggle for Survival," *Caijing* (July 5): 24.

Liang Qizi 梁其姿 (1997) *Shishan yu wenhua: MingQing de cishan zuzhi* 施善與文化明清的慈善組織, Taipei: Lianjing 聯經.

Lin Mingang 林闽钢 (2003) "Woguo Nongcun Yanglao Shixian Fangshi de Shentao 我国农村养老实现方式的探讨," *Zhongguo Nongcun Jingji* 中国农村经济 3 (March). Available online: www.usc.cuhk.edu.hk/wk_wzdetails.asp?id=2543 (accessed May 29, 2007).

Lin Wanyi 林萬億 (2000) *Fuli guojia: lishi bijiao de fenxi* 福利國家. 歷史比較的分析, Taipei: Juliu Tushu 巨流圖書.

Mackey, Michael (2005) "The New Chinese Philanthropy." *Asia Times Online* (May 14).

Médecins sans frontières (2007) "Que fait MSF? Pays d'intervention: Chine." Available online: www.msf.fr/site/themes.nsf/pages/chine (accessed May 28, 2007).

Mercy Corps (2007) "Mercy Corps: China." Available online: www.mercycorps.org/items/318/ (accessed May 28, 2007).

Merrien, François-Xavier (2000) *L'état-providence*, 2nd ed., Paris: Presses universitaires de France.

Minzhengbu (2005) "Gang Ao Tai shiwu 港澳台事务." Available online: www.mca.gov.cn/artical/index.asp?currentid=196&parentid=20 (accessed May 28, 2007).

Murphy, Rachel (2002) *How Migrant Labor is Changing Rural China*, Cambridge: Cambridge University Press.

Naughton, Barry J. and Yang, Dali L. (2004) "Introduction," in Naughton, Barry J. and Yang, Dali L. (eds.), *Holding China Together: Diversity and National Integration in the Post-Deng Era*, London: Cambridge University Press: 1–25.

Ogden, Suzanne (2002) *Inklings of Democracy in China*, Cambridge: Harvard University Press.

OXFAM (2004) "Oxfam Hong Kong—Situation Report No 1: Report on Floods, the People's Republic of China" (July 22). Available online: www.reliefweb.int/rw/rwb.nsf/AllDocsByUNID/5ef78cc6e8984ab785256eda0077113c (accessed May 28, 2007).

Pei Minxin (1998) "Chinese Civic Organizations: An Empirical Analysis," *Modern China*, 24(3) (July): 285–318.

Phillion, Stephen (1998) "Chinese Welfare State Regimes," *Journal of Contemporary Asia*, 28(4): 518–36.

Ramesh, M. (2000) "The State and Social Security in Indonesia and Thailand," *Journal of Contemporary Asia*, 30(4): 534–61.

Saich, Tony (2000) "Negotiating the State: The Development of Social Organizations in China," *The China Quarterly*, 161: 124–41.

Shi Yuxiao 施育晓 (2005) "Dishouru Renshi Zhufang Zhengce: Guoji Bijiao Jiqi Qishi 低收入人士住房政策：国际比较及其启示," *Zhongguo Zhengfu Menhu Wangzhan* 中国政府门户网战 (December 31). Available online: www.gov.cn/ztzl/2005-12/31/content_143724.htm (accessed May 29, 2007).

Shih, June and Young, Nick (2003) "From Remittance to Endowment: New Spirits of Philanthropy Abroad," *China Development Brief*, 6(2) (October).

Song Binwen 宋斌文 , Xiong Yuhong 熊宇虹 and Zhang Qiang 张强 (2005) "Dangqian Nongmin Yiliao Baozhang de Xianzhuang Fenxi yu Duici Gouxiang 当前农民医疗保障的现状分析与对策构想 ," [The Analysis on Rural Welfare and Suggestion], *Guoji Yilian Yisheng Daobao*, 9 (September 1): 11–15.

Taiwan shiwu bangongshi (2005) "Jiaoyu keji jiaoliu 教育科技交流 ." Available online: www.gwytb.gov.cn/jlwl/lajl2.asp (accessed May 28, 2007).

Tang Jun 唐钧 (2004) "Shehui zhengce xueshu fazhan baogao 社会政策学科发展报告 ," *Shehui zhengce wang*. Available online: www.sociology.cass.cn/shxw/shzc/P020040112538758123567.pdf (accessed May 29, 2007).

Tittmuss, Richard (1958) *Essays on the Welfare State*, London: Allen and Unwin.

Tzu Chi Foundation (2005) *Dalu Zengzai* 大陆赈灾 . Available online: www2.tzuchi.org.tw/tc-charity/html/ch-relieve.htm (accessed May 28, 2007).

—— (2001a) *Ciji Nianjian* 慈济年鑑 , *2000*, Taipei: Ciji Wenhua Chubanshe.

—— (2001b) "Tzu Chi Services: International Relief." Available online: www.tzuchi.org/global/services/relief.html (accessed May 28, 2007).

—— (2000a) *Bu hui da ai liang'an qing* 不悔大爱两岸情 , Taipei: Ciji wenhua zhiye zhongxin.

—— (2000b) *Ciji Nianjian* 慈济年鑑 , *1999*, Taipei: Ciji Wenhua Chubanshe.

—— (2000c) *Qiangjiu zainan de yongzhe* 抢救灾难的勇者 , Taipei: Ciji wenhua zhiye zhongxin.

—— (1999) *Ai zai liang'an jian huidang* 爱在两岸间回荡 , Taipei: Ciji wenhua zhiye zhongxin.

UN Office for the Coordination of Humanitarian Affairs (2004) "China: Floods OCHA Situation Report No. 1" (July 22). Available online: www.reliefweb.int/w/rwb.nsf/6686f45896f15dbc852567ae00530132/3bc095e50f31578885256ed900554e66?OpenDocument (accessed May 28, 2007).

UN Department of Humanitarian Affairs (1991) "China: Floods, June 1991, United Nations Disaster Relief Operations Reports 1–9" (June 25). Available online: www.reliefweb.int/rw/RWB.NSF/db900SID/OCHA-64CRBM?OpenDocument&r=3&cc=chn&emid=ACOS-635NNF (accessed May 28, 2007).

Wang Mengkui 王梦奎 (ed.) (2001) *Zhongguo shehui baozhang tizhi gaige* 中国社会保障体制改革 , Beijing: Zhongguo fazhan chubanshe.

Wang Ming 王名 (2004) *Zhongguo feizhengfu gonggong bumen: Qinghua fazhan yanjiu baogao 2003* 中国非政府公共部门 2003, Beijing: Qinghua chubanshe.

Watts, Jonathan (2004) "China Admits First Rise in Poverty Since 1978," *Guardian* (July 20).

Xu Dianqing 徐滇庆 , Yin Zunsheng 尹尊声 and Zheng Yuxin 郑玉歆 (eds.) (1999) *Zhongguo shehui baozhang zhidu gaige* 中国社会保障制度改革 , Beijing: Jingji kexue chubanshe.

Xu Yuebin (2001) "Family Support for Old People in Rural China," *Social Policy and Administration*, 35(3) (July): 307–20.

Yang Zhong (2003) *Local Government and Politics in China: Challenges from Below*, Armonk, NY: M. E. Sharpe.

Zhang Yan 张彦 and Chen Hongxia 陈红霞 (1999) *Shehui Baozhang Gailun* 社会保障概论 , Nanjing: Nanjing daxue chubanshe.

Zhao Ling Yun (1999) "Hubei: Rising Abruptly over Central China?" in Hendrischke, Hans and Feng, Chongyi (eds.), *The Political Economy of China's Provinces*, London: Routledge, pp. 155–78.

Zhao Liqing 趙黎青 (1999) "Fei Zhengfu Zuzhi: Zuzhi Chuangxin he Zhidu Chuangxin 非政府組織——組織創新和制度創新," *Jianghai Xuekan* 江海學刊, 6(204) (November): 45–52.

Zhao Man 赵曼 (2003) *Shehui baozhangxue* 社会保障学, Beijing: Zhongguo caizheng jingji chubanshe.

Zhonghua cishan zonghui (2003) "Mingyu Juwen 名誉顾问." Available online: www.chinacharity.cn/wzwznrscrvlet?xh=62&flbm–myzw&url=zhjs&lx=1 (accessed May 29, 2007).

Zhongguo fupin xinxi (2005) *Kedi gaikuang* 客地概况, "Zhongguo fupin kaifa fuwu zhongxin 中国扶贫开发服务中心." Available online: www.help-poverty.org.cn/help web2/gaikuang/gaikuang.htm (accessed May 28, 2007).

Zweig, David (2002) *Internationalizing China: Domestic Interests and Global Linkages*, Ithaca, NY: Cornell University Press.

6 The Hong Kong Special Administrative Region

Implications for world order[1]

Susan J. Henders

Territorial self-government arrangements are widely used to manage political tensions in many states where sub-state territorial communities claim distinct identities. Although the degree, scope, and institutional form of territorial self-government vary, autonomy arrangements have been used in states as diverse as Canada (for mainly francophone Quebec and First Nations communities), the Philippines (for parts of Muslim-claimed Mindanao), and post-communist Russia, Moldova, and Georgia. In the People's Republic of China (PRC), the concern of the present volume, grants of formal territorial autonomy have been a state building and maintenance strategy aimed at securing and legitimating regime authority in minority nationality areas. In the Han heartland, they have more recently been deployed as a means of managing market reforms and China's integration with global capitalism while also resolving territorial disputes. Following upon the "special economic zones" of the late 1970s, the authorities of the PRC proposed the "one country, two systems" policy to entice Taiwan back to the motherland. In the 1980s, they promised a version of this territorial autonomy regime to Hong Kong and Macau. The aim was to take back the territories, ending China's humiliation at the hands of European imperialists, while legitimating and protecting Communist party rule and Hong Kong-style capitalism, the engine of China's post-Mao market reforms.[2]

This chapter looks at the consequences of the territorial autonomy arrangement in the Hong Kong Special Administrative Region (HKSAR), understood as a set of institutions and discourses that attempt to reproduce political and economic power simultaneously at multiple levels, in Hong Kong, in China, and in the world order. On the one hand, by allowing Hong Kong some measure of autonomy, the PRC Government has creatively adapted the rigid practices of sovereignty and the homogeneous distribution of territorial political authority associated with the modern territorial state, to reflect some of the diversity and demands for self-rule within its borders. As a form of state adaptation and part of ongoing efforts to maintain state legitimacy, the territorial autonomy arrangement in Hong Kong would seem to be pushing China towards territorial-political pluralism and values potentially supportive of long-term liberal democratic development. On the other hand, the territorial autonomy arrangement in Hong Kong fosters socio-economic and political exclusion, perpetuating patterns established under British rule. Hong Kong is not only formally undemocratic, it also has one of the widest income inequalities among developed economies. Its political and socio-economic disparities are marked by the intersecting lines of class, gender, race and ethnicity. These inequalities exist, in part, because "one country, two systems" entrenches an ideology of *ethno-patriotic economism,* which legitimates the political domination of a alliance of PRC authorities and Hong Kong big business elites in Hong Kong, the post-Mao political-economic order, and, by implication, the wider capitalist state system.

The first section of the chapter briefly examines the policymakers' motives behind the "one country, two systems" territorial autonomy policy and conventional analysis of the immediate impact of the arrangement on stability and the legitimacy of PRC rule in Hong Kong. The second section then critically examines the conceptual assumptions that underlie such assessments, which stress only the role of autonomy arrangements in protecting vulnerable distinct communities from the threat of *external interference,* thereby preserving local identity and values. The critique exposes the lesser-known *internal* political effects of territorial autonomy arrangements and why they run the risk of reproducing exclusions based on class, ethnic, racial, gender, and class differences. Subsequent sections explore the institutional and discursive means by which existing power relations in the HKSAR are legitimated and exclusionary citizenship practices reproduced under "one country, two systems." By way of a conclusion, the chapter briefly considers the extent to which and the conditions under which formal democratization, including improvements in civil and political rights protection, would result in more inclusive internal citizenship practices in the territory. The analysis is largely based on the rich secondary literature that is now bringing the insights of critical social science to the study of Hong Kong, supplemented by an analysis of key legal texts.

The HKSAR as a legitimation strategy of the late Cold War

The "one country, two systems" formula for Hong Kong is a consequence of the Chinese post-Mao leadership determining that resolving the Hong Kong question peacefully, through a negotiated, internationally recognized agreement, would legitimate its rule over Hong Kong and reinforce its economic modernization objectives. By legitimate rule, I mean, following Beetham (1991: 3), rule that is regarded by key groups in China, Hong Kong, Britain, and the international community as having been acquired and exercised in a manner consistent with justifiable rules. As Foot (1995: 5) notes, "Legitimacy is important to the exercise of power because it represents the moral or normative aspect, and affects the costs associated with a power relationship." Legitimacy, according to Beetham (1991: 27–35), reduces a regime's need to use incentives and sanctions to maintain compliance with the prevailing power relations by appealing to subordinates and other key actors as moral and not merely self-interested parties. However, in exchange, the regime must respect to an acceptable degree the limits imposed on its power by the values and principles held by these actors. If PRC leaders wanted the benefits of having its rule in Hong Kong considered legitimate, it had to accept some constraints on its power—or at least appear to do so. The territorial autonomy regime for Hong Kong was essentially that package of constraints, expressed in an international legal agreement—the 1984 Sino-British Joint Declaration, or JD. In this way, the regime employed the legitimacy of a recognizable legal form to foster international and local confidence in Hong Kong's future autonomy and continued economic and political viability and to increase the British Government's willingness to hand over Hong Kong.

Coming prior to the end of the Cold War, in the early years of China's economic opening to the outside world and market reforms, the JD was widely hailed by world economic and political leaders, journalists and academics from liberal democracies as an innovative autonomy strategy reflecting the new primarily economic pragmatism of China's post-Mao leaders (see Domes 1988). As US Secretary of State George Schultz commented on the British Government pledge to depart Hong Kong in July 1997 and the PRC pledge to set up the HKSAR:

> The agreement will provide a solid foundation for Hong Kong's enduring future progress . . . We expect American business communities, both in the United States and Hong Kong, will see in this agreement good reason for sustained confidence in the future of Hong Kong as an attractive and thriving commercial centre.
>
> (quoted in Costa 1993: 851 n.181)

The HKSAR would be, in world terms, a creative departure from the modern state model, with its preference for centralization, a homogenous distribution of territorial political authority, and rigid practices of sovereignty (see Hannum 1990; Lapidoth 1997; Davis 1989). The HKSAR model was also rightly lauded as an important laboratory for political liberalization in China and beyond (Davis 2001). The degree of *de facto* political autonomy permitted the HKSAR would be weak. However, the promise to protect, for fifty years, Hong Kong's capitalist system, rule of law, independent judiciary, limited direct elections, and civil and political rights protections was remarkable, for China remained an avowed Leninist party-state and had only begun to experiment with capitalism. The JD, followed by the Basic Law (hereafter BL), granted Hong Kong a high degree of autonomy in economic, social, and cultural affairs under a government made up of local inhabitants. By making this promise, Chinese leaders sought to legitimate their reincorporation of Hong Kong into China and provide a model by which

Taiwan people would agree to follow suit. They also wanted international credibility for their bid to establish China as a status quo major power and, last but by no means least, to protect Hong Kong-style capitalism and legitimate their rule in the territory. Deemed one of the Asian tigers, the Hong Kong economy had seen an average GDP growth of 8.5 percent annually from 1974–84 (Hong Kong Government 1995). By the early 1980s, Hong Kong had become one of the world's major transhipment ports and largest trading economies; a major global financial centre in terms of external banking transactions and stock market capitalization; an important regional headquarters for foreign firms; and the world's largest port in terms of container throughput. Not coincidentally, it had also emerged as the single largest source of investment capital for the Chinese economy.

Under the JD and BL, Hong Kong would continue functioning as the juridically separate economy it had been under British rule, its monetary, trade, customs, fiscal, and financial institutions unregulated by PRC authorities. Hong Kong would maintain its free port and international financial centre status; its separate customs jurisdiction; and its right to maintain economic and cultural relations with outside states, regions, and relevant intergovernmental organizations dealing with economic and cultural matters.[3] It is remarkable and indicative of the flexibility in sovereignty practices in the contemporary states system and global capitalism, that Chinese, British, and other governments permitted Hong Kong to develop, and then maintain after 1997, this high degree of international legal personality. Most other non-central governments with substantial involvement in intergovernmental organizations are either states-in-waiting or associated states with a recognized right to declare independence (Henders 2001; 2000).

In the short term, the "one country, two systems" strategy was a success by these measures. With the major exception of the immediate aftermath of the 1989 Tiananmen Massacre, the autonomy package helped sustain investor confidence, high economic growth, and political stability in the territory prior to the handover to PRC rule. By the mid-1990s, GDP per capita in Hong Kong was approximately US$ 22,000, higher than the UK or Australia and second in Asia only to Japan. The Hong Kong economy continued to pump capital into the Pearl River Delta and beyond. As the shock of Tiananmen declined and China's capitalist opening continued through the 1990s, there was some optimism that the PRC Government would abide by the autonomy agreement, despite the lack of constitutionalist protections for the autonomy arrangement. Indeed, in the first years of the HKSAR, many analysts pointed to the relative lack of obvious meddling by the central government. As some of the most perceptive of these analysts put it: "to date it has been in the interest of the Chinese Government to maintain a façade of autonomy in Hong Kong, and in practice pessimists have thus been confounded . . . In the first five years political autonomy in Hong Kong has been both fatally compromised, and, at the same time, a living political reality" (Holliday *et al.* 2002: 455).

Reconceptualizing territorial autonomy

Underlying many analyses that focus on PRC interference in Hong Kong is the questionable assumption that territorial autonomy concessions are mainly a means of protecting a distinct territorial community from external threats in order to preserve its particular identity.[4] Using this approach, often only implicitly, many analyses of Hong Kong autonomy focus on whether, to what degree, and how PRC authorities assert their preferences into what are supposed to be autonomous Hong Kong institutions (e.g. Vickers 2001). The politics of autonomy in Hong Kong is understood as "skirmishes along the 'one country, two systems' boundary" (Overholt 2001). The frontier in question is assumed to be an obvious marker delineating two territorial communities with significantly distinct identities. Autonomy is measured by how many times the PRC authorities or their proxies in Hong Kong impose PRC preferences on the territory, or to what extent Hong Kong remains substantially as it was under British rule, its political stability and economic prosperity intact. Relatively little attention is paid to whether Hong Kong people *all* benefit equally from and, therefore, want to preserve the status quo ante (in this case, replacing British colonial with PRC rule). The collective identity of Hong Kong is assumed to be discrete, fixed, internally homogenous, and internally uncontested or, at least, that internal differences and tensions pale in comparison with the differences and tensions between Hong Kong and the mainland. That there is a singular Hong Kong identity that can be preserved under the protective glass of self-rule remains an unexamined premise.

Such interpretations also hide the ways in which the most powerful *locally* use territorial autonomy arrangements to preserve their privileges, reproducing an unjust status quo that may also serve the needs of the state for stability and legitimacy. They do so partly by representing autonomy as a means to protect the community and its most cherished values from outside and internal threats. They aim to entrench in the institutions of self-rule an understanding of the community and its values that reproduces and legitimates their own interests particularly in the face of *internal* challengers. Thus, the politics of territorial autonomy has an important internal dimension in addition to the provision of "external protection," to use Kymlicka's term (1996), for Hong Kong and legitimation for the PRC political-economic order. This is a politics marked by *internal contestation, in a context of unequal power, over the very identity of the distinct community, its core values, and its membership.* At its heart are debates over *what vision of community should be reflected in and protected by the institutions of self-rule.* This is a contest for political power and over citizenship practices in the HKSAR, over their degree of political, socio-economic and cultural inclusiveness.[5] At its heart is the question of the very values that define Hong Kong as a community: "[r]esistance in this sense is not merely about the building of a defensive mechanism in reaction to dominant institutions, but is also a re-definition of the 'Hong Kong people' and 'Chinese people'" (Fung 2001: 594).

Consequently, territorial autonomy arrangements such as those for the HKSAR do challenge the exclusionary assumption that state-level identities are homogenous, coherent, and fixed. They do so by recognizing distinct territorial communities within the state and granting them a measure of self-rule vis-à-vis the central authorities, helping to legitimate the state and hold it together in the face of these alternative power centres. However, territorial autonomy arrangements also potentially reproduce at the regional level these same understandings of identity that make the modern state dysfunctional and exclusionary. That is, they too often constitute the identity of the territorial community, like that of the "nation-state," as fixed, discrete, and prior to politics, when it is, in fact, internally contested, fuzzy around the edges, an effect of politics and constitutive of political power. The following sections explain how the "one country, two systems" autonomy arrangement reproduces Hong Kong as just such a community, coherently defined by ethno-patriotic economism.[6] By reinforcing this ideology, the structures and processes of the autonomy arrangement reinforce the power of the ruling PRC state–Hong Kong big business alliance and legitimate inequalities based on ethnicity, race, gender, and class that marginalize so many in Hong Kong, not to mention in China itself (though the latter are beyond the scope of the present analysis).

Economism and inequality

The ethos of ethno-patriotic economism represents Hong Kong people as the apolitical epitome of "*homo economicus*" and as patriotic Han Chinese who, for both nationalistic and pragmatic reasons, related to China's political, military, and economic might, accept the authoritarian leadership of the PRC party-state. Reproduced in the JD, the BL, and other public discourses, the dominance of ethno-patriotic economism depoliticizes Hong Kong society and naturalizes its significant internal inequalities. Entrenched in the institutions of the HKSAR, ethno-patriotic economism perpetuates the idea that, with hard work and some luck, anyone can get rich and that a meaningful public social safety net is an unnecessary burden that would undermine prosperity.[7] Ethno-patriotic economism also legitimates the continuation of Hong Kong's long-standing business-dominated, authoritarian political system,[8] and an instrumental approach to the rule of law and civil and political rights. In short, the ideology treats Hong Kong people largely as market actors and subjects, not as citizens with a range of social, economic, political, and civil rights in both public and private spheres (see Ghai 2001).

Economistic discourses are not new to political legitimating practices in Hong Kong. The present one adapts representations of Hong Kong that elites used to legitimate British rule and Hong Kong's highly unequal society in the colonial past. This narrative cast Hong Kong people as utilitarian, politically apathetic, and family-centred.[9] They were said to want minimal government, focused on creating the free-market conditions for capitalism to produce economic prosperity. Governments were not to interfere in Chinese Hong Kong society, but, in keeping with local values, leave charities and the family to provide for the vulnerable and for hard times. The emphasis on family as a self-reliant economic unit continued even as the post-war Hong Kong Government invested in social entitlement programs, particularly in the wake of the legitimacy crisis associated with the 1966/1967 riots (Ho 2004: 29–34).[10] As living standards were improving for many in the high growth 1970s and 1980s, government could spend some money on social welfare while still maintaining its traditional low tax policy (see Chan 2003). It did so, not because of a belief in citizenship in the sense the term is used here, but because it was functional for capitalism and essential to the political legitimacy of what was not only an undemocratic, but also a colonial government. Moreover, the government believed that, by maintaining public welfare provisions at a level that sustained inequality, it created incentives for work and self-sufficiency (Chau and Yu 1999: 89–91).

Meanwhile, the Hong Kong British Government and business elites continued to depoliticize Hong Kong people. In both the formal and informal political realms, Hong Kong people were active in political campaigns with goals such as the defence of Chinese national dignity; anti-racism; the use of the Chinese language in public institutions; women's rights; freedom of association; and economic fairness and equity.[11] Nevertheless, government elites blamed political activism and demands for a more inclusive society on "troublemakers," denied its political character, and warned of "political sensitivity" given the territory's delicate position in the Cold War and in the rivalry between the PRC government and Republic of China elites in Taiwan (Lam 2004: 39–40). In the 1980s depoliticization became harder to achieve. The emergence of the 1997 handover question, the introduction of limited direct elections, and economic restructuring as industrial jobs were moved to lower wage markets in China meant that political involvement was more widespread and sustained (Lam 2004). Still, the rags-to-riches version of Hong Kong history remained a dominant public discourse in which:

> the hardships of poverty have been, so to speak, petrified, distanced as a faraway historical period—archaeologically termed the Age of Poverty—and thus, in effect, removed from the present-day social memory of Hong Kong. In this way, poverty and the impoverished are suppressed by this glittering totem and are effectively removed from the social agenda.
>
> (Cheung 2000: 1)

Since the handover, the HKSAR Government has perpetuated the econ-omism ethos. It regularly trumpets Hong Kong's annual ranking as "the world's freest economy" by the Cato, Fraser, and other similar think thanks (HK Economic and Trade Office 2003; HKSAR Government 2004). While the "economic miracle" narrative of pre-1997 years has declined, a victim of the recession wrought by the Asian Financial Crisis and SARS, the government still boasts of growth rates averaging 4.9 percent in real terms in the last two decades (despite the post-1997 slump) and an economy and per capita GDP more than doubling in size such that it is now "higher than many Western countries" (HKSAR Government 2004). The government attributes the achievements to the territory's "hardworking, adaptable and well-educated workforce" and its "entrepreneurial flair . . . the bedrock of Hong Kong's productivity and creativity" (HKSAR Government 2004; see also Ku and Pun 2004).

What the economism ethos hides is that the recent decades of high economic growth have also been a period of growing economic inequality. Notably, this was so even before the post-1997 recession. While living standards improved for many in the 1970s and 1980s, except for the 1966–71 period, income inequality measured by Gini coefficients increased steadily. It reached 0.525 in 2001, up from levels of 0.476 in 1991, 0.45 in 1981, and 0.43 in 1971 (Sing 2004b; Zhao, Zhang and Sit 2004: 452).[12] Throughout the 1980s, the top 20 percent of households controlled more than half the territorial income, an unusual degree of inequality amongst developed countries which is, however, not uncommon amongst developing economies. Compared with Hong Kong's 0.525 (2001) Gini coefficient, those in Canada were 0.315 (1994), 0.46 in the U.S. (1999), 0.53 in Britain (2000), 0.351 in South Korea (2002), and 0.481 in Singapore (2000), while they were 0.45 in China (2002), 0.461 in the Philippines (2000), and 0.601 in Brazil (1995) (Zhao *et al.* 2004: 446–7, 457; Sautman 2004: 128).

There were several reasons for deepening inequality. Jobs were lost in the manufacturing sector as Hong Kong capitalists chasing cheaper labor moved their factories across the border. Nearly 400,000 manufacturing jobs disappeared between 1991 and 2001 alone, though the drain began earlier (Chiu and Lui 2004). By 1995, unemployment had already hit 3.5 percent, the highest official rate in ten years. Hong Kong Federation of Trade Union surveys estimated it was closer to 13 percent in reality (So 1999: 205). By 1995, the welfare roll had risen to more than 100,000 people, up from 83,000 in mid-1993, and inflation was more than 9 percent. With the post-1997 recession, official unemployment rates climbed to 6.3 percent in 1999 and remained high (Chan 2003; Zhao *et al.* 2004: 460). Wages fell further and low-paid, fragmented, and part-time work continued to increase in the ever more important service sector. The Hong Kong Social Security Society estimated that in 1999 there were more than one million people (nearly one in seven residents) living in poverty (based on a poverty line of half the median income). About 360,000 of these were not unemployed, but working poor (Chan 2003; see also Social and Economic Policy Institute 2001). The middle class also suffered losses in property and stock market investments.

The growing inequalities are gendered, as women are overrepresented at the lower income levels (a later section looks at their ethnic and racial dimensions). Many middle-aged female factory workers who lost their jobs found they lacked the skills needed to transfer to service sector jobs. The numbers of mostly female foreign domestic workers (FDWs) continued to increase. Overall, restructuring has been accompanied by the feminization of low wage, low-skilled jobs in the Hong Kong service sector (Chiu and Liu 2004; see also Zhao *et al.* 2004: 459).

The economism ethos continues to propagate the myth that this is all temporary to the extent that it addresses these inequalities at all. However, inequality appears to be becoming a structural, rather than a cyclical phenomenon: "It looks unlikely that Hong Kong will ever go back to the days when full employment is the norm rather than the exception. Furthermore, depressing [*sic*] wages mean that what unskilled workers are earning is already hardly enough to support a family" (Chow c.2004: 12–13). Even so, public social welfare programmes have not caught up. They continue to provide insufficient support for low-income individuals and families, or even middle class families, thrown out of work. As the post-1997 recession took hold, there were daily demonstrations outside government offices (So 1999: 205–6). When half a million people took to the streets in each of the July 1 protests of 2003 and 2004, defying their apathetic label, many voiced discontent with the HKSAR government and, specifically, Chief Executive Tung's handling of the SARS crisis and the economic downturn, in addition to important civil and political rights questions: a draconian proposed anti-subversion law and even the government failure to move ahead on democratization. These large-scale protests occurred against a background of other major public demonstrations by professionals and workers demanding reforms and policies to address pressing economic needs (Chan 2003; Sing 2004b).

Autonomy as institutionalized inequality

Hong Kong's autonomy process has played an important role in reproducing these inequalities, allowing the HKSAR government largely to portray the current state of affairs as exceptional. Maintaining Hong Kong's "previous capitalist system and way of life . . . unchanged for 50 years" (BL Art 5) involves far more than ensuring the continuation of the territory's economic autonomy in fiscal, monetary, and trade/customs matters; its free port status; participation in global economic governance; independent judiciary; private property; and the common law. It also involves legitimating the very socio-economic and cultural discourses and institutional features of the Hong Kong economy and political system that produce inequality: its nearly complete reliance on the market to distribute wealth; its low taxes; its assigning to families and charitable institutions the role of social safety net provider, with the government taking but a residual role; and its authoritarian executive-led, business dominated, political system. The latter aimed to ensure disadvantaged voters did not rock the boat with demands for meaningful social, economic and political citizenship.

It is no coincidence that Hong Kong big business elites dominated the ranks of local BL drafters. The criticism that social services professionals and unions made of the socio-economic side of their anti-citizenship agenda got little media attention compared with the attention given the promises of eventual democratization and protection for liberal institutions. Ideological and class divisions and preoccupation with immigration plans also weakened the ability of non-business BL drafters to challenge the economism ethos, as did the very hegemony of the latter (see So 1999: Ch. 143*ff*). Consequently, reflecting the JD, the BL gave constitutional status to what had become golden principles in Hong Kong from early colonial times: the requirement that the Hong Kong government maintain a balanced budget, low taxes, and prudent fiscal reserves (Chan 1998: 280–1; BL Arts 107, 108, 111). The BL provides for a partially democratically elected legislature to counter the fact that the Chief Executive would be virtually handpicked by the central government. It says that the Legislative Council "shall be constituted by election," with the "ultimate aim" being "the election of all the members of the Legislative Council by universal suffrage" (Art. 68[1] and [2]). However, the vague wording protects the anti-democratic preferences of PRC leaders and vocal Hong Kong business elites. The latter have long been opposed to democratization, arguing that it would provoke confrontations with China and encourage demands for an expensive expansion of social programs the territory can ill afford and that, in any case, do not reflect Hong Kong values (see So 1999: 20; Sing 2004a: Ch. 4).

By constituting Hong Kong as a laissez-faire economy, the JD and BL also deflect attention from the selectivity of free-market practices in the territory and their impact on income and power distribution. As critics have pointed out, Hong Kong's laissez-faire reputation is only deserved when it comes to external tariffs and trade and, internally, with respect to social entitlements and some aspects of labour markets. In other areas, such as the financial, entertainment and some other services sectors, the domestic economy is a complex of cartels and monopolies (Overholt 2001: 10). Historically, government and property developers have colluded to keep property prices high, generating business profits and filling government coffers (all land is government owned) ("Asia: A High-Rise Bust," *The Economist*, June 27, 1998). At the peak, the government provided social housing to nearly half the territory's workers. Even so, the high cost of housing and land, in addition to low wages for many, restructuring, and skeletal social programmes, were and remain the foundation of economic inequalities in Hong Kong. "The wealth divide between those who own some property and those who do not is so great that wealthy Hong Kong's social structure is as deeply divided as any Third World country's" (Overholt 2001: 13). The BL perpetuates the system of land leases and related rights that underlies these inequalities (Arts 120–3). It also constitutes and legitimates long-established spheres of active government non-interference and often less acknowledged active interference in the economy. The latter includes the requirement that the HKSAR government "provide an appropriate economic and legal environment for the maintenance of the status of Hong Kong as an international financial centre" (Art. 109) and that it encourage investment, technological progress, and new industries (Art. 118). More often cited by advocates of laissez-faire economies are the actively negative obligations of HKSAR authorities to refrain from imposing exchange controls (Art. 112), from imposing tariffs that would remove its free port status (Art. 114), and from impeding the free flow of goods, intangible assets, and capital (Art. 115).

Even JD and BL protections for Hong Kong's international legal personality contribute to maintaining inequalities. On the one hand, the continued application to Hong Kong through China of such human rights treaties as the International Covenant on Civil and Political Rights and the International Covenant on Economic, Social and Cultural Rights provides important resources to those struggling to advance citizenship in the territory (Henders 2004: 128–31). On the other hand, the majority of international commitments undertaken by the HKSAR Government or by the PRC authorities on its behalf reinforce a neo-liberal international economic regime whose costs and benefits are unequally shared across the territory. Hong Kong authorities were, in the British years, a founding member of the World Trade Organization, and they remain a stanch supporter. However, as we have seen, the benefits of trade and investment liberalization have mainly gone to local capitalists and middle class managers, not ordinary workers. Notably, the HKSAR Government, like the Hong Kong British Government before it, continues *not* to enforce clauses protecting such rights as freedom of association vis-à-vis trade unions and to collective bargaining in International Labour Organization (ILO) and other human rights conventions applicable to Hong Kong (Hong Kong Human Rights Commission 1998; Social and Economic Policy Institute 2001). Days before the handover, the Hong Kong Legislative Council passed last minute laws aimed at weakening prohibitions against trade unionism and collective bargaining. After 1997, these provisions were struck down by the big business and pro-China dominated Provisional Legislative Council (HKSAR Provisional Legislative Council 1997). Following complaints by the Hong Kong Confederation of Trade Unions, the ILO Committee on Freedom of Association declared in 1998 that the PRC government, on behalf of the HKSAR authorities, was in "non-compliance" with ILO Conventions 87 (on Freedom of Association and Protection) and 98 (on the Right to Organize and Collective Bargaining Convention) ("SAR Government Violates International Labour Conventions," *Hong Kong Voice of Democracy,* November 21, 1998; "ALU Interviews Lee Cheuk Yan," October 3, 2002). Efforts by opposition legislators to establish a legal minimum wage have since been defeated in the Legislative Council

Journalists and scholars have given a lot of justified attention to the precariousness of Hong Kong's autonomy vis-à-vis Chinese authorities and to its survival as a distinct semi-liberal community, given the *de facto* veto of PRC authorities over political institutions and court rulings. The PRC central government, not independent courts, has the authority to approve amendments to and interpret the BL (Arts 158, 159) and, in effect, determine the constitutionality of HKSAR laws. The central government also appoints the SAR chief executive after "elections or . . . consultations held locally" (Art. 45) in which its choice is assured. Hong Kong autonomy is, indeed, functionally broad, but shallow and fragile in law and political practice. However, the emphasis on autonomy as a way to protect Hong Kong from China hides the extent to which the political and identity border with China is already penetrated by ties between PRC state and Hong Kong Chinese business elites, built upon patronage and a coincidence of interests.

The transition to PRC rule saw many former pro-British business elites publicly declare their loyalty to the PRC government and gain important positions in the post-1997 government—and access to lucrative business ventures in China—as rewards. By the mid-1990s, a Hong Kong Chinese big business alliance with Beijing had displaced the expatriate business alliance with London of the colonial years as the keystone of the Hong Kong political-economic order (So 1999: 203). Selected by China, leading local capitalists and/or pro-Beijing members dominated the Preparatory Committee selected by the PRC government to prepare the new HKSAR government. In keeping with the BL, they selected and, in many cases, "self-selected" the Selection Committee, which chose the first Chief Executive for appointment by PRC authorities, as well as the Provisional Legislature (see Sing 2004a: 156–7). Tung Chee-hwa, appropriately a shipping magnate whose company had once been bailed out financially by the PRC government, surrounded himself with an executive dominated by wealthy Hong Kong Chinese business men (Sautman 2004: 128–9). After 1997, the Provisional Legislature reversed the expansion of direct elections attempted by the last British governor and cancelled or annulled many of the improvements in social programmes and (as noted above) the labor protection bills passed just prior to the handover (So 1999: 186, 215, 228–9).[13] Protesters labelled the provisional legislature the "tycoon dictatorship" (So 1999: 231).

The system of contained democracy installed after 1997 aimed to perpetuate and legitimate this exclusionary order. Following elections in 2000 and 2004, big business and other pro-China representatives continued to dominate the Legislative Council and, backed by the BL, undermine its ability to check the big business and pro-China executive. The enforcement of BL Annex II meant that, in 2004, half of its sixty members were elected by limited-membership functional constituencies mostly composed of professional and business associations. Homemakers, FDWs,[14] the unemployed, the majority of Hong Kong workers and others deemed to have no "function" in the productive sphere were denied a vote for the functional constituency seats (Hong Kong Women's Coalition for Beijing '95 1997: 392–3). The other thirty legislative seats were selected through competitive multi-party elections in geographic constituencies based on universal adult suffrage. However, the electoral system was designed to disadvantage the democratic opposition that had swept the partial elections held prior to 1997. Moreover, the BL requires that bills, motions, or amendments to government bills introduced by individual legislators have the support of the majority of both functional and geographic constituency legislators. This ensures that big business elites and their allies dominate law making (Sing 2004a: 158–68). In short:

> Beijing and London, together with the local business establishment, planned a government that they all hoped would combine representative deliberativeness with authoritarian decisiveness . . . The legislature itself was a carefully engineered body, chosen through complex, multilayered procedures designed to ensure that it would be dominated for a least ten years by economic and managerial experts who would steer well clear of anything resembling economically risky populism.
>
> (Overholt 2001: 5)

With the onset of the Asian financial crisis and the subsequent economic disasters that rocked Hong Kong, the stock and property market bubbles burst and unemployment skyrocketed. As the size of Hong Kong's welfare rolls climbed, government and business elites stepped up their representation of Hong Kong people as aggressively self-reliant individuals and families in a global city facing intense international competitiveness. The message was clear: Hong Kong could not afford a welfare state—and did not really need it (see Ho 2004: 343). The new HKSAR Government had promised improvements in government home-ownership schemes and public education, a mandatory retirement fund, and a commission for the elderly and elderly allowance increases (So 1999: 239–40). However, with welfare costs growing (despite low benefits levels) and revenues from land sales and taxes falling (see Chow c.2004), the emphasis shifted. It focused on limiting increases in social spending and reducing access to welfare through such neo-liberal policies as workfare and measures to assist self-reliance, regulations that reinforce the family as the economic and welfare provisioning unit, and a continuation of pre-1997 reforms based on the market provisioning of welfare services (Chan, 2003; Chow c.2004; Chan 1998). In keeping with the economism ethos, welfare recipients were portrayed and often treated as outsiders who lacked the resilience and self-reliance of Hong Kong people (Hui 2004: 216–17; Chan 1998: 283–5).

The discourse of economism has overshadowed the extent to which Hong Kong people have over the decades demanded equality and a more inclusive community. At least since the 1966/1967 riots, social workers have been one of the most vocal proponents of welfare rights as a means to a more just society. Pressure groups focusing on these issues increased their activism from the late 1980s in particular (Chow c.2004). The narrative of economism —including its influence amongst the middle classes—has inhibited the ability of activists to garner the sustained public support necessary to get issues of economic injustice on the political agenda, particularly *as citizenship issues* understood in terms of rights that create obligations for the state and other actors. Economism, with its emphasis on consumerism and consumption, gets little criticism partly because so many people grew up comparatively poor and, until the 1970s, were also refugees from China—money was one of the few things one could count on (Mathews and Lui 2001: 9–11). The Hong Kong People's Alliance on the WTO sees this history and the current dependence on the PRC economy as ongoing barriers to ideological change that would support more inclusive citizenship:

> Given that Hong Kong has historically been a very open economy, and that many Hong Kong people are individualistic, there is a lot of faith in [sic] free market should work. Competition, squeezing out, the drive for efficiency at the cost of working conditions—these are all realities that many Hong Kong people have lived, and consider "natural," given that many have their roots in refugee families from China, who came with nothing to their name and little to expect from the past colonial government.
>
> As Hong Kong still plays a role as a "trading agent" between China and the world . . . Hong Kong people identify very much with China's future, and generally want to see China benefiting from more open markets . . . This is a real-life issue for many of HK's middle-lower class populace, many of whose wages depend on importing or exporting goods or services.
>
> (HKPA n.d.)

Ethno-patriotism and inequality

The unjust status quo entrenched in the institutions of Hong Kong self-rule is one marked not only by class and gender, but also by exclusion linked with ethnicity and race. An ethos of ethno-patriotism helps legitimate and naturalize this state of affairs, while also reinforcing the nationalist credentials of the PRC regime. The patriotic side of this ideology is well documented. In the "one country, two systems" dominant discourse, Hong Kong people are represented as "patriotic Chinese and Hong Kong loving" (*aiguo aigang*).[15] The PRC authorities present the "one country, two systems" policy as a patriotic state-building strategy. It is a means to bring an end to colonial rule on Chinese soil, while completing the unification of the Chinese nation-state blocked by the Nationalists with respect to Taiwan. In the JD (1), the PRC Government declares that "to recover the Hong Kong area . . . is the common aspiration of *the entire Chinese people*" (emphasis added) and that "upholding national unity and territorial integrity" is one of its basic policies regarding the territory (JD (2)). The first sentence in the BL also represents "one country, two systems" as a national reunification strategy, declaring that "Hong Kong has been part of the territory of China since ancient times" (BL Preamble).

Furthermore, the autonomy process clearly aims to facilitate the decolonization and the re-nationalization of Hong Kong. Less noted in the literature has been the extent to which this patriotism is *ethnic* or *racial* in character, the ways in which the autonomy process justifies the exclusion of people from political power based on these presumed characteristics. As Barry Sautman (2004) has astutely pointed out in his pioneering work on this subject, post-1997 Hong Kong is a "quasi-ethnocracy" in which the Hong Kong ethnic Chinese have replaced white European expatriates as the rulers.[16] This is despite China's official status as a multi-national state and despite Hong Kong's own increasing diversity.

The 2001 census estimates the non-ethnic Chinese population of the territory was 5.1 percent, or approximately 350,000 individuals. This included some 170,000–200,000 FDWs with foreign passports (predominantly from the Philippines, but also from Indonesia, Thailand, and other countries); approximately 20,000 people of south Asian descent (Indian, Sri Lankan, Nepalese, and others), many Hong Kong born; a small minority of long-term "foreign" residents who think of themselves as Hong Kong people; and other "foreigners" who have resided in Hong Kong for shorter periods. Even amongst the so-called ethnic Chinese majority, there are many differences of dialect, place of birth, (multiple) nationality and "flexible citizenship" practices (Ong 1999; Henders 2004). Many Hong Kong people are foreign born and/or possess US, British, Canadian, or other non-PRC nationality. An estimated 100,000 Hong Kong-born individuals now live in the mainland. Some 340,000 Hong Kong residents (roughly 5 percent) are new migrants from the mainland (Sautman 2004: 115–16, 121–6).

Much of this growing diversity has been fuelled by structural changes in Hong Kong's economy associated with economic globalization. With the deindustrialization of Hong Kong has come more low-wage service jobs and an increasing demand for migrant workers willing to do them. Most of these have come as FDWs and unskilled workers from mainland China and elsewhere in the region, although smaller numbers of more highly skilled workers have been admitted through employment visas. The result is a quasi-ethnic or racial and gendered division of labour. Non-ethnic Chinese (mostly individuals from the Philippines, Indonesia, Thailand, and south Asia) and recent mainland migrants are overrepresented in low-wage service sector work and separated from the rest of the population by a widening income gap (Chiu and Lui 2004: 1878–83). Women are overrepresented in these socio-economically and politically marginalized groups. Individuals in these groups are not only more likely to be poor, but more likely to face discrimination or exclusion in the workplace, in accessing public services, and in society at large (Sautman 2004: 121ff).

FDWs technically have the same rights and freedoms as other workers under the BL (Art. 25). However, in practice the HKSAR Government limits their rights and encourages their social, economic, and political marginalization, backed by widespread social discrimination. Most are legally denied the possibility of permanent residency, welfare benefits, and union rights and must leave Hong Kong if they lose their jobs. Though many have resided in Hong Kong for ten or fifteen years, they are not allowed long-term visas and are not allowed to bring their families to the territory. They cannot change job categories and must leave Hong Kong within two weeks of losing their job, making it difficult to change employers.

These policy conditions and practices encourage abuses and exploitative conditions on FDWs in Hong Kong. At the same time, there are increasing reports of FDWs deprived of vacation leaves, adequate food, and cases of physical, verbal, and psychological abuse inflicted on them by their employers.

(Migrants Rights International, 2003; see also Bell 2001)

The Coalition for Migrants Rights regards these policies as a direct violation of the ILO Conventions to which the HKSAR Government is a signatory through China. Ironically, the PRC Government aimed to enhance its status as a law-abiding member of the club of major states by supporting the continuation of Hong Kong's international human and labor rights obligations established in the British years. However, the ongoing selectivity of these commitments and of their enforcement points to the inequalities legitimated by Hong Kong's international legal personality in the current world order.

Comparatively recent arrivals from the mainland are not always ethnically or racially distinct from the majority, but are often "racialized" in the sense of being treated as members of a separate cultural group of second-class citizens, due to their presumed inferiority, lower education levels, and relative poverty (Sautman 2004: 115–16, 121–6; see Pun and Wu 2004; Leung, H.C. 2004). Recent mainland immigrants earn on average HK$6,000 to HK$12,000 monthly, the latter about 64 percent of the median household income. This marginalization has a gender dimension too. As Sautman (2004: 126) points out, surveys suggest that as many as 70 percent of new mainland migrant women are unemployed and, amongst those working, 75 percent worked for sixty three hours a week and 80 percent earned HK$6,000 monthly or less.

Additionally, long-standing government immigration policies disadvantage ordinary families divided by the mainland border by inhibiting their reunification and opportunities to share income and social reproduction responsibilities. The policies also block access to social services and fail to protect residents from discriminatory treatment, with considerable public support from permanent residents. This has particularly devastating effects on female single parents and married women with children. There is little affordable daycare in Hong Kong and many recently created benefits programmes, such as Comprehensive Society Security Assistance and the Mandatory Provident Fund for retirement income, tie benefits to the lifetime paid employment patterns typical of men, to the presumption that women doing unpaid work are married to men with sufficient incomes, and to the income levels of spouses. The introduction of welfare-to-work programmes after 2000 has further stigmatized social service users in a society dominated by the self-sufficiency and rags-to-riches ethos, reinforcing the view that newer mainland immigrants do not share Hong Kong values and are a culture apart (Leung L-C. 2004: 183–5).

A number of other structural features of Hong Kong self-rule help reproduce a state of affairs where a small group of mostly male, rich, ethnic-Chinese business elites dominate the political system and economy and where the ethnic Chinese middle class largely colludes to marginalize the ethnicized, racialized, and gendered other. The PRC nationality law as applied in Hong Kong under the BL (Annex III) largely reserves PRC nationality to Hong Kong ethnic Chinese permanent residents. Non-ethnic Chinese are typically permitted to naturalize only if they have near relatives who are Chinese and if they are settled in China and renounce their nationality in other states. The latter requirement is not applied to Hong Kong Chinese given PRC nationality in 1997. Non-ethnic Chinese permanent residents of Hong Kong, even if they are locally born, normally cannot get an SAR passport. A non-ethnic Chinese permanent resident loses this status if they live abroad for more than three years, whereas a PRC national with Hong Kong permanent residency (including the right to vote, to stand for election, and not to be deported) never loses right of abode in Hong Kong. Unlike Chinese nationals, a non-ethnic Chinese person claiming permanent residency must make Hong Kong her or his sole place of residence (Sautman 2004: 125; BL Art. 24).

A similarly ethnicized understanding of citizenship and narrow nationality-based determination of loyalty to the state pervades the political system, reinforcing exclusion. Under the BL, all the top positions in Hong Kong's political and judicial system, including 80 percent of the Legislative Council seats, must be held by PRC citizens who are permanent HKSAR residents without right of abode in a foreign country. In some cases, they are also required to have lived in Hong Kong for a continuous period of not less than fifteen years (BL Arts 43, 55, 61, 67, 71, 90, 101). In addition to excluding most non-ethnic Chinese residents from full political participation, this provision also excludes many ethnic Chinese residents. Its provisions fly in the face of the "flexible citizenship" patterns of many Hong Kong middle-class families who have sought passports, educational opportunities, and professional and business advancement in other states. This seems natural only if "one country, two systems" is mainly about decolonization, re-nationalization, and protecting the distinct *ethnic Chinese* identity of Hong Kong, papering over divisions of class, gender, race, and ethnic exclusion and multi-layered, multiple identities amongst Chinese nationals in Hong Kong and "othering" non-ethnic Chinese residents.

This exclusionary outcome is perpetuated by an authoritarian political system and laissez-faire economic policies and is naturalized by the ethos of ethno-patriotic economism. The first Chief Executive, Tung Chee-hwa, spoke of Hong Kong as a place defined by "Chinese values" such as a deference to authority, mutual care in the family, especially the elderly, and hard work

(HKSAR Government 1997; see also Chan 2003; Sautman 2004). Those who do not earn their own way, who use the territory's skeletal social programmes, or challenge the political status quo are the un-Chinese, un-patriotic other. In this way, the ethnic contours of the institutions of self-rule reinforce economism and ethno-patriotism, while legitimating Chinese rule in Hong Kong and the wider political-economic order.

Further, ethno-patriotic economism is underpinned by and reinforces the growing economic integration of the HKSAR with the mainland, fostered by both the PRC and HKSAR Governments as well as global market forces, speeded up by China's entry into the WTO. By 2000, mainland–Hong Kong trade accounted for more than one-third of total trade transactions in the HKSAR. China was Hong Kong's second biggest investor and was present in a growing number of sectors. By 2001 Hong Kong residents were making 53 million trips into mainland China a year, against only 29 million in 1996; and mainland Chinese were making 4.4 million trips to the SAR compared to only 2.4 in 1996 (Holliday *et al.* 2002: 461). Increasing numbers of Hong Kong professionals were working in the mainland, while the Hong Kong economy was increasingly dependent on mainland tourists and investors. Since the post-1997 economic downtown, this integration has brought much needed job and investment opportunities for Hong Kong workers and capitalists. As a consequence, many individuals increasingly regard mainland markets, jobs, investment opportunities, and tourists as the key to reviving Hong Kong's economy and their personal economic fortunes (Kueh and Ng 2002: 407).

Democratization and its limits

The "one country, two systems" policy has contributed to building a world political economic order more accommodative of distinctive sub-state territorial communities. It has also reinforced the external and internal legitimacy of the post-Mao regime by bolstering its nationalist and capitalist credentials and its identity as a status quo world power. It has allowed the capitalist, (semi-)liberal institutions of Hong Kong, a product of its particular history and experience of colonialism, to survive within an authoritarian state that is still marketizing and whose government is little tolerant of liberal civil and political rights. As such, it has demonstrated that both world order and the modern state form, including in its post-socialist Leninist variation, can be adapted to recognize the distinctive identities of sub-state territorial communities and their role as non-state power centres. However, at the same time, Hong Kong's autonomy process has also allowed local pro-China and business elites, backed by the PRC and British Governments, to use the ideology and institutions of self-rule to reproduce and legitimate the class, gender, racial and ethnic inequalities that scar one of the world's richest societies and one of the supposed economic success stories of East Asia. That dominant ideologies and formal political institutions, local, state, and global, act together to legitimate inequality is hardly unique to Hong Kong. What is less common, as well as seldom noted, are the ways in which the discourses and institutions of territorial autonomy and collective identity legitimate an internally exclusionary order, while simultaneously reinforcing state legitimacy and world order. No doubt these effects of the "one country, two systems" autonomy regime are in some respects unique to Hong Kong. However, the Hong Kong experience may be of wider significance, given the growing role of self-government arrangements in managing tensions in culturally plural societies that are simultaneously adapting to and shaping the global economy. This is an important subject for further research, as is a fuller analysis of the resistance to exclusion in Hong Kong.

Meanwhile, in closing, it is worth briefly considering the role that formal democratization of the HKSAR might play in promoting a more emancipatory autonomy process, leaving aside the important question of whether and how this democratization might come about. The HKSAR case suggests two hypotheses for further research. The first is that formal democracy—understood as a political system where regular, competitive, free, and fair elections based on universal adult suffrage, backed by the full enjoyment of civil and political rights, are used to select an executive and legislature with binding decision-making authority—is a prerequisite to creating emancipatory forms of self-rule for sub-state territorial communities. Hong Kong provides evidence of this, in that public contestation over Hong Kong identity and values exists because those resisting ethno-patriotic economism take advantage of the limited elected seats in the Legislative Council, free speech and association and other rights to articulate another understanding of what Hong Kong is and can become. The second hypothesis is that formal democratization alone cannot promote more inclusive self-rule vis-à-vis those marginalized by gender, racial, ethnic, and class inequalities. Formal democracy would be unlikely to expand the number of female elected representatives, for instance, unless structural and ideological barriers to gender equality were addressed (Hong Kong Women's Coalition for Beijing '95 1997: 392; Ng c 2000). Given the underdeveloped state of denizenship rights in much of the world, including Hong Kong, there is little chance that FDWs and other migrants without permanent residency would be given the right to vote or run for office. Moreover, enhancing civil and political rights protection would do little on their own to advance rights in private realms such as homes and workplaces. To make inclusive self-rule meaningful for the least powerful members of society, the poor, ethnic and racialized (migrant) workers, and marginalized women and girls need substantive socio-economic and cultural rights and freedoms, including material means and a supportive discursive climate. It would require that Hong Kong opposition groups move beyond their dominant focus on the struggle for democracy and civil and political rights, to also include economic, social, and cultural empowerment for all Hong Kong residents (see Sing 2004a: 102ff; Ch. 7, 8; So 1999: 179–80, 244–6; Sing 2004b). The ethos of ethno-patriotic economism and its embeddedness in the HKSAR autonomy arrangement, underpinned by world political economic order and the Chinese regime's legitimacy needs, remains a major barrier to a more egalitarian outcome.

Notes

1 I wish to thank Jennifer Catallo and Lauren Turner for their resourceful and good-humoured research assistance in the preparation of this article.
2 This is akin to what Aiwa Ong (1999) has termed "graduated sovereignty," a strategy used by south-east Asian post-developmental states under late capitalism in which "citizens in zones that are differently articulated to global production and financial circuits are subjected to different kinds of surveillance and in practice enjoy different sets of civil, political, and economic rights. By thus calibrating its control over sovereignty to the challenges of global capital, the so-called tiger state develops a system of graduated zones that also projects against pockets of political unrest" (pp. 215–26).
3 On Hong Kong's international status as a highly autonomous non-state entity, see Tang (1993) and Davis (1989), Ch 5.
4 Amongst the exceptions are Holliday, Ngok, and Yep (2002).
5 Citizenship is more than legal status with related rights and duties. It includes the recognition of identity and requires political, socio-economic, and cultural conditions in which meaningful participation in political community, civil society, and public spheres is possible, including but not limited to representation (see Wong 2002, esp. pp. 64–5). Citizenship is not synonymous with nationality, which is a legal status and relationship with the state conferred by the state through laws and regulations. Sub-state public authorities, including those of autonomous regions, play important roles in addition to the state in determining who enjoys citizenship in all its dimensions, as do civil society and economic actors.
6 On "the gospel of patriotic capitalism" and its promotion through popular culture, see Law (2000: 213–14).
7 For example, see Overholt (2001).
8 On business-government ties under British colonialism, see Jones (1995: 167); Scott (1998).
9 For a critical analysis of the work of Lau Siu-kai in this regard, see Lam Wai-man (2004).
10 Reforms included a slow expansion and improvement in public housing, public health care at modest fees, free primary school education (later expanded to nine years), minimal labour laws to protect workers against the worst abuses, and bare-bones social assistance for the very destitute (see Leung 2004 in Ku and Pun: 103).
11 See Lam, Wai-man (2004), who provides an excellent account of Hong Kong history that demonstrates the mythology of political apathy. See also Klein (1995).
12 Gini coefficients are common indicators of income inequality, where 0 represents perfect equality of income and 1 is perfect inequality.
13 Following Patten's increase in social programme spending and support for caps on imported labour in his 1996 budget address, the legislature in late June 1997 proposed seven private members' bills that protected employees' rights to consultation, representation, and collective bargaining; protected trade unions; demanded extra statutory holidays; demanded measures against age discrimination, and changes to laws on dismissal and compensation schemes for occupational injuries (So 1999: 23).

14   Women's groups have demanded the abolition of the functional constituency system
     on the grounds that it denies political citizenship to those with less wealth and lower
     social status and is discriminatory for women (Leung Lai-ching 2004: 188).
15   The narrative of Chinese patriotism is also reinforced through civic education in
     schools and public campaigns (see Tse 2004) and popular culture (see Mathews
     and Lui 2001).
16   On the racist foundations of British colonial rule, see Klein (1995).

Bibliography

"Asia: A High-rise Bust," *The Economist*, June 27, 1998.

"ALU Interviews Lee Cheuk Yan," October 3, 2002. Available online: www.amrc.org.
hk/4403.htm (accessed June 15, 2005).

Beetham, David (1991), *The Legitimation of Power*, London: Macmillan.

Bell, Daniel A. (2001) "Equal Rights for Foreign Resident Workers: The Case of Filipina
Domestic Workers in Hong Kong and Singapore," *Dissent* (Fall): 26–34.

Chan Chak-Kwan (1998) "Welfare Policies and the Construction of Welfare Relations in a Residual Welfare State: The Case of Hong Kong," *Social Policy and
Administration*, 32(3): 278–91.

Chan, Raymond K. H. (2003) "The Sustainability of the Asian Welfare System after the
Financial Crisis," *Asian Journal of Social Science*, 31(2): 172–97.

Chau, Ruby C. M. and Sam W. K. Yu (1999) "Social Welfare and Economic Development in China and Hong Kong," *Critical Social Policy*, 19(1): 87–107.

Cheung Siu-keung (2000) "Speaking Out: Days in the Lives of Three Hong Kong
Cage Dwellers," *Positions: East Asia Cultures Critique*, 8(1): 235–62.

Chiu, Stephen W. K. and Lui, Tai-lok (2004) "Testing the Global City–Social
Polarization Thesis: Hong Kong Since the 1990s," *Urban Studies*, 41(10): 1863–88.

Chow, Nelson (*c*.2004) "Social Welfare in Hong Kong—Post 1997" (mimeo).

Costa, Christopher K. (1993) "One Country, Two Foreign Policies: United States
Relations with Hong Kong After July 1, 1997," *Villanova Law Review*, 38: 825–70.

Davis, Michael C. (2001) "Representing the Local in a Global Age: The Case for a
Confederal Solution to China's Territorial Conflicts," Paper presented to the
Conference on "Globalization and Its Challenges in the 21st Century," International
Studies Association, Hong Kong Global Conference, July 2001.

Davis, Michael C. (1989) *Constitutional Confrontation in Hong Kong. Issues and
Implications of the Basic Law*, London: Macmillan.

Domes, Jürgen (1988) "Introduction," in *Hong Kong: A Chinese and International
Concern*, Boulder, CO: Westview, pp. 1–6.

Foot, Rosemary (1995) *The Practice of Power: US Relations with China Since 1949*,
Oxford: Oxford University Press.

Fung, Anthony (2001) "What Makes the Local? A Brief Consideration of the
Rejuvenation of Hong Kong Identity," *Cultural Studies*, 15(3/4): 591–601.

Ghai, Yash (2001) "Citizenship and Politics in the HKSAR: The Constitutional
Framework," *Citizenship Studies*, 5(2): 143–64.

Hannum, Hurst (1990) *Autonomy, Sovereignty, and Self-Determination: The Accommodation of Conflicting Rights*, Philadelphia, PA: University of Pennsylvania Press.

Henders, Susan J. (2004) "The Self-Government of Unbounded Communities," in
Laycock, David (ed.), *Representation and Democratic Theory*, Vancouver: University of British Columbia Press, pp. 119–40.

—— (2001) "So What if It's Not a Gamble? Post-Westphalian Politics in Macau," *Pacific Affairs*, 74(3) (Fall): 342–60.

—— (2000) "Hong Kong and Macau in Intergovernmental Organizations," *Policy Options*, 21(1) (January–February): 88–9.

Ho, Denny Kwok-Leung (2004) "Citizenship as a Form of Governance: A Historical Overview," in Ku, Agnes S. and Pun Ngai (eds.), *Remaking Citizenship in Hong Kong: Community, Nation, and the Global City*, London: Routledge, pp. 19–36.

Holliday, Ian, Ngok, Ma and Yep, Ray (2002) "A High Degree of Autonomy? Hong Kong Special Administrative Region, 1997–2002," *The Political Quarterly*, 74(4) (October): 455–64.

Hong Kong Economic and Trade Office (2003) "Hong Kong Tops Free Economy List Again," Hong Kong Update (September), Toronto.

Hong Kong Government (1995), *Background Facts*, London: Hong Kong Government Office, August.

Hong Kong Human Rights Commission (1998) "Submission to the United Nations Committee on Economic, Social, and Cultural Rights on Hong Kong Human Rights Situation after the Change of Sovereignty," Hong Kong: HKHRC, April. Available online: www.hkhrc.org.hk/homepage/index_e.htm (accessed April 9, 2005).

Hong Kong People's Alliance on WTO (n.d.) "HKPA Background," Hong Kong: HKPA. Available online: www.hkpa-wto.org/ (accessed May 26, 2005).

HKSAR Government (1997) "Policy Address: Building Hong Kong for a New Era," Hong Kong: HKSAR Government.

HKSAR Government (2004) "About Hong Kong," Hong Kong: HKSAR, October. Available online: www.info.gov.hk/info/hkbrief/eng/ahk.htm (accessed May 26, 2005).

HKSAR Provisional Legislative Council (1997) "Legislative Provisions (Suspension of Operation) Bill 1997," July 9, Hong Kong: HKSAR Government. Available online: www.info.gov.hk/isd/speech/1997bill.htm (accessed April 9, 2005).

Hong Kong Women's Coalition for Beijing '95 (1997) "Alternative Report on Women in Hong Kong," in Cheung, Fanny M. (ed.), *EnGendering Hong Kong Society: A Gender Perspective of Women's Status*, Hong Kong: Chinese University Press, pp. 385–94.

Hui Po-Keung (2004) "In Search of Communal Economic Subject: Reflections on a Local Community Currency Project," in Ku Agnes S. and Pun, Ngai (eds.), *Remaking Citizenship in Hong Kong: Community, Nation, and the Global City*, London: Routledge, pp. 215–34.

Joint Declaration of the Government of the United Kingdom of Great Britain and Northern Ireland and the Government of the People's Republic of China on the Question of Hong Kong, 1984.

Jones, Carol (1995) "The New Territories Inheritance Law: Colonialization and the Elites," in Pearson, Veronica and Leung, Benjamin K. P. (eds.), *Women in Hong Kong*, Hong Kong: Oxford University Press, pp. 167–92.

Klein, Richard (1995) "Law and Racism in an Asian Setting: An Analysis of the British Rule of Hong Kong," *Hastings International and Comparative Law Review*, 18(1): 223–76.

Kymlicka, Will (1996) *Multicultural Citizenship: A Liberal Theory of Minority Rights*, Oxford: Oxford University Press.

Ku, Agnes S. and Pun Ngai (2004) "Introduction: Remaking Citizenship in Hong Kong" in Ku, Agnes S. and Pun Ngai (eds.), *Remaking Citizenship in Hong Kong: Community, Nation, and the Global City*, London: Routledge, pp. 1–16.

Kueh, Y. Y. and Ng, Raymond C. W. (2002) "The Interplay of the 'China Factor' and US Dollar Peg in the Hong Kong Economy," *The China Quarterly*, 170 (June): 387–412.

Lam Wai-man (2004) *Understanding Political Culture in Hong Kong: The Paradox of Activism and Depoliticization*, Armonk, NY: M. E. Sharpe.

Lapidoth, Ruth (1997) *Autonomy: Flexible Solutions to Ethnic Conflict*, Washington, DC: US Institute of Peace Press.

Law Wing-sang (2000) "Northbound Colonialism: A Politics of Post-PC Hong Kong," *Positions: East Asia Cultures Critique*, 8(1): 201–33.

Leung, Beatrice (2001) "Church–State Relations in Hong Kong and Macau: From Colonial Rule to Chinese Rule," in *Citizenship Studies*, 5(2): 203–19.

Leung Hon-Chu (2004), "Politics of Incorporation and Exclusion: Immigration and Citizenship Issues," in Agnes S. Ku and Pun Ngai (eds.), *Remaking Citizenship in Hong Kong: Community, Nation, and the Global City*, London: Routledge, pp. 97–114.

Leung Lai-Ching (2004) "Engendering Citizenship," in Ku, Agnes S. and Pun Ngai (eds.), *Remaking Citizenship in Hong Kong: Community, Nation, and the Global City*, London: Routledge, pp. 175–94.

Mathews, Gordon and Liu Tai-lok (2001) "Introduction" in Mathews, Gordon and Liu, Tai-lok (eds.), *Consuming Hong Kong*, Hong Kong: Hong Kong University Press, pp. 1–21.

Migrants Rights International (2003) MRI and Migrant Forum in Asia (MFA) Symposium: "Asian Migrant Workers: Issues, Needs and Responses," Parallel Event to the 59th Session of the Commission on Human Rights, Palais des Nations, Geneva, April 7. Available online: www.migrantwatch.org/mri/whats_new/mri_mfa_symposium.htm (accessed June 6, 2005).

Ng, Catherine W. (*c.*2000), "Women and Electoral Politics in Hong Kong: Institutional Factors for Under-participation and Under-representation," Hong Kong: Citizens Party. Available online: www.citizensparty.org/community/eo/women.htm (accessed March 23, 2002).

Ong Aiwa (1999) *Flexible Citizenship: The Cultural Politics of Transnationality*, Durham: Duke University Press.

Overholt, William H. (2001) "Hong Kong: The Perils of Semi-Democracy," *Journal of Democracy*, 12(4) (October): 5–18.

People's Republic of China (1990) The Basic Law of the Hong Kong Special Administrative Region of the People's Republic of China, April 4.

Pun Ngai and Wu Ka-Ming (2004) "Lived Citizenship and Lower-Class Chinese Migrant Women: A Global City Without its People," in Ku, Agnes S. and Pun Ngai (eds.), *Remaking Citizenship in Hong Kong: Community, Nation, and the Global City*, London: Routledge, pp. 139–54.

"SAR Government Violates International Labour Coventions," *Hong Kong Voice of Democracy*, November 9, 1998.

Sautman, Barry (2004) "Hong Kong as a Semi-Ethnocracy: 'Race,' Migration and Citizenship in a Globalized Region," in Ku, Agnes S. and Pun, Ngai (eds.), *Remaking Citizenship in Hong Kong: Community, Nation, and the Global City*, London: Routledge, pp. 115–38.

Scott, Ian (1998) "Introduction," in Scott, Ian (ed.), *Institutional Change and the Political Transition in Hong Kong*, London: Macmillan, pp. 1–25.

Sing Ming (2004a), *Hong Kong's Torturous Democratization*, London: Routledge Curzon.

—— (2004b) "Weak Labor Movements and Opposition Parties: Hong Kong and Singapore (1)," *Journal of Contemporary Asia*, 34(4): 449–64.

—— (2001) "The Problem of Legitimacy of the Post-Handover Hong Kong Government," *International Journal of Public Administration*, 24(9) (September): 847ff.

So, Alvin Y. (1999) *Hong Kong's Embattled Democracy: A Societal Analysis*, Baltimore, MD, and London: John Hopkins University Press.

Social and Economic Policy Institute (2001), "Current Labour Market Conditions in Hong Kong," Global Policy Network, March. Available online: www.globalpolicy network.org (accessed March 3, 2005).

Tang, James T. H. (1993) "Hong Kong's International Status," *Pacific Review*, 6(3): 205–15.

Tse, Thomas Kwan-Choi (2004) "Civic Education and the Making of Deformed Citizenry. From British Colony to Chinese SAR," in Ku, Agnes S. and Pun, Ngai (eds.), *Remaking Citizenship in Hong Kong: Community, Nation, and the Global City*, London: Routledge, pp. 54–73.

Vickers, Simon (2001) "'More Colonial Again'—The Post-1997 Culture of Hong Kong's Governing Elite," *International Journal of Public Administration*, 24(9) (September): 951ff.

Wong, Lloyd (2002) "Transnationalism, Diasporic Communities, and Changing Identity: Implications for Canadian Citizenship," in Cameron, David R. and Stein, Janice Gross (eds.), *Street Protests and Fantasy Parks: Globalization, Culture, and the State*, Vancouver: University of British Columbia Press, pp. 49–87.

Zhao Xiaobin, Li Zhang and Tak, Kelvin Sit O. (2004) "Income Inequalities under Economic Restructuring in Hong Kong," *Asian Survey*, 44(3): 442–73.

7 The uses of the past
History and legitimacy

Diana Lary

"Gu wei jin yong"
古为今用
"The past is to be used by the present"

In 2000, the world celebrated the start of the new millennium. Booming, self-confident new China marked the event with the rest of the world. In Beijing the government sponsored the Millennium Monument, a dramatic semi-circular, rotating structure. The monument celebrates the millennium, and at the same time fulfils a critical historical role. It traces China's history and culture back to pre-history, it connects the present to the earliest origins of man, and it gives this connection a mystical, as well as a concrete form.

> The Monument is a grand structure ingeniously combining the spirit of traditional Chinese culture with modern architectural art, and integrating architecture, landscaping, sculpture, mural painting, and various other art forms. It will not only be an eternal memory of the turn of the millennium, but also serve as a centre for cultural, artistic, and scientific exhibitions both at home and abroad, as well as an inspiration in patriotism. Inside the southern entrance to the Monument is the Plaza of Holy Fire, one metre below ground and 960 square metres in area, standing for China's vast territory of 9,600,000 square kilometres. With the gentle centripetal rise of the ground suggesting the rise of the Chinese nation, the Holy Fire of China is located right in the middle of the Plaza. The fire originated at the site of Peking man at Zhoukoudian, Beijing, and is fed on natural gas. The ever-burning flames, rising some 45 centimetres high, are a token of the unceasing creativity of the Chinese civilization.
>
> (Beijing 2008 Olympic Games Official website)

In the building attached to the monument is a vast round chamber, the outer wall lined with the official version of Chinese history carved in golden stone, in deep bas-relief. The carvings start with the mythical culture heroes, go on through a legion of iconic figures, most of them from the world of culture, and end with the figure of Deng Xiaoping, flanked by a colophon in the calligraphy of Jiang Zemin. The wall has an overwhelming message: it shows the historical inevitability of contemporary China, the unbroken march from the distant past to the present, and its glorious culmination in the present government. History proves the right of the government to rule; history has been put at the service of the state.

History, the state and legitimacy

One of the products of the intellectual foment of nineteenth-century Europe was scientific history, usually encapsulated in the rather pedestrian statement of Leopold von Ranke that he wanted to discover "what had actually happened" (*wie es eigentlich gewesen ist*). This meant the search for objectivity, the basing of historical research on the analysis of documents, to establish an objective truth. The belief in the use of documentary sources, carefully and accurately analysed, still dominates western academic history and though there has long since been a recognition that interpretation is critical, the idea that the purpose of history might be to justify a contemporary government is still anathema.

The official Chinese view of history is quite different. Chinese governments have always taken the past very seriously, and seen it as one of the key factors in proving a particular regime's right to rule. To do this the state needs to control history. One of the major state projects for the past 2,000 years has been the writing of history. Almost every government has employed a large contingent of historians, men of the highest intellectual calibre. These men have compiled over the last two millennia the twenty-four official histories (*zhengshi* 正史). These are not histories for popular consumption—indeed, they may never have been read at all by anyone beyond the few people with a requirement to know the official view.[1] The histories were compiled as a repository of the official truth.

The need for an official version of the past assumes the need to control historians. Traditionally this control was harsh. Sima Qian (司马迁), the Grand Historian and the compiler of the *Historical Record (Shiji* 史纪 *)*, the first comprehensive history, was also the first historian to fall victim of the state. He was castrated at the order of the emperor Han Wudi, in 96 BC. Wu Han (吴晗), the historian and deputy mayor of Beijing, who lived 2,000 years later, was the most recent historian to be destroyed by the state. He was driven to death[2] during the Cultural Revolution, after his article *Hai Rui dismissed from office (Hai Rui baguan* 海瑞罢官 *)*, the story of an honest official in the Ming Dynasty, was perceived to be a criticism of Mao Zedong.

Wu Han's fate was especially poignant because in his youth Chinese historians and archaeologists had begun to do scientific research that would transform the study of Chinese history—and reject many of the traditional interpretations. This work was done by a generation of brilliant, western-trained scholars who worked in China's new universities. In the 1920s and 1930s archaeologists discovered hominids near Beijing (Peking Man); the capital of the Shang Dynasty at Anyang, a dynasty previously existing only in myth; and oracle bones; with the earliest form of Chinese writing. Their work was nationalist in that they wanted to build a new, modern China that would value the past but not be dominated by it. It was also internationalist in that many of the scholars worked with foreign collaborators.[3]

The work was broken off by the Japanese invasion of 1937, when many of China's universities were forced to move deep in to the interior, far from the archives and the archaeological sites. It did not resume at the end of the war, because the chaos of the Civil War prevented any serious academic research. After 1949, the practice of scientific history was replaced by a new historical straitjacket; Marxism-Leninism, another western import, forced Chinese historians to apply the mechanistic determinism of Marxism to a history it did not fit. This approach was itself abandoned with the start of the Cultural Revolution. In the post-reform era a new slogan started to dominate the academic practice of history, "seeking truth from facts" (*shishi qiushi* 实事求是). This slogan remains very influential in academic history; China's present historians work to very high standards of research and strive for accuracy. But their work is now only one of the forms of history. There is a separation between this modern, scientific form of history, and the state's official history.

The current official approach to history is very much in the pattern of traditional history. The state presents a vision of history that confirms its right to rule, that gives it legitimacy. The state sponsors grandiose and expensive projects to underline the greatness of China, and the greatness of the present government. These include the repair and rebuilding of ancient monuments[4] and the financing of massive works of teaching, research and entertainment, all directed at the common goal of underlining the glory of the Chinese past, and appealing to a population that may share this view. It is much more comfortable and reassuring for people to be proud of their past; and there is enormous scope within China's rich history for pride in the past.

Confucius revived

One of the recent state projects is the revival of traditional China's greatest sage, Confucius. The Ministry of Education sponsors one hundred Confucian Institutes around the world. Its website states: "[Confucius'] doctrine has a very important influence throughout the world and to name this institute after him shows the longevity and profundity of Chinese language and culture. It also embodies the developing trend of the integration of Chinese language and culture into the world in the new century."

The irony of the Confucius revival is that it comes only three decades after the vicious attacks on the sage in the "Criticize Lin Biao, Criticize Confucius" (*Pi Lin Pi Kong* 批林批孔) Campaign of 1972.[5] The revival would make Mao turn in his grave—if he had been buried, instead of providing a daily offence to Confucian practice by lying unburied in the middle of Beijing; by tradition, he should be ensconced in a tomb outside the city.

The revival can be explained by a need to fill the ideological vacuum left by the collapse of Marxism, and by a desire to inspire people with a belief system less threatening than some of the new religious currents sweeping the country. It may also speak to the question of legitimacy; the present leadership has only the flimsy ideology of "socialism with Chinese characteristics" upon which to base its claim to ideological legitimacy. Confucianism may bolster the leaders' position by doing what it has traditionally been designed to do: inspire respect for experience, and encourage a natural deference for leadership in the family, the community and the state. Deference is the most effective tool of efficient government, one most leaders anywhere in the world long for; it not only makes it easy for them to rule, but the deferential behaviour of their subjects convinces them that they really should be rulers.

The Qing history

The present government has returned to traditional practice in another striking way. In 2002 the government announced a massive ten-year project, to write the official history of the Qing dynasty. 600 million *yuan* (RMB) (CN$100,000,000) was set aside for the project, and 400 scholars are employed full time on the project. The end product will be so massive that it will take 10,000 days (without holidays) for a person to read the volumes straight through (*The Epoch Times*, September 10, 2004). The first volume is due to be published in 2009, for the sixtieth anniversary of the establishment of the People's Republic.

There is a deeply serious purpose to this project, aside from the glorification of the past. It will prove conclusively two major points. One is the present government's political legitimacy, based on a proper succession. The government is the legitimate heir of the last imperial dynasty. By precedent, Beijing should be compiling the history of the Republic, its immediate predecessor. But by commissioning the Qing History, the Republic is consigned to a historical limbo as an interregnum, not a proper dynasty. The People's Republic becomes the heir of the Qing and associates itself with the Three Great Emperors, Kangxi, Rongzheng and Qianlong, now the subjects of a major exhibition that is touring the world.

Second, the history will establish that the government in Beijing is the legitimate ruler of Xinjiang, Tibet, Taiwan—all territories brought fully under Chinese rule by Qing conquests. We can safely say "will," because in the writing of an official history there is no fear that conclusions other than those acceptable to the current government will be reached.

The Han Wudi (汉武帝) saga

Over the past decade or so, Chinese television has shown increasing numbers of historical dramas, usually multi-episode serials that deal not with the sad episodes of Chinese history, but with the glories of the past. Central China Television (CCTV) is an arm of the state propaganda machine, so that major series shown there can be assumed to follow the official line. The fifty-eight part serial on the life and times of Han Wudi, which was aired in 2005, had a budget of RMB50,000,000 (CN$9,000,000), and was described as "a hit among soap opera fans across the country." It was also profit-making; shortly after the series started, CCTV had already made RMB120,000,000 (CN$19,000,000) from the sale of advertisements alone, before the sale of DVDs started (China Heritage Project, September 2005). Han expanded China to the west and the south. His brutality is overlooked; this was the emperor who ordered that Sima Qian be castrated.[6]

The three projects discussed here derive from ancient history and are designed principally to inspire pride in the state and gratitude for the government's work to promote the glorious past. The contemporary state would rather encourage this kind of uplifting project than deal with what has been at times a tragic modern history. It is better to ignore some topics. The first and only museum of the Cultural Revolution, which opened for the fortieth anniversary of the start of the ten years of turbulence, is a private one, founded by a local official in Shantou. For the government, which still espouses the ideology in force during the Cultural Revolution, an official commemoration of the victims of the period would amount to self-incrimination.

This is also the case with other tragic periods since 1949 (Land Reform, the Great Leap Forward, the famine that followed it). They can be discussed in literature (known as the *literature of scars)* or in film, but not in history, neither official history nor academic history.

One period that used to be taboo is now officially commemorated— the War of Resistance. This year will be the seventieth anniversary of the Rape of Nanjing. In December, a huge new museum will open in Nanjing, almost four times the size of the present museum. It will cost almost 500,000,000 RMB. This museum is one of eighteen museums now devoted to the war, most of which include references to the role of the Guomindang and its armies (*China Daily*, September 27, 2006) a subject that was taboo until very recently.

These and other historical projects will reach their apogee during the event that most underlines China's contemporary status in the world, the 2008 Olympics. But they will continue thereafter. The state can never ignore history, because to forget it might mean losing control of the past. The challenges to this control are always there, sometimes lurking, sometimes open.

Discreet dissension

One major source of challenge to official history is the popular tradition. A different version of history is carried in stories and legends, the most important of which is *The Romance of the Three Kingdoms (Sanguo yanyi* 三国演义 *).* Here the heroes are not emperors, but intelligent, resourceful commoners such as Zhuge Liang (诸葛亮). This version is replicated in many forms of popular entertainment—opera, theatre, and martial arts. This challenge can easily be dealt with by the state. It is tolerated, but consigned to a lower level of culture, the Little Tradition, and then left alone.

Other challenges are more difficult, because they are often indirect and subtle. These challenges involve the ancient Chinese tradition of allegory. Chinese poets, artists and writers have long experience in using allegory and allusion to criticize the government of the day. Wu Han was doing this when he mentioned the name of Hai Rui. The use of allegory makes it essential that anyone involved in the public world in China must know history—otherwise they might miss the allusions, possibly with devastating effects.

Some of the most important contemporary practitioners of the art are filmmakers, who make films whose entertainment value covers deep and complex messages. Zhang Yimou's 1994 film *To Live (* 活着 *)* is the life story of a couple from the 1930s to the 1970s—and also a film of deep sadness, about the awful disruptions of modern history, not a few of which can be ascribed to the mistakes of the Communist Party. Chen Kaige's 1998 film, *The Emperor and the Assassin (* 荆柯刺秦王 *),* is a spectacular portrayal of the first emperor—and also an allegory on the violence and savagery that periodically engulfs China, most recently in the Cultural Revolution. Zhang Yimou's 2002 version of the same story, *Hero (* 英雄 *),* comes even closer to the bone; the hero, played by Jet Li, has the opportunity to assassinate the first emperor, but decides to sacrifice himself instead, for the greater glory of China. The message is that it was Qin Shihuang's brutality that created the glory of the Chinese empire. The price to be paid for its creation is the death of the hero; the last scene of the film shows a man-shaped space surrounded by thousands of arrows.

Allegorical challenges to the state can be dealt with in a number of ways. One is simply to censor films or not allow them to be shown. Another is to make it difficult for people to make films, by putting pressure on film studios. A third is to co-opt the critics: Zhang Yimou's current project is to direct the opening ceremonies of the 2008 Olympics.

Contesting histories

The state has a repertoire of means of dealing with its critics in the artistic world. It has greater difficulty in dealing with another, more insidious challenge, the devotion of many Chinese to the history of their own regions, often at the cost of the state narrative. These regional versions of history seldom attack the state; they ignore it, or bypass it.

Regional histories

The contemporary state, like its predecessors, faces huge problems in controlling its vast lands and in persuading its disparate people that they all belong in China. Its success is not guaranteed. Many regions have an attachment to their own histories, and deep convictions about how they diverge from the state's history. They, too, use the past to justify the present and make tacit statements about their own historical autonomy. They often go back to the remote past, truncating the period between the time when many of the regions had little to do with the central government, and the present period when this relationship is imposed on them. Many regions have found discreet but powerful ways of celebrating their own origins—and at the same time challenging the Centre.

The regions know better than to challenge the Centre directly, given the vituperative charges and attacks from the Centre that might follow. The challenges are cautious, and rely on implication rather than bold statement. One discreet statement is the sponsoring of regional history projects—by the regions' own governments, by cities or by prominent citizens. Some of the projects are books, others films—and, more and more often, museums. Newly rich Guangdong, the powerhouse of economic growth over the past two decades, has filled Guangzhou with proud references to the region's own past.

No reference is more lavish or more potent than the Tomb of the King of Nanyue (南粤王墓), on Liberation Street in the centre of Guangzhou. The tomb is more than 2,000 years old. It was discovered accidentally in 1983, during excavation for a construction project. Nothing was accidental after that; the tomb became a project of regional history. Public and private donations poured in from Cantonese who loved their region, including many from Hong Kong. A spectacular building went up. Underground, the tomb was lovingly reconstructed. Above ground a huge museum was built, a tribute to the great and distinct history of Guangdong and the Cantonese. Its exhibition treats Nanyue as the centre of a rich world, stretching to Vietnam and Southeast Asia. The north, the Han, scarcely exists. And it makes Nanyue the direct ancestor of present day Guangdong. There is a play on two characters both pronounced *yue*, one the character for the ancient Yue peoples 越 , the other an alternative character for the Cantonese 粤 . Using the first as a loan word for the second implies that the free-standing state in Guangdong 2,000 years ago is the linear predecessor of the present-day Guangdong (Lary 1996).

The interest in regional history found in Guangdong is replicated in all the major regions of China. But the state still trumps the region if the discovery or the artefact is important enough. Sichuan's ancient cultures, associated with the states of Shu and Ba, suffered a double blow. Its wonderful ancient bronzes, found at Sanxingdui, have been ascribed as "treasures of ancient China," rather than artefacts of an independent culture. And at the same time some of the most important sites have been drowned as the waters behind the Three Gorges Dam have risen. But at least their history is known. Other regions have seen their histories suppressed.

Suppressed histories

The western border regions were visited sporadically by Chinese forces from the second century BCE onwards, but were brought under the direct control of Beijing only in the eighteenth century, as a result of the Qianlong Emperor's military campaigns. In the late Qing and during the Republican period, Chinese governments lost control in practical terms, but never abandoned the principle of Chinese rule. After 1949, Beijing resumed tough control, by the use of military conquest followed by the stationing of large People's Liberation Army (PLA) garrisons and the establishment of vast military farms (*bingtuan* 兵团). History was also crucial as a tool of control, and this meant rewriting the history of the outlying regions in terms of the Chinese presence there, sporadic as it was. The regions and the indigenous people were denied their own histories. This denial of the past is the only way to cope with the obvious truth that these regions have their own quite separate histories and traditions.

This can mean awkward adjustments even to the Chinese tradition, for the sake of present use, as for example in the claims that China can take credit for the Mongol Khans Ghenghis and his grandson Khublai, who are seen as Chinese national heroes instead of the ferocious conquerors of the whole Eurasian continent, including China. This "ownership" of Mongol history identifies major Mongol sites, including Ghenghis' putative tomb, as being in China (in Inner Mongolia). But at least the Mongol past lives on; other "minority" areas are treated with greater disdain.

Xinjiang

Xinjiang (新疆) means the new territories; this was the name given to the homeland of the Uighurs after the Qianlong conquest. The Uighurs are a Turkic people, closely connected to Central Asia and to Turkey. They have a strong sense of their own history, a recent memory of virtual autonomy in the Republic, and an even more recent memory of maltreatment during the Mao era. They have seen waves of Han immigrants settle in their region. Across the borders, in the former Soviet Union, the Russians have departed and the new states have reasserted their own traditional identities. The changes in Central Asia have strengthened the Uighurs' identity.

There are hard and soft frontiers between China and the neighbouring states: the hard frontier is military, a series of defended lines on the map. The soft frontier is a zone of close cultural and commercial connections as recognized by the Shanghai Agreement that aims to join the Central Asian states and China in a pact against terrorism and unrest.

The Uighurs do not have a formal, official voice in their own history. Their history has been submerged into Chinese history. Their artefacts are ignored. The almost miraculous mummies, some of them 2,000 years old, found in the desert in the last twenty years, are displayed in a series of ramshackle cases at the back of the local museum; very little research has been done on them. This seems to be because some of them are clearly Caucasian, an origin that severely challenges any idea of long-term Chinese presence (Mair 2000). Some of their sites have even been appropriated. Outside Kashgar, the tomb of the Khoja family, one of the great Uighur families, is referred to in Chinese as the tomb of the Fragrant Concubine (Xiang Fei 香妃). She was a junior member of the Khoja family, an unwilling concubine of Qianlong—and she is not buried in the tomb.

The Uighurs, like other non-Han ethnic groups in Western China, cannot be allowed an autonomous history. One of the reasons for this has nothing directly to do with them and their relations with the Centre but everything to do with the one outlying region not directly controlled from Beijing.

Taiwan history

One of the most aggravating aspects of the current Taiwan situation, to Beijing, is that Taiwan insists on having its own past, a past that has little to do with the Mainland. The past few years have seen the uncovering of a Taiwan past that focuses only on the island—the history of the aboriginal peoples, the study of Taiwanese culture. This work is carried out in institutes and colleges funded by the government. Running through the work is the theme of how brief Taiwan's connection to China was, from the mid-seventeenth century to 1895, when the island was ceded to Japan.

The earliest overt claims to a distinct history focused on the tragedy that occurred in 1947, just after China had resumed control of Taiwan. Ererba (二二八 February 28) was the backdrop for an immensely influential film by Hou Hsiao-hsien, *City of Sorrows* (*Beijing chengshi* 悲情城市). The film showed what many Taiwanese believed, that the island had been occupied rather than liberated in 1945. The official investigation into Ererba led to bitter criticism of the Guomindang, and to the erection of a monument to the thousands who had been killed in the centre of Taibei.[7]

Since the Democratic Peoples Party came to power in 2000, and the possibility that Taiwan would declare independence, the focus on Taiwan's history has grown more intense. The Palace Museum, the greatest museum of Chinese art in the world, is undergoing a makeover that is intended to make it more "relevant" to Taiwanese, and less a commemoration of Chinese past. The renovation is regarded with trepidation by those who loved the previous museum for the sublime beauty of its contents. For Beijing the revamping is less of an effrontery than the fact that the treasures are in Taiwan at all, rather than in their rightful home in the Palace Museum in Beijing.

Another recent development in Taiwanese history seems destined to please some people, in Taiwan and Japan, and outrage many others. There is a leaning towards a reassessment of the Japanese occupation and the growth of a positive view of the colonial period, a view supported by Japan, where the idea of Taiwan as a "model colony" is seen as a counter-balance to the stories of Japanese atrocities elsewhere in Asia. In China, where historical work, museums and TV series paint the Japanese occupation of the Mainland in blacker and blacker tones, the idea that the Japanese could be "good colonialists" is anathema. Reassessing the Japanese period will almost certainly lead to a new round of conflict between the Mainland and Taiwan.

That conflict may be bitter, and murky, heavily involved with contemporary politics. There is a contrasting historical issue, one that appears at first glance to be quite positive and uncontroversial, since all sides take a strongly positive view, and that is the status of Zheng Chenggong. The impression is illusory. There are many positive views of Zheng, each with a quite different premise, a quite different symbolic value, and a quite different contemporary usage —except that all use Zheng to promote their claims to legitimacy and sovereignty.

The universal symbol of legitimacy—Zheng Chenggong (郑成功)

Zheng Chenggong lived three and a half centuries ago, at the end of the Ming Dynasty and the beginning of the Qing Dynasty. The historical Zheng Chenggong is an insubstantial figure. He left no writings, no personal records, no portrait. The known facts about his life are few. He was born in 1624. His father was a maritime adventurer (i.e. pirate) from the southern part of Fujian Province, Minnan (闽南), who became a major regional power-holder. His son was born in Japan and spent his earliest years there with his mother; he joined his father as a grown boy. He was educated by Confucian tutors, and may have passed some level of the imperial examinations.

In the 1640s the Zhengs were involved in resistance to the Manchus as they swept south on their conquest of China. The resistance failed. In 1661, father and son parted company. The father capitulated to the Qing; the son sailed across to the southern tip of Taiwan, evicted the Dutch from their settlement of Zeelandia and started to build his own power base on the island, in Tainan, planning for a return to the Mainland. Zheng represented an enormous threat to the Qing, large enough that the coastal zones of Guangdong and of Fujian were cleared of inhabitants to prevent there being any Mainland support for his return. Zheng died in 1663, at a suspiciously early age. Almost everything else about his life story is a matter of speculation and interpretation. And he has been interpreted in many different ways, each designed to give legitimacy to the interpreter, a historical proof of the rightness of their present position.

The Beijing view: a hero of national reunification

On the Mainland Zheng Chenggong is the flag-bearer for the reunification of Taiwan with the Mainland. Since 1949 Zheng has been promoted at the highest levels of the People's Republic as a symbol of the legitimacy of the PRC's claim to Taiwan, his eviction of the Dutch from Tainan cited as the first example in which Chinese soil was rescued from foreign occupation. During the Taiwan Straits crises in the 1950s, when war across the Straits, either a Mainland invasion of Taiwan or a Guomindang assault on the Mainland, seemed very likely, Zheng was promoted as a hero of reunification. A stele on Gulangyu, the island just off Xiamen, was dedicated to him by Guo Moruo, the most official of official Communist intellectuals. Guo also wrote an ultra-patriotic, not to say xenophobic, poem about Zheng in 1961:

> Taiwan has been a part of China since ancient days
> The Han nation and the tribe of Gaoshan are brothers
> How can we allow foreigners to sully the country
> Or shameless thieves its riches and wealth steal?
> Great feats indeed to drive the Dutch invaders out.
> O Lord of Given name you are the nation's hero.
>
> (Changingtrip.com)

Zheng faded out during the Cultural Revolution, when the convulsions on the Mainland erased external concerns, but since stability and calm have been re-established, Beijing has promoted Zheng strongly, as a hero of reunification. In 1995 Zheng's portrait appeared on a fifty yuan coin. In 2000 an epic film was made of his life. Zheng Chenggong was marked by dramatic license rather than historical accuracy; the film's blurb describes Zheng as passing the imperial examinations in the capital Nanjing, though Beijing was the capital when Zheng was alive. The People's Liberation Army has adopted him as a military hero, publishing works that celebrate his military skills in the campaign against the Dutch (Wang 1997). This is the image that dominates on Gulangyu—the martial hero set on the military conquest of an inalienable part of China.[8]

Zheng celebrations take many forms. In May 2002, there were major celebrations for the three hundred and fortieth anniversary of Zheng's recovery of Taiwan from the Dutch, when 8,000 people took part in a special ceremony in Nan'an (南 安县), the Zheng ancestral home west of Quanzhou. The participants included senior government officials from Beijing, as well as local people and descendents of Zheng "from across the world"—including a number from Taiwan. The keynote speaker was Wang Fuqing, deputy director of the Taiwan Affairs Office in the State Council, who made a less than subtle connection between Zheng and the present situation (*People's Daily Online*, May 27, 2002).

This was an important event in the exchanges across the Taiwan Straits. It helped promote Zheng's great patriotism, but it also advanced relations across the Straits and helped fight advocates of Taiwan independence.

The Minnan view: a regional culture hero

Zheng Zhenggong has also been co-opted by people who have agendas other than a Beijing-dominated, unified China. The weighty messages from Beijing are political and speak of the nation and national unity. There are subtle claims to ownership of the Zheng legend, claims that come from regional local origins.

In his ancestral home Zheng is a Minnan hero. Quanzhou and the counties round it are the ancestral homes of much of the Taiwan population, who moved over to Taiwan from the seventeenth century onwards. They continued to speak the Minnan dialect, to worship the Minnan deities and to eat Minnan food. Until the arbitrary separation of Minnan and Taiwan when the island was handed to Japan, the two were really one place separated by a short stretch of sea. The two areas were reunited in 1945, but four years later the separation was reimposed at the end of the Civil War, when the defeated Nationalists hunkered down in Taiwan.

Minnan is the home region of the overseas Chinese populations in much of Southeast Asia, the descendents of the emigrants who left the region from the seventeenth century onwards to move to the Nanyang (南洋 , the Southern Oceans). Many of these people maintained ties to the region; and these ties, disrupted after 1949, have been reinvigorated over the past twenty years.

In Minnan, Zheng Chenggong embodies the characteristics Minnan people prize in themselves. He was bold and daring, he made his own rules, and was as happy operating outside a state or legal structure as within one. He was part of the maritime, outgoing world of Minnan, a world of fishermen, pirates, traders and everything in between. These people had been looking to the outside world for centuries. There were few dividing lines between legal and illegal maritime activities, little concern over what the state regarded as legal or illegal. The Minnan people went their own way.

In Minnan Zheng Chenggong is an object of serious academic study. Xiamen University, the leading educational institution, has a research group for the study of his life *(Xiamen daxue Zheng Chenggong lishi diaocha yanjiuzu* 厦门大学郑成功历史调查研究组 *)*. The famous Minnan historian Fu Yiling was director of the Society to Study Zheng Chenggong (*Zheng Chenggong yanjiu xuehui* 郑成功研究学会). These academic efforts are part of a larger focus on the history of the Minnan/Taiwan region, which includes a specialization on the ancient Baiyue cultures, and on more recent MinTai culture. (*MinTai wenhua yanjiu* 闽台文化研究) (see Fu 1997; 1984). These regional specializations were, in the radical Mao era, considered "splitism," "attempts to break up the country," and "feudal remnants." The Society was closed down for twenty years, from 1902 to 1982.

Zheng's resurrection is paralleled in the flowering of popular culture. Minnan has one of the richest regional cultures in China. The physical forms of this culture—temples, lineage halls and shrines, genealogies—were attacked during the Cultural Revolution, and many were destroyed. The outward symbols of deep culture could be destroyed, but their roots could not. Family, lineage and clan symbols have been restored over the past two decades. Lineage halls, memorials to ancestors, graves have been rebuilt; the Zheng ancestral hall in Nan'an has been lavishly restored. Lineages have also re-edited their genealogies, finding copies that survived the wholesale burning of genealogies in the Cultural Revolution, and having them updated. No project is more ambitious than the plan to produce a fifty-volume genealogy of the Zheng clan. The new version of the genealogy will cover the Zheng clan over more than a thousand years. It is due to be completed by 2010 (*People's Daily Online*, November 23, 2002).

A Taiwan view: the hero of independence

In Taiwan Zheng Chenggong is a hero of independence, the ultimate Taiwanese hero, the man who made Taiwan a home for his own people, Minnan settlers. Zheng set up his base in Tainan, the city that was the capital of the island from 1663 to 1885, when political power was moved to Taipei. Tainan is still the most independentist city in Taiwan, the home base of President Ch'en Shui-pien. Zheng is the "father of Taiwan," the creator of its first autonomous government. He left China to make a new society for his people on Taiwan, in much the same way that European adventurers and dissidents left the Old World of Europe to settle in the New World.

Zheng is embedded in Taiwanese culture in ways that go beyond ancestral connections and political history. He has an intimate association with Mazu (妈祖), the most popular deity in Taiwan. He brought the first icon of Mazu to Taiwan from her mother shrine in Meizhou (Fujian). Mazu, also known as Tianhou, the goddess of the seas, is the patron saint of seafarers in southern China. She is effectively the patron saint of Taiwan. There are over eight hundred Mazu temples and shrines in Taiwan.

Mazu has always been susceptible to political manipulation, and continues to be so. She plays a delicate role in the intricate triangular relationship between Taiwan, Beijing and Fujian. In 1997 the major Mazu image from Meizhou was sent on a tour of Taiwan, and spent a hundred days there. She travelled in splendour, and was met at every stage by adoring crowds. The political messages that came with her stressed her help in letting Qing forces take over Taiwan and bring Taiwan back to the motherland (Bosco and Ho 1999).

Zheng Chenggong, for the independentists, is the unquestioned hero of independence. He symbolizes the power of the will, of commitment and of continuity—and of the triumph of right over might.

The Guomindang view: the saviour of the Mainland in waiting

Zheng has served other masters in the contemporary manipulation of history. He was used as a symbol of the hope of reunification by the Guomindang after Taiwan became their last hold-out in 1949. Taiwan became the place of temporary refuge before the eventual return to the Mainland, as it was claimed to have been for Zheng in the early Qing. The Guomindang saw itself as having been ousted from the Mainland by an alien conspiracy, led by the Soviet Union.[9]

Zheng's image has not endured in the Guomindang camp. As the years have gone by, and the prospect of reunification has dimmed, so did the role of Zheng Zhenggong as a national hero. The Guomindang's loss of the presidency of Taiwan in 2000, to the leader of the independence party Ch'en Shui-pien, finally put an end to Zheng's standing with the Guomindang.

The Tainan view: a local hero

Zheng Chenggong is a local hero in Tainan, a city of temples, historic sites—and a centre of art, literature, music and excellent food. The Tainan people thank Zheng for setting the style for all this richness; in his entourage when he arrived in Tainan were a thousand artists, writers, musicians, and chefs.

The view from Tainan is that the city is the true capital of Taiwan. Taipei is brash and new, a creation of the Japanese and then of the Guomindang. Tainan is the authentic, historic Taiwan. Tainan's science and technology industries are at the cutting edge of modernity, but this modernity is set in a venerable setting. Tainan honours Zheng Chenggong for founding the city and for giving it an edge over any other city in Taiwan—for making it, as the official guide says, "the beginning of Taiwan's history" (Tainan City Government 2007). The people of the city have used their energy and creativity to promote the connection. Most of the historic sites in the town are connected to Zheng, and his story is told again and again, in film, fiction, comic books and paintings. He is a cult figure.

The Japanese view: a distaff hero

There is a Japanese claim on Zheng Chenggong: his mother was Japanese. Zheng's life story became the stuff of one of Japan's most famous plays, *Kokusen'ya kassen (The Battles of Koxinga)*, by Chikamatsu Monzaemon. The play made Zheng as famous in Japan as the Scot Macbeth was in England after Shakespeare made him into a tragic hero.

Zheng's use by Japan as a political symbol came later on, when his maternal connection seemed to offer a potent advantage—i.e. when the Japanese became the masters of Taiwan and were looking for anything which seemed to carry some promise of their legitimacy there. Zheng's mother was made a heroine of maternal love and sacrifice. A Shinto addition was put on to

Zheng's shrine in Tainan to show that he was now construed as the son of a Japanese mother.

Concluding views

The historic Zheng is obscured by the myths, legends and dramatic tales that surround him. Some of these myths can be deconstructed and brought down to earth. The reasons for his attack on the Dutch, for example, can be seen not as an early example of inflamed nationalism, but rather as a more prosaic recognition that he could not defeat the Manchus, and that since he was about to be thrown out of Fujian he would do much better going across the water. Careful research might shrink his force from the astronomical 8,000 war junks and 240,000 men often cited to a more credible and much smaller size. An explanation of his life course might reveal a more mundane story—death from malaria, for example. But is there any point to deconstruction? One outcome of deconstruction would be to make his story very brief. Almost everything known about Zheng is mythic; stripping away myth from reality would be guaranteed to upset most of the many different devotees of Zheng and please no one.

We may never know the objective truth about Zheng Chenggong, but what the passionate versions of his life tell us is that history really matters, and that the present is justified in terms of the past. As long as history is equated with legitimacy, it will be dangerous to ignore history or to discount China's fascination with her past.

Notes

1   E. P. Wilkinson, lecture at Faculty of Oriental Studies, Cambridge University, November 16, 2006.
2   Wu Han was viciously attacked for his supposed attack on Mao (which had actually been written several years before), and then jailed. His death may have been suicide.
3   The Canadian missionary Arthur Menzies worked actively on the oracle bones project, and the French Jesuit Pierre Teilhard de Chardin worked on Peking Man, along with the Swedish archaeologist J. G. Andersson and the Canadian professor of Anatomy, Davidson Black.
4   Many of these had been damaged or destroyed during the Cultural Revolution.
5   Lin Biao, once named as Mao Zedong's close comrade in arms and chosen successor, parted company with Mao in a mysterious incident that ended with Lin dead in a plane crash in Mongolia.
6   The episode was filmed for the series, as was Sima's later life. The director apologized for the mistake of not making the actor who played Sima shave off his moustache for the later episodes, after criticism that a castrated man should not have facial hair.
7   The man held most responsible for Ererba, General Chen Yi, was long dead, executed by the Guomindang as a communist spy just before the Mainland fell to the Communists in 1949.
8   Gulangyu itself has become a symbol of military accomplishment. A TV game show is set there, a cross between *Jeopardy* and *Who wants to be a Millionaire*.

All the contestants are soldiers from the local garrison, and many of the questions are about military affairs.

9 For an excellent study of the manipulation of Zheng Chenggong in Taiwan, see Croizier (1977). Note that Koxinga is the name used for Zheng in contemporary Western sources.

Bibliography

Beijing 2008 Olympic Games Official website, "The China Millennium Monument." Available online: http://en.beijing2008.cn/65/70/article211987065.shtml (accessed May 22, 2007).

Bosco, Joseph and Ho Puay-peng (1999) *Temples of the Empress of Heaven*, Hong Kong: Oxford University Press.

Changingtrip.com, "Garden of the Sea—Gu'Lang'Yu." Available online: www.changing trip.com/english/50sight/34.asp (accessed May 22, 2007).

China Heritage Project (2005) "The Rebirth of Serious Historical Drama?," *China Heritage Newsletter*, 3 (September). Available online: www.chinaheritagenewsletter. org/articles.php?searchterm=003_hanwudi.inc&issue=003 (accessed May 27, 2007)

"China Recompiles Qing Dynasty History Costing 600 Million Yuan," *The Epoch Times*, September 10, 2004. Available online: http://en.epochtimes.com/news/4-9-10/23177.html (accessed May 22, 2007)

Croizier, Ralph (1977) *Koxinga and Chinese Nationalism: History, Myth and the Hero*, Cambridge, MA: Harvard University Press.

Fu Yiling (ed.) (1997) *Research on Min/Tai Culture* [*Fujiansheng yanhuang wenhua yanjiuhui. MinTai wenhua yanjiu* 闽台文化研究], Xiamen: Fujian renmin chubanshe.

—— (1984) *Collected Articles on Research on Zheng Chenggong* [*Zheng Chenggong yanjiu lunwenji* 郑成功研究论文集], Xiamen: Fujian renmin chubanshe.

Hanban [Office of the Chinese Language Council International] website, "Confucius Institutes." Available online: www.hanban.edu.cn/en_hanban/kzxy.php (accessed May 22, 2007).

Lary, Diana (1996) "The Tomb of the King of Nanyue—The Contemporary Agenda of History: Scholarship and Identity," *Modern China* (January).

"Records Tracing Zheng Chengong's Family Tree," *People's Daily Online* November 23, 2002. Available online: http://english.people.com.cn/200211/23/eng20021123_107333.shtml (accessed May 22, 2007).

"Renovation Details of Memorial Hall Revealed," *China Daily*, September 27, 2006. Available online: www.chinadaily.com.cn/cndy/2006–09/27/content_697526.htm (accessed May 27, 2007).

Mair, Victor (2000) *Tarim Mummies: Ancient China and the Mystery of the Earliest Peoples from the West*, New York: Thames and Hudson.

"Meeting Commemorates Zheng Chenggong Recovering Taiwan," *People's Daily Online*, May 27, 2002. Available online: http://english.people.com.cn/200205/27/eng20020527_96503.shtml (accessed May 22, 2007).

Tainan City Government (2007). "Introduction: History." Available online: www.tncg. gov.tw/tour.asp?sub1=01&sub2=03&lang=E (accessed May 27, 2007).

Wang Xuedong (1997) *The Bloody Battle for the Island of Taiwan: Zheng Zhenggong Takes Back Taiwan* [*Xuezhan Taiwandao: Zheng Zhenggong shouhui Taiwan* 血战台湾岛郑成功收回台湾], Beijing: Jiefangjun chubanshe.

The "Beijing Consensus" and China's quest for legitimacy on the international stage

Charles Burton

The quest for legitimacy by the Chinese government

The cosmology of ancient China identified the temporal and natural orders. Thus harmony prevailed in nature when harmony prevailed in human relations of which the most fundamental relation was that of filial piety. The Emperor therefore ruled by ritualized ceremonies to placate Heaven and by regulating the social order through the restraint of his personal virtue. The Emperor's virtue radiated out and was reflected down by the upright conduct of his hierarchy of officials. This was the ideal at least. But in the natural course of dynastic succession the degree of virtue upheld by successive generations decayed. Corrupted rule then led to concomitant decline in the natural order. The resultant floods and pestilence and rapacious taxation left the people no option but to have to break from social harmony and join in rebellion against the established authority. The dynastic histories record that when a dynasty reaches the nadir of its rule that things are so disharmonious that in addition to the tragedy of famine and rampant immorality at all levels due to the generalized decay in virtue, there are also earthquakes, volcanoes erupt, women give birth to cows and birds start to fly backwards. Then, following a civil war, Heaven transfers its Mandate to a new and vigorous dynasty with renewed virtue and the capacity to engage in prudent governance. Harmony is again restored and nature again provides ample grain for the granaries and the burden of taxation is tolerable once again. This narrative of the legitimacy of the rule of emperors in dynastic succession served China well over twenty-four dynasties for 3,000 years. But it could not survive the challenge of Western scientific alternative ways of understanding man and his world that started to threaten the bases of legitimacy for China's political and social order in the nineteenth century.

In China's thirty-year-long "Mao era" dating from the establishment of the People's Republic in 1949, the legitimacy of the rule of the Chinese Communist Party (CCP) was based on the Marxian interpretation of history. The Party's rule was vaunted as a necessary condition of China's inevitable revolutionary progress from the bourgeois to the socialist form of organization, which would ultimately lead to utopian Communism. But as China's socialist planned economy failed to achieve the high rates of growth in productivity that are part and parcel of the Marxist theory of revolution, the bases for the Party's assumption of state power were called into question. While Party General Secretary Hu Yaobang, in the mid-1980s, asserted that "we cannot expect Marxism to solve all the questions of the day," most intellectuals had come to the conclusion Marxism could not solve anything at all. They urged that the Party had to come up with a new justification to legitimate its continuing in power after its Marxist program had been so devastatingly discredited by economic failure and the insanity of the Great Leap Forward and Cultural Revolution campaigns. A group of intellectuals associated with the Premier of the State Council, Zhao Ziyang, proposed a new formulation, the doctrine of "neo-authoritarianism" (see Sautman 1992). This doctrine drew on Marxism-Leninism, Stalinism, and Mao Zedong Thought not at all, but was rather inspired by the Harvard University's Samuel Huntington's (1968) classic *Political Order in Changing Societies*, whose thesis is that the political order is threatened when the level of mobilization exceeds the level of institutionalization within a society. Neo-authoritarianism's legitimating basis was that China would commit to an eventual transition to a legitimate democracy but for the foreseeable future it was necessary to maintain the power of enlightened elements of the current political régime until conditions for a stable democratization were ripe. But this doctrine faded from acceptable discourse in China after Mr. Zhao was purged from power in the wake of the June 4 "Tiananmen Incident" in 1989.

Since the United Nations (UN) was established sixty years ago the most accepted criteria for measuring state legitimacy has become membership in the UN. One of the conditions of UN membership is acknowledgement of the Universal Declaration of Human Rights. Assessment of régime legitimacy is more and more associated with the degree to which national régimes' domestic practices are compliant with the articles of the major UN Covenants, in particular the International Covenant on Civil and Political Rights. This discourse has even been extended to suggest that national régimes can even be deemed illegitimate due to grievous flaunting of UN standards that measure the relative virtue of governments *de facto*, and in terms of this emerging body of international law, *de jure*, must forfeit sovereignty over the territory under their authority. The September 2005 UN Reform Outcome Document declared that the UN should "affirm that every sovereign government has a 'responsibility to protect' its citizens and those within its jurisdiction from genocide, mass killing, and massive and sustained human rights violations" (UN 2005). The failure of régimes to comply with these evolving international standards for régime legitimacy thus provides a legal and ethical basis for "humanitarian intervention," outside invasion being the penultimate abrogation of national assertions of state sovereignty based on régime legitimacy.

China signed the International Covenant on Civil and Political Rights in 1998. This act of signing this very critical UN instrument could be interpreted as a device for the Chinese Communist authorities to buttress the legitimacy of the current Chinese régime. Signing the Covenant indicates intention to become compliant with its provisions. But accountability for domestic non-compliance with the Covenant through obligatory reporting to the relevant Committee of the UN does not go into effect until China ratifies the International Covenant on Civil and Political Rights. This is not likely to happen within the foreseeable future because China is in fact not compliant with many of the central elements of the International Covenant on Civil and Political Rights with regard to freedom of association, freedom of expression and freedom of the Chinese people to choose their government by free and fair elections.

With regard to the latter, experiments with elections at the village level in China began in the late 1980s. At the time and for some years afterwards these elections were seen by Western liberal thinkers as indicative that Chinese farmers, because they were now producing for markets as individual economic actors rather than as members of the masses organized into People's Communes as they had been before, would come to identify themselves as autonomous members of society entitled to political rights. The expectation was that the village elections would prove instrumental in the rise of a sense of citizenship among the peasantry that could lead to the spread of civil society in China (see Wu 1997). The village elections would act as a catalyst and "inevitably" lead to increasing demands for election of political leaders at higher levels, eventually leading to China having an elected President. So China would thereby eventually obtain a legitimate government based on election by the people. However, fifteen years on the elections have hardly expanded to the township level and show no signs of anything that could be interpreted as leading to governments in China legitimated by an election mandate within the foreseeable future.

Over the years liberal Western scholars also looked to the possibility that China would genuinely implement the National Constitution of the People's Republic of China promulgated in 1982.[1] This document calls for the National People's Congress (NPC) to function as the supreme organ of state power. There have been some signs over the years that suggested that the NPC would gradually assume a role consistent with its mandate as set out in the Chinese constitution. This sort of thinking was prevalent over the period of Peng Zhen and then Qiao Shi's chairmanships of the NPC. But the consensus among scholars today is that the stymied attempts to expand the authorities of the NPC reflected more the jockeying for augmented personal authority in the Chinese Communist power structure on the parts of Peng Zhen and Qiao Shi than being indicative of genuine response to social pressure for China to democratize and genuinely implement constitutionalism (see Nathan 2006 and Tanner 1999). In the Fourth Amendment to China's National Constitution promulgated in 2004 its Article 33 even had a third paragraph amended to the effect that: "The State respects and preserves human rights." But as the power of the State is evidently in reality invested in the Standing Committee of the

Politburo of the Central Committee of the CCP and not the NPC, the assertion that China respects and preserves human rights may be more about seeking legitimacy for the Party's rule than an indication of a domestic policy re-orientation away from the "people's democratic dictatorship" under the leadership of the CCP toward a liberal democratic system wherein the rights of the individual citizen are paramount.

Similarly since the late 1990s, the Chinese Ministry of Foreign Affairs has engaged in annual government-to-government bilateral human rights dialogues with at least eleven Western nations as well as the EU and Japan (see Woodman and Samdup 2005). The purpose of these bilateral human rights dialogues is to allow Western governments to engage in "quiet diplomacy" with a view to encouraging the Chinese régime to come into compliance with UN-determined human rights norms. It could be argued that the Chinese Government's stated intention to work with the West to improve its human rights-related domestic practices provides legitimacy for the Chinese régime *per se*. But after ten years and close to two hundred dialogue sessions there is no evidence that these dialogues have had any significant impact on any of China's government agency's policies and practices. The police, security agencies, censors of books, magazines, TV, films and internet and Party agencies do not appear to have been much touched by the Western government's aspirations to promote liberal democracy in China. A major factor in the lack of discernible progress with regard to respect for human rights in China is that the agency of the Chinese Government responsible for the human rights dialogues is the Chinese Ministry of Foreign Affairs which has as its mandate the promotion of China's interests abroad, but no mandate to promote social justice in China domestically.[2]

So the political legitimacy of China's current régime could be called into question because of the Chinese régime's failure to comply with international norms for domestic protection of the rights of Chinese citizens as defined by the UN. Despite this, China's rapid economic development has become the envy of the developing nations. Despite negative aspects in China's development such as official corruption, increasing polarization of wealth, environmental degradation, commoditization of women, etc., developing nations envy and aspire to the high economic growth rates that China seemingly effortlessly achieves year after year. It has led to the pressing question for other Third World nations: Why has China's economy taken off in recent years while ours has not? Is it related to the fact that China's political and legal institutions are in fact not compliant with the criteria demanded of the UN's human rights covenants? Is China now legitimized by a mode of authoritarian rule and development that is at odds with "the Washington Consensus" that liberal democratic political orders are the *sine qua non* for successful participation in the global economy? In response to this concern, professor at Tsinghua University, Joshua Cooper Ramo, has proposed the concept of a "Beijing Consensus" as an alternate legitimating paradigm for the Chinese political status quo. The Beijing Consensus rejects fundamental neo-liberal assumptions such as the superiority and legitimacy of polities based on separation of the powers of the executive, legislature and judiciary (Ramo 2004).[3]

China's development model is characterized by theorists of development as falling into the category of "state-led development."[4] However, this sort of classification has little explicatory value because most of the developing nations also followed a model of "state-led development" in the 50s, 60s and 70s, but with severely contrasting results to those experienced in China. So while "state-led" development has arguably been outstandingly successful in China, it has not led to prosperity in Africa. But while the Chinese experience would suggest that under the correct conditions, "state-led development" can be extraordinarily efficacious, in recent years throughout the developing world this model has been replaced by the neo-liberal development paradigm promoted by the "Washington Consensus" institutions: the World Bank, International Monetary Fund (IMF) and World Trade Organization (WTO). This neo-liberal model up to now has shown no meaningful evidence of lifting nations out of poverty and negative economic growth. But it has led to weakening state capacity to provide people with social benefits such as health care and educational services due to the Bretton Woods institutions' demands that states cut tax and allocate a greater proportion of government revenues to debt repayment. For example a clear statement of the "Washington Consensus" expectations are expressed in the documents supporting the New Partnership for Africa's Development (NEPAD) (Manuel 2003) which is strongly endorsed by the African Development Bank, Economic Commission for Africa, the Food and Agricultural Organization, the United Nations Environment Program, the World Bank, and the International Monetary Fund. The NEPAD explicitly rejects the developmental virtue of state-led development in favour of liberal democratic political-economic systems designed to draw on the power of market economic forces to fundamentally transform societies to engender high economic growth rates. But this NEPAD program is likely not to engender the anticipated results in the region. There is strong empirical evidence that the Chinese model, on the other hand, can lead to strongly improved economic indicators over a sustained period. Nevertheless, it is the doctrine of Western nations that they should send developmental aid money to poor nations whose régimes commit to liberal democracy and free markets as it is the current received wisdom that the régimes with these characteristics will ultimately enjoy political legitimacy, political, economic and social stability, are non-belligerent and amenable to participation in globalized trade and investment. To Western nations the CCP's current "opening and reform" policies under the rubric of "socialism with Chinese characteristics" while arguably very successful to date are based on a system that lacks political legitimacy, so it cannot be a desirable option for the development of other lands. So China finds itself perceived by the West in a paradoxical way, as on the one hand a régime that has delivered admirable results in developmental term, but on the other, at the same time, a régime that fails to meet the internationally respected criteria for designation as a legitimate régime because it is by no stretch of the imagination a democracy, as "democracy" is understood in the West.

The Chinese Communist Party's quest for alternative sources of legitimacy

Indeed, to many in the West, China's post-Mao rise is disconcerting. Should we welcome or fear China's growing economic power? Is the current Chinese régime legitimate, stable, peaceful and willing to participate fairly in the globalized economy as it claims in its own self-defence? Reflecting this uncertainty about the meaning of China's development for the West, journalistic writing often characterizes China's economic transformation in tantalizing prose calculated to both shock and awe the reader. For example in a single recent *New York Times Magazine* article it is observed that China currently has more than 15,000 highway projects in the works which will add 162,000 kilometres of road to the country. The article suggests that this many kilometres would circle the planet at the equator four times (Fishman 2004: 27). Then the writer notes us that there are 300 million mobile telephone subscribers in China today with 5 million new subscribers joining the network every month (Fishman 2004: 27). Later on the same article quotes a policy brief issued by the Carnegie Endowment for International Peace that makes the extraordinary assertion that "if all US jobs were moved to China, there would still be surplus labour in China" (Fishman 2004: 46).[5] But on the other hand there is also the idea that China's economic boom fuels Western prosperity by providing a huge and rapidly growing export market for our goods and services as well as providing our shops with cheaply produced Chinese imports that keep our own living costs down. But then maybe all those Chinese imports are "hollowing out" our own economy? What's the good of cheap goods in the shops if it leads to unemployment domestically? And can China's economic rise sustain indefinitely, or is it the case as one Canadian specialist has put it that: "China is one giant Enron?"[6] So one is hard-pressed to know for sure if China's rise benefits them but threatens us, or benefits both us and them.

Then there is the issue of human rights. Is China's economic boom at the cost of gross violations of Chinese citizens' civil and political and economic, social and cultural rights by the Government of the People's Republic of China led by the CCP? If so, how can we accept the moral legitimacy of such a régime?

Finally, there is the issue of China's strengthening military. Could China's rise lead to things going very wrong in security relations in the region? That is to say, will superpower rivalry between China and the US eventually lead to war over North Korea and Taiwan? Could the US lose that war? Could the PRC régime legitimate itself through military supremacy?

But nevertheless to developing nations still in the throes of poverty, China's rise is a source of fascination and great admiration. What can the Third World learn from China's development and how is China's enormous success related to the methodology of the political rule of the CCP? Could their own régimes enhance their political legitimacy if they re-make themselves based on the new authoritarian norms of the "Beijng Consensus"?

Particularly since the 1989 Tiananmen Incident, the CCP is perceived by many in the West as a fundamentally malevolent institution of doubtful political legitimacy. It is seen as instrumental in enforcing restrictions on freedom of expression, suppressing citizens' political rights, unfairly imprisoning political dissidents and a wide range of other violations of universal human rights as defined in the UN Human Rights Covenants. But what has been the role and function of the Party in China's post-Mao economic rise? Has the Party played an instrumental role in the astonishing success of China's economic development over the past twenty-five years? That is to say that if one re-defines the "old China" as the revolutionary China of the Mao era between 1949 and 1976 before the implementation of the policies of opening and reform, would it be true to say that "without the Communist Party there would be no New China" today? The other options would be that the CCP's policies have had no impact on China's economic rise one way or another; that China's economic rise would have occurred with or without them. Or even a third possibility that the Chinese Communist Party's policies have inhibited China's economic rise and that China would be an even stronger and richer nation if the Communist Party was not running the Chinese Government. Another variant interpretation of the role of the CCP in China's economic rise would be that the policies of the CCP were instrumental in the transition of China's economy and social system from a Stalinist model to a free market model in the 80s, but that China would do better after the transition if a different political party with liberal democratic policies was able to come to the fore. This last has long been an expectation among political scientists in the West. For example, Condoleezza Rice, when she was a professor of political science at Stanford in 1999, said: "The Chinese Communists are living on borrowed time; economic liberalization is going to create pressure for political freedom" (quoted in Heilbrunn 1999: 22). So the assumption is that the CCP-led régime is not a legitimate régime but that a liberal democratic régime will inevitably displace the Chinese Communists and that that successor régime will be a legitimate one and attendant benefits for China will follow. But as will be argued below there is no empirical evidence that China's economic liberalization has led to pressure for political freedom.

The Chinese Communist Party and development as a source of legitimacy

Clearly China has not met the liberal-democratic preconditions for régime legitimacy and successful economic development approved by the World

Bank, IMF and the other multilateral agencies who have endorsed the NEPAD, but all the same China has experienced higher rates of sustained growth over more than twenty years than has ever been achieved by any nation before. So if China has failed to meet the liberal-democratic preconditions for development endorsed by the World Bank, IMF and the other multilateral agencies what have been the factors that have led to its extraordinary rise? Is it due to the unique role that the CCP plays in China's government, economic management, and society?

The Chinese Communist Party was initially formed as the vanguard of the proletariat to lead China's workers, peasants and soldiers in a revolution that would end in utopian Communism. To this end all education and media in China were brought into conformity with Marxist ideology and all non-Marxist expressions were strictly prohibited. The Party assumed leadership over all social organizations to ensure that all of their activities were consistent with furthering the Revolution.

Today the legitimating ideology for the rule of CCP is still the inevitability of the ultimate realization of Communism, but according to the Constitution of the Communist Party of China (CPC) amended and adopted at the Sixteenth CPC National Congress on November 14, 2002, the segment of society that the Party represents is no longer limited to the proletariat. It says that:

> Any Chinese worker, farmer, member of the armed forces, intellectual or any advanced element of other social strata who has reached the age of eighteen and who accepts the Party's Program and Constitution and is willing to join and work actively in one of the Party organizations, carry out the Party's decisions and pay membership dues regularly may apply for membership in the Communist Party of China.
>
> The Communist Party of China is the vanguard both of the Chinese working class and of the Chinese people and the Chinese nation. It is the core of leadership for the cause of socialism with Chinese characteristics and represents the development trend of China's advanced productive forces, the orientation of China's advanced culture and the fundamental interests of the overwhelming majority of the Chinese people. The realization of communism is the highest ideal and ultimate goal of the Party.
>
> (Constitution of the CPC 2002)

But the realization of Communism is not something that any of us can expect to see within our lifetimes. As the document explains:

> China is at the primary stage of socialism and will remain so for a long period of time. This is a historical stage which cannot be skipped in socialist modernization in China that is backward economically and culturally. It will last for over a hundred years. In socialist construction we must proceed from our specific conditions and take the path to

socialism with Chinese characteristics. At the present stage, the principal contradiction in Chinese society is one between the ever-growing material and cultural needs of the people and the low level of production. Owing to both domestic circumstances and foreign influences, class struggle will continue to exist within a certain scope for a long time and may possibly grow acute under certain conditions, but it is no longer the principal contradiction. In building socialism, our basic task is to further release and develop the productive forces and achieve socialist modernization step by step by carrying out reform in those aspects and links of the production relations and the superstructure that do not conform to the development of the productive forces.

(Constitution of the CPC 2002)

So the function of the Party today is to engender economic growth.

But according to the Party Constitution the political principles underlying this program of economic development are still the same ones identified by Deng Xiaoping a quarter of a century ago. The Constitution indicates:

The Four Cardinal Principles—to keep to the socialist road and to uphold the people's democratic dictatorship, leadership by the Communist Party of China, and Marxism-Leninism and Mao Zedong Thought—are the foundation on which to build our country. Throughout the course of socialist modernization we must adhere to the Four Cardinal Principles and combat bourgeois liberalization.

(Constitution of the CPC 2002)

This last point about combating bourgeois liberalization is significant because as noted above it is precisely commitment to "bourgeois liberalization" that is the legitimating precondition that the NEPAD demands of African nations before the World Bank, IMF, FAO and the rest will agree to release further development loans. So the CCP's pre-conditions for China's development are in this aspect diametrically opposed to those liberal-democratic pre-conditions that define régime legitimacy as espoused by the Bretton Woods institutions under the "Washington Consensus."

Moreover, insofar as the transparency in political and economic affairs that the NEPAD requires of African nations seeking further external develop-mental funding, the CCP does not support transparency in political economic affairs in the sense that the press is not free to expose official policy shortcomings or wrongdoing, except as authorized by the Ministry of Propaganda of the Central Committee of the CCP. Secrecy is the watchword of the CCP's approach to development. There is therefore no independent press in China. As the CCP's Constitution (2002) indicates: "Newspapers, journals and other means of publicity run by Party organizations at all levels must disseminate the line, principles, policies and decisions of the Party."

As all Chinese media are only licensed on condition that they are answerable to the Ministry of Propaganda of the Central Committee of the Chinese Communist Party, it is clear that the Party's program is explicitly opposed to freedom of expression in China.

Since the abandonment of orthodox Marxist ideology by the Party after 1978, the function of censorship has shifted away from ensuring that nothing is written that calls into question Marx's theories of history and economics to simply ensuring that nothing is written that challenges the bases of authority for the rule of China by the CCP. So, while writing on philosophy and history are no longer subject to the sort of intense vetting that they once were, and fiction and popular culture no longer has to focus on revolutionary themes, entire topics of potentially high interest to Chinese citizens such as the June 4, 1989 incident, or economic malfeasance by the families of the ruling elite, or the political debate among Chinese power holders over determination of national policy initiatives, or the determination of who will succeed to political offices, are not allowed to be written. Moreover, due to advances in modern technology the censorship is more insidious than it used to be. While in the earlier period censors had to actively listen to telephone conversations and physically steam open envelopes, today, mathematical algorithms make monitoring all e-mail relatively easy, digital switches leave a clear trail and voice recognition technologies and sophisticated scanners mean that telephone calls and faxes and letters are more amenable to mass-scale monitoring than before. Internet access is monitored and sites that include materials that the censors feel challenges the legitimacy of the CCP's rule are systematically blocked. True political freedom in China remains a superficial illusion.

The NEPAD Action Plan on the other hand includes the declaration:

> At the beginning of the new century and millennium, we reaffirm our commitment to the promotion of democracy and its core values in our respective countries. In particular, we undertake to work with renewed determination to enforce:
>
> — the rule of law;
> — the equality of all citizens before the law and liberty of the individual;
> — individual and collective freedoms, including the right to form and join political parties and trade unions, in conformity with the constitution;
> — equality of opportunity for all;
> — the inalienable right of the individual to participate by means of free, credible and democratic political processes in periodically electing their leaders for a fixed term of office; and
> — adherence to the separation of powers, including the protection of the independence of the judiciary and of effective parliaments.
>
> (NEPAD 2006)

The CCP's program arguably does not fulfil any of these criteria. For example, all organizations in China must be registered with the Ministry of Civil Affairs, which imposes rigid criteria that no independent political party or independent trade union has been able to fulfil to date. For example there is the stipulation that only one organization can assume functional responsibility for the same social concern in the same area. This makes it very difficult for new organizations to be legally formed as Communist Party-affiliated mass organizations have already staked out all the social territory. So far civil society has not grown in China to the extent some western social scientists predicted ten years ago. It is similar to the village elections which many in the West felt would lead to pressure for elections at higher levels (see Yu 2002).

The Party does not believe in rule of law in the sense of the sanctity of legal process that is the foundation of the Western system. The 2002 Party Constitution refers to "the combination of ruling the country by law and ruling the country by virtue." Law is a means to mechanization of centrally-ordained policy's implementation. But the law is not superior to the judgements of leading officials who are by virtue of their Party membership deemed to be in the "vanguard." As the Constitution (2002) notes: "Members of the Communist Party of China are vanguard fighters of the Chinese working class imbued with communist consciousness."

The form of democracy that the CCP expounds is "democratic centralism" which is characterized in the Party Constitution (2002) as "democracy under centralized guidance." It explains further that "correct centralism must be practiced so as to ensure concerted action in the whole Party and prompt effective implementation of its decisions" (Constitution of the CPC 2002). The key here is that the Party makes the decisions and they are expected to be implemented regardless of the popular will. The system is not really strongly characterized by democracy, in the sense of democracy as a form of government in which ordinary citizens take part in governing. It is more like oligarchy, a form of government where most political power effectively rests with a small segment of society (typically the most powerful, whether by wealth, military strength, ruthlessness, or political influence); the word oligarchy deriving from the Greek for "few" and "rule."

Insofar as some political theorists have argued that all societies are inevitably oligarchies regardless of the supposed political system, it is worth exploring what positive values the CCP espouses aside from engendering economic development.

First of all the Party Constitution (2002) indicates that "Members of the Communist Party of China must serve the people wholeheartedly, dedicate their whole lives to the realization of communism, and be ready to make any personal sacrifices."

But then, as noted above, the realization of communism is "a long historical process" that will take "over a hundred years," so the practical implications for current Party members in dedicating their whole lives to something that will only be achievable long after their deaths is difficult to discern.

The Constitution does note that Communist Party members:

> adhere to the principle that the interests of the Party and the people stand above everything else, subordinating their personal interests to the interests of the Party and the people, being the first to bear hardships and the last to enjoy comforts, working selflessly for the public interests and working to contribute more.
>
> (Constitution of the CPC 2002)

Clearly this is a specious claim as the evidence indicates that Party members are not typically the elements in Chinese society that are the "last to enjoy comforts." For the most part the members of the Party live lives of privilege. The Party Constitution also refers to the notion that Party members show "moral integrity" but this is also an area where overwhelming evidence suggests otherwise. Nevertheless, while subjectively one might judge that CCP officials are more venal in personal conduct than members of ruling parties in other political systems, this is likely more a matter of degree than substantial difference.

Nationalism as an alternative to legitimacy

Of more significance is the function of Party defined in the Constitution to inspire "patriotism, community spirit" and to enhance the people's sense of "national dignity, self-confidence and self reliance." Moreover the Party identifies itself with all the people. The relevant clauses from the Party Constitution are as follows:

> The Communist Party of China upholds and promotes relations of equality, unity and mutual assistance among all ethnic groups in the country, upholds and constantly improves the system of regional ethnic autonomy, actively trains and promotes cadres from among ethnic minorities, and helps them with economic and cultural development in the areas inhabited by ethnic minorities so as to achieve common prosperity and all-round progress for all ethnic groups.
>
> The Communist Party of China unites with all workers, farmers and intellectuals, and with all the democratic parties, personages without party affiliation and the patriotic forces of all ethnic groups in China in further expanding and fortifying the broadest possible patriotic united front.
>
> (Constitution of the CPC 2002)

Arguably it is in these aspects of promoting patriotism and social solidarity that the CCP has played a significant role in engendering conditions that have led to China's sustained economic take-off, which along with Party's assertion that its authoritarian rule is essential to social stability are critical aspects in the Party's current claims to political legitimacy.

Joseph Levenson's (1968) argument in his classic trilogy of books published as a set under the title *Confucian China and Its Modern Fate* was that China adopted Marxism in response to the devastating blow to national pride that resulted from the humiliations inflicted on China by nineteenth-century Western and Japanese imperialism starting with the Opium Wars in the 1830s. The idea was that Marxist ideology allowed China to perceive that by establishing socialism, it would achieve superiority over the capitalist West and Japan who would be left behind in the inferior bourgeois stage of development. Moreover, the theory was that the socialist planned economy would engender higher economic growth rates than free-market capitalism. However, this formulation was proved thoroughly bankrupt by 1966 when the CCP launched, with great fanfare, the ill-conceived and socially disastrous Great Proletarian Cultural Revolution Campaign. The subsequent April 5, 1976 Tiananmen Incident led the CCP to realize that it could lose its power if Marxist ideology as the guide to its economic program was not abandoned. The poster plastered to the Monument to the Martyrs in the centre of the Square containing the phrase "mouthing empty phrases about the realization of Communism will not satisfy the people's desires" was too true to be ignored.

But despite the cumulative process of unfulfilled expectations that marked the first thirty years of Communist Party rule of China, there was always a general confidence among the Chinese public at large in the notion that China had once been the world's greatest economic force and greatest civilization and that the dishonor that China had suffered at the hands of foreigners in the nineteenth century was a relatively minor episode in a glorious history that spans millennia. The Cultural Revolution marked the low point in China's reaction to the humiliations of the Western and Japanese imperialism. By the late 1970s, there was a consensus among Chinese that the adoption of the Soviet model had clearly been based on miscalculation and now the time had come to set things right again. So the basis of CPC's legitimacy was transformed from overseeing class struggle to achieve communism to the Party maintaining that its political function has always been to oversee and direct China's rise to nationalist power and global triumph.[7] The Party is now dedicated to restoring China to greatness as a power in the world and thereby redressing all past humiliations. Under its leadership, despite some setbacks after 1949, the Chinese people will "Rise up!" It is in this context that the CCP's mandate articulated in the 2002 Party Constitution to engender "patriotism, community spirit" and to enhance the people's sense of "national dignity, self-confidence and self reliance" is so significant. China is blessed by strong social solidarity and social cohesiveness. It has allowed for meaningful reform that has allowed significant elements of the power élite to suffer meaningful dislocation for the overall good of the whole.[8]

This is in strong contrast to the nations involved in the NEPAD who suffer from severe social cleavages based on tribal and religious identities and a feeling of cultural inferiority to the great civilizations of the former colonial masters. Their interpretation of African history reinforces a victim mentality and passivity in the face of tyrannies, kleptocracies and economic mismanagement. This has inhibited the development of the patriotism and community spirit and "national dignity, self-confidence and self reliance" that has been the basis for China's rise. So while China's régime can make its claim to legitimacy based on the promise of delivering on nationalistic aspirations to a comprehensive rise to global authority, in contrast African régimes are inherently unstable and illegitimate because they are weak.

Conclusion

In the more than 20 years since the CCP *de facto* abandoned Marxist dogma in the face of the failure of its Mao-era Stalinist economic policies, the nature of the relationship of the Party to its core constituency of workers and peasants has become more and more ambiguous, and régime legitimacy has therefore decayed. Polarization of wealth between rural and urban, and interior and coastal continues apace. Concomitantly workers in state-owned industry suffer from high rates of unemployment and loss of their "life-time guarantee" of housing and social welfare benefits. Dramatic drops in agricultural commodity prices as well as crippling taxation by bloated and corrupt local bureaucracies have led to considerable discontent among farmers. There is a deep and pervasive popular cynicism about the current leadership of the Communist Party's professed policy priority to address the pressing concerns of the workers dispossessed by the failing state industries and the problem of desperate poverty in much of China's rural area. These perceptions pose a strong challenge to the legitimacy of the CCP's rule of China.

But among many Chinese citizens there is a prevailing view that while the rule of the CCP has led to these social shortcomings due to the Party's identifying its interests with China's rising corporate élite, this is a necessary cost for China's continuing economic strengthening overall. The repression of political freedoms is seen as irksome, but unavoidable. It is seen as the price paid to fulfil the greater end of a continuing rise of China to global economic and cultural dominance—the fulfillment of a great historical mandate going back to China's period of great glory before relative decline started to set in just some hundreds of years ago.

But whether the Communist Party's authoritarian rule is essential to China's continued rise to power is open to question. So basing the legitimacy of the Party's rule on the proposition that only the CCP can lead China to great prosperity and national prestige as a dominant world power could be much open to challenge. Indeed the actual form of political organization in developing nations appears to be neither cause nor result of economic and cultural renaissance. There is no evident correlation between system of political organization and economic growth rates in the Third World.

It is becoming clear that the rise of a middle class in China is not having the democratizing effect that Chinese and Western theorists had hypothesized (see Yu 2003). But China may eventually chose liberal democracy as a means to resolve in a thoroughgoing way the structural injustices of the current system based on the maintenance of the privilege of the Chinese Communist Party. The Chinese Communist Party may lose the legitimating basis for its rule and be replaced by a régime that derives its legitimacy from strong identification with the indicators defined by the UN Covenants to assess the good in national governments. If so, China would not necessarily suffer from the sorts of devastating social, political and economic disorder that many fear would be the unavoidable cost of such political change. Indeed a more just society based on a democratic government whose rule is seen as virtuously legitimate, domestically and abroad, could strengthen China's social solidarity, national pride and unified sense of purpose.

Notes

1   This document can be found online. Available: http://english.people.com.cn/ constitution/constitution.html (accessed February 23, 2007).
2   This point is made in a report written by me but released by the Canadian Department of Foreign Affairs and International Trade (2006).
3   For an earlier study see Perkins (1997).
4   More sophisticated analysis has been done. For example see White (1996).
5   The article itself entitled "Job Anxiety is Real and It's Global" can be found online. Available: www.ceip.org/files/pdf/Policybrief30.pdf (accessed August 9, 2004).
6   This observation was made at a meeting at the Department of Foreign Affairs in Ottawa on May 9, 2005, but as the meeting was held under "Chatham House Rules" the speaker cannot be identified.
7   For discussion the development of China as a nation since Liang Qichao's formulations in the early twentieth century to today see Moskalev (2003; 2002).
8   A very strong argument for this is made in Gries (2004).

Bibliography

Canadian Department of Foreign Affairs and International Trade (2006) "Assessment of the Canada–China Bilateral Human Rights Dialogue." Available online: http://spartan.ac.brocku.ca/~cburton/Assessment%20of%20the%20Canada-China%20Bilateral%20Human%20Rights%20Dialogue%2019APR06.pdf (accessed February 23, 2007).
Constitution of the CPC (2002). Available online: www.learnworld.com/COURSES/P141/CCP-Constitution-Nov-2002.html (accessed August 30, 2004).
Fishman, Ted C. (2004) "The Chinese Century," *New York Times Magazine* (July 4).
Gries, Peter Hays (2004) *China's New Nationalism: Pride, Politics and Diplomacy*, Berkeley, CA: University of California Press.
Heilbrunn, Jacob (1999) "The Unrealistic Realism of Bush's Foreign Policy Tutors," *The New Republic* (September 27).
Huntington, Samuel (1968) *Political Order in Changing Societies*, New Haven, CT: Yale University Press.
Levenson, Joseph (1968) *Confucian China and Its Modern Fate: A Trilogy*, Berkeley, CA: University of California Press.

Manuel, Trevor A. (2003) "L'Afrique et le consensus de Washington: Trouver la bonne voie" [Africa and the Washington Consensus: Finding the Right Way], *Finances et développement* (September).

Moskalev, Alexei (2003) "Doctrine of the Chinese Nation" (Part Two), *Far Eastern Affairs*, 31(1): 64–82

—— (2002) "Doctrine of the Chinese Nation" (Part One), *Far Eastern Affairs*, 30(4): 78–98.

Nathan, Andrew (2006) "China's Constitutionalist Option," in Dittmer, Lowell and Liu, Guoli (eds.), *China's Deep Reform*, Toronto: Rowman and Littlefield.

NEPAD (2006) *Action Plans*. Available online: www.nepad.org/2005/files/action plans.php (accessed May 29, 2007)

Perkins, Dwight (1997) "History, Politics, and the Sources of Economic Growth: China and the East Asian Way of Growth," in Itoh, Fumio (ed.), *China in the Twenty-first Century: Politics Economics and Society*, Tokyo: United Nations University Press.

Ramo, Joshua Cooper (2004) *The Beijing Consensus*, London: The Foreign Policy Centre. Available online: http://fpc.org.uk/fsblob/244.pdf (accessed February 23, 2007).

Sautman, Barry (1992) "Sirens of the Strongman: Neo-Authoritarianism in Recent Chinese Political Theory," *China Quarterly*, 129 (March): 72–102.

Tanner, Murray Scot (1999) *The Politics of Lawmaking in Post-Mao China: Institutions, Processes and Democratic Prospects*, Oxford: Clarendon Press.

UN [Report of the Secretary-General] (2005) "In Larger Freedom: Towards Development, Security and Human Rights for All." Available online: www.un.org/larger freedom/ (accessed June 29, 2006).

White, Gordon (1996) "The Chinese Development Model: A Virtuous Paradigm?," *Oxford Development Studies* (June): 169–81.

Woodman, Sophia and Samdup, Carole (2005) "Canada's Bilateral Human Rights Dialogue with China: Considerations for a Policy Review," Briefing Paper released by the International Centre for Human Rights and Democratic Development. Available online: www.dd-rd.ca/site/_PDF/publications/asia/chinabilateraldialogue. pdf (accessed February 23, 2007).

Wu Guoguang (1997) "Why in the Rural Villages, Is It the Peasants: An Exception to the Failure of China's Democratization" [Weishenme zai nongcun, weishenme shi nongmin: Zhongguo minzhuhua shibai zhongde yige liwai], in Chen Mingtong and Zheng Yongnian (eds.), *Basic-Level Elections and Political and Social Change on Both Sides of the Taiwan Straits* [*Liang'an jicen xuanju he zhengzhi yu shehuide biandong*], Taipei: Yuean.

Yu Keping (2003) *Incremental Democracy and Good Governance: Chinese Politics in Transition* [*Zenglian minzhu yushanshi: zhuangbianzhongde zhongguo zhengzhi*], Beijing: Shehui Kexue Wenxian Chubanshe.

—— (2002) *The Emerging Civil Society and Its Significance to Governance in Reform China*, Beijing: Shehui kexue wenxian chubanshe.

9 The developmentalism/ globalization conundrum in Chinese governance

Marc Lanteigne

Introduction: enter globalization

This chapter argues that the Chinese state stands at the crossroads between the pursuit of its selective embrace of globalization and its desire to maintain a developmentalist model of economic growth. The policy towards globalization followed by President Hu Jintao can be viewed as a natural outgrowth of the attempts by Deng Xiaoping in the late 1970s to move China away from the largely isolationist policies of the late-Mao era. At the same time, modern China's current approach to globalization is considerably more complex than in the Dengist era, addressing issues far more numerous than solely economic reform. In addressing the challenge of globalization, the Chinese party-state has sought to gain from openness while simultaneously preventing potentially harmful influences from entering the country, a problem reminiscent of Deng's alleged aphorism about how difficult it is to open a window without letting in flies. Nevertheless, with the modern Chinese Communist Party (CCP) staking much of its political survival on its ability to provide ongoing and expanded economic benefits to more and more Chinese citizens, the party-state's approach to globalization must continue to be one of considerable caution.

On the surface, it can be argued that the Chinese state has adjusted to globalization's many challenges very well despite numerous potential pitfalls. The idea that China is completely in control of its economic globalization policies is backed up by the power of the numbers. Between 1978 and 2005, the country's Gross Domestic Product growth averaged about 9.6 percent annually despite some potentially damaging shocks just after the turn of the century (Naughton 2007: 140). The Asian Financial Crisis of 1997–8 spared China, due to the half-closed nature of the country's economy, and in fact allowed the country to gain much political capital in Asia after it assisted with the recovery of stricken states in Southeast Asia and later through its support behind mechanisms, such as the ASEAN-Plus-Three regime, dedicated to preventing further regional economic crises (Moore and Yang 2001). In 2002–3, the Severe Acute Respiratory Syndrome (SARS) epidemic, which had its origins in southern China but spread to other parts of Asia and then to North America, also had the potential to seriously derail the country's economic growth and international confidence. Yet the economic effects of SARS were transitory at best, and Beijing responded to international criticism of its early handling of the incident with tougher bureaucratic responsibility rules and the sacking or forced resignation of numerous high-ranking civil servants accused of mishandling information about the crisis (Lam 2006: 139–40). China's market size and increasing confidence in its ability to participate in the shaping of international trade, has resulted in the country now being commonly linked with Brazil, India, and Russia as one of the four most powerful emerging markets, the so-called 'BRIC' states. This quartet of states has been distinguished not only by its large size and population, but also its growing economic power, its ability to affect politics on a regional level and at times internationally, as well as its potential challenge to Western-led international economic norms (Wilson and Purushothaman 2003; Khalip 2006). China's inclusion in this category further serves to illustrate a state adjusting to globalization while continuing to develop as a strong economic power.

There are also positive signs of China's adaptation to globalization from an institutional viewpoint. After a long negotiating process, Beijing acceded to the World Trade Organization (WTO) in December 2001. In addition to the international-level benefits of having a more direct say in the course of the global economy and the development of liberalized trade, the benefits of membership for Chinese governance was also apparent. A new layer of pressures, this time external, was placed on various actors in the Chinese economy to accelerate the reforms of the 1990s and to better address politically and economically sensitive areas, including flexible links between state-owned enterprises (SOEs) and the government, as well as the country's burgeoning financial sector (Wang, Y. 2006: 43). During the five years since Beijing's accession, the CCP wasted little time in immersing itself in the regime's ongoing process of improving trade relations, a task further complicated by increasing developed/developing world divides which have threatened to scuttle the tempestuous Doha Round of international trade negotiations. At the same time, China has also taken on other approaches to improving its international economic contacts, seeking out participation in trade regimes such as the Asia Pacific Economic Cooperation (APEC) forum, and preferential trade agreements (PTAs) with its Asian neighbours and also seeking productive trade deals well beyond Asia, in Europe, Latin America and Africa. Long seen as a latent economic power, Beijing has endeavoured since the 1990s to translate its potential into more tangible economic returns.

From a business viewpoint, the CCP today has adopted and expanded Deng's 'open door' policies, encouraging foreign investment by 'inviting in' (*qingjinlai* 请进来) foreign firms at an accelerated rate. More recently, Beijing has promoted the 'walking out' (*zouchuqu* 走出去) of Chinese firms into international markets, as well as the development of commodity and service industries capable of competing globally (Shi 2001: 119–25). The walking out programs have produced some high-profile successes, including the purchase of IBM's personal computer division by China's Lenovo in 2004, as well as some notable setbacks, the most notorious being the politically charged, and unsuccessful, acquisition of Unocal, an American energy firm, by the China National Offshore Oil Corporation (CNOOC), in 2005 (Kynge 2006: 163–76). At the same time, in relation to the Asian developmentalist economies of the 1970s and 1980s, Beijing has had less luck compared to Japan and South Korea in developing truly global brands. Nevertheless, Beijing's increasing visibility in business, financial and trade circles has firmly entrenched the so-called 'China Inc.' mystique around the world (for example, see Studwell 2002 and Fishman 2005). The Chinese leadership is now looking towards August 2008, when the country is expected to host its official 'coming out' party in the form of the Summer Olympics, an event designed to attract greater foreign investment and further underscore China's re-entry into the world economy.

However, the economic rewards brought to China from increased economic globalization have resulted both in heightened risks to Chinese governance and the possibility of a considerable backlash from numerous quarters. The rewards of China's opening have been unevenly distributed, with some segments of the population benefiting greatly from increased access to global markets, capital and information and others, especially in the interior, left out of the process. The impact of such unbalanced growth has resulted in numerous incidents of protests and riots. As a result of these domestic-level tensions, there are concerns that China will be unable to sustain its economic growth rate in the wake of formidable obstacles, including a still-unreformed financial system, the urban–rural gap, and increasing energy demand, which have prompted Beijing to compete with the USA and other Western actors for international goods and materials.

Part of the complexity of attempting to measure and analyse the effects of globalization on the Chinese party-state is that the core concept of globalization has been subject to much interpretation. There are many varieties of globalization, including economic, technological, social, cultural and philosophical. As well, subsets of globalization study, including the questions of 'grobalization' and 'glocalization', both of which will be discussed later in the chapter in regards to China, further add to the sphere of current and potential research. To examine how the Chinese party-state has been affected by all of globalization's facets would be well beyond the scope of this chapter, but conclusions can be drawn in the area of how interdependence, via the increasing trade links between Beijing and other actors, has affected the question of governance in modern China. A deeper question to be addressed when considering China's economic future is how the party-state will manage this type of economic globalization as it continues to increasingly affect China's economic and political dimensions.

Globalization has had a 'transformative' effect on China, as it has upon many other states. To measure a state's transformative abilities is to gauge how well the said state is able to adjust to constant shocks and pressures from international actors by adaptation, creating new forms of governance to adjust to an atmosphere of perpetual change (Weiss 1999: 4–5). Rather than examining whether the Chinese state is being weakened by globalization forces, it is far more useful to determine how the party-state has been transformed as a result of these pressures, and more pointedly how these changes are being accepted and with what degree of resistance. It can be argued that there has been much opposition in Beijing to changes brought about by globalization, which may affect the security and stability of the party-state. This has created an almost à la carte approach by Beijing to economic globalization itself, namely taking the good and eschewing the rest as much as possible. This has also been described as the model of state-guided, 'selective importation' of international goods and ideas, primarily Western (Zheng, Y. 2004: 40–1). Thus China is determined to ensure that its own globalization process is overseen by the state in the hope of maintaining stability.

By adopting modified developmentalist economic policies, the CCP has attempted to prevent the forces of globalization from undermining its legitimacy and sparking greater chaos. As part of its policy of economic reforms, Beijing borrowed heavily from the East Asian economic models in Japan, South Korea, Taiwan, Hong Kong, and Singapore in creating a modified developmental state, defined as a system which places the state at the centre of the reform process, a state which has the power to regulate and micromanage the key economic and political relationships which support sustained economic growth (Chang 1999: 183; see also Johnson 1982: 3–24). The state 'picks winners' by concerning itself greatly with which economic actors best help the process of growth and maintains strong connections between government and economic actors, including private firms. Despite China's growing enthusiasm for globalization, the CCP is committed to preventing economic liberalization from undermining Party authority and wearing down the state, and maintaining an economic policy of modified developmentalism can be viewed as a defence against this outcome.

However, it is uncertain whether China's current selectivity towards globalization can be maintained while the country continues to employ a modified developmental model to ensure constant economic growth and development. China's discerning approach to globalization is becoming increasingly incompatible with its desire to maintain a state-guided developmentalist model of economic reform. Nonetheless, it is in China's current interests to maintain the developmental model as it continues its path of economic reform, especially since there remain many potential pitfalls for Beijing to address before it can assume the mantle of global economic power. It is uncertain whether the CCP will be able to continue moulding and channelling globalization as a means to maintain its leading role in the country's socio-economic life without sacrificing its commanding role over the macro-economic tools necessary for development. Moreover, there are the greater questions of whether developmentalism and acceptance of global-ization can continue to exist in tandem within the Chinese socio-economic structure, and what effects these two policies will have on future Chinese governance. Finally, there is also the issue of the degree to which the reforming Chinese party-state accepts and understands the often contradictory processes of globalization itself.

From the 'open door' to globalization thinking

Before examining the state of China's relationship with the current global-ization phenomenon, it is important to briefly survey the policy processes that permitted China to arrive at its current stage of economic opening and interdependence. In this case, globalization is defined using the concept explained by Bueno de Mesquita as 'the international process that leads to the worldwide integration of market-driven exchanges in goods, services and capital.'(2003: 407) The very concept of globalization (*qianqiuhua* 全球化) was not officially acknowledged by the Chinese party-state until well into the administration of Jiang Zemin in the 1990s, when policy speeches made mention of its challenge to China's international affairs. This move underscored the importance of trade to China's rapidly evolving post-cold war foreign policy priorities. After describing the international economic system as an 'interdependent whole' in 1994, then-Foreign Minister Qian Qichen used the term 'economic globalization' for the first time in his 'State of the World Message' in September 1996, a year before Jiang himself would first mention the term in his report to the Fifteenth Communist Party Congress (Kim 2006: 282–4). Beijing's interpretation of globalization at that time was seen as qualified at best, with much focus on its specific economic effects. Moreover, China's addressing of globalization was undertaken despite a long legacy of holding to a staunchly Westphalian view of the anarchic nature of the international system and the absolute need for state sovereignty, a viewpoint which had become increasingly at odds with the growing economic interdependence in the international system (Deng 1998: 311–14).

Moreover, China had to understand the role of emerging globalization not while outside of it, but while already surrounded and well immersed in it (Deckers 2004: 104). Nonetheless, despite progress in economic reforms in China in the 1980s the country had yet to address its Maoist-era concerns with excessive international engagement, especially concerns with inter-state regimes which by that time had become both well-established and domin-ated by great economic powers, particularly the USA. However, China's increasing foreign policy confidence, along with the need to enlist foreign actors to continue the country's economic recovery, mitigated some of these fears. Despite the late arrival of 'globalization' into the Chinese political lexicon, it has been argued that the concepts of globalization theory were well entrenched in Deng's rationales for economic reform while at the same time preserving the party-state and the paramount role of the CCP. The 1980s were a time of rediscovery of the benefits of Western goods and ideas within the larger conundrum of the pursuit of 'modernity' and thinking which moved beyond communist traditions (Dirlik 2002: 27). This change was ideally suited to Deng Xiaoping's plans for instituting reforms to the country and party-state while taking advantage of far more favourable international conditions than his predecessor had to experience.

The balancing act between maintaining state stability and economic opening became even more tenuous after 1989, when Deng had to preserve the reform agenda in the face of international condemnation and sanctions. Deng's post-Tiananmen reforms stressed the need to avoid 'peaceful evolution' (*heping yanbian* 和平演变), a long-standing political euphemism for China becoming subservient to the West not through force but rather through an externally-controlled erosion of China's distinct identity (see Whiting 1995). Thus reform became a dyadic process, with reform being pursued on one side and bolstering the party-state on the other, with both processes proclaimed as being necessary to bring about modernity in China (Hughes 1997: 104–9). This particular approach of grafting nationalism with economic liberaliza-tion has been referred to as 'nationalist globalism', namely the theory that economic opening was not only beneficial to the state but also quite com-patible with said state's core values and ideas. The successful implementation of this policy creates much more space for a regime to tinker with and adjust to the reform process without concerns by opposition forces that the economy and the identity of the state were becoming increasingly subordinate to global political and economic forces. This term was used to describe India's policy of adapting to globalization in the 1990s after a long period of Nehruvian policies of controlled markets (Amalgir 2003). However, the idea is very much relevant to Deng's post-1989 policies of open door reform and setting the stage for China's own immersion into the globalization vortex.

Within a milieu of greater international stability as well as a nationalist globalist approach, Deng was better able to implement the sweeping reforms he felt China needed. By the middle of the decade, the need for Chinese citizens to 'become rich' had been embedded in Deng's strategy and the Special Economic Zone (SEZ) policies, allowing for pockets of liberalized joint ventures and international trade contacts, had been expanded in the name of removing the doctrine of Maoist isolation (Baum 1994: 164–5). The idea of the permanence of these reforms underscored the need for open door policies to permit China's economic re-entry into the global market while still maintaining security. Self-reliance and autarky were increasingly viewed by the Deng regime as unworkable and as a result of the economic damage created by the Great Leap Forward and Cultural Revolution eras, China could ill-afford further inward-looking economic planning. However, in order to adjust to these new realities, not only was much structural change required, including the expanding SEZ program but new laws and regulations were also necessary to accommodate foreign economic actors and controlled decentralization of state authority to further allow for trade liberalization (Shirk 1993: 47–50). China's international pull as a giant market and potential economic pivot has gained the country much recognition as a latent, emerging market and economic powerhouse. However, well after the Deng era, institutional and legal reform continues as the Chinese party-state engages in an ongoing game of catch-up with the globalizing market, a project that has occupied much of its governance.

The Jiang government attempted to consolidate and then expand China's open door policies despite the international aftershocks of the Tiananmen incident in 1989. This process took place at the same time, however, as the collapse of the Soviet Union and, more critical to this study, the failure of the communist economic system in many parts of the former-Soviet world, thus producing a host of new states seeking to enter the market. New actors emerged in the international system as economic and communications links, having expanded considerably in the West during the Cold War, could now take on a truly global dimension. However, contrary to the embracing of globalization in the thinking of many states, the Chinese government was comparatively slow in grafting its ideas on foreign and domestic policy. It was in a speech by Jiang in September 1997 that the concept was first articulated, and since that time much policy debate on globalization has been primarily through an economic lens, namely the growing interconnectedness of markets and the best way China can take advantage of them (Moore 1999: 65–8). This included the need for China to accede to the WTO in order to become accepted globally as a trading state and to take part in the increasingly complicated formation of international trade rules.

Even more importantly, with Maoist economics being discredited, the CCP needed to craft an ideological alternative to socialism in order to ensure that it would not be swept aside in the name of reform. Its solution was a form of 'pragmatic nationalism,' a common staple of Chinese policy since Deng Xiaoping. This variation of nationalism stresses the need for ongoing economic development, and such development being contingent upon the maintenance of political stability and order. The party-state was thus framed as the only apparatus capable of providing the twinned virtues of political stability and economic growth (Zhao 2004: 29–31). A variation on this idea has been 'techno-nationalism', suggesting the strong role of the scientific and technical backgrounds of many current Chinese policymakers (including those in the CCP Standing Committee, the Party's inner circle) on modern governance (Hughes 2006: 33–4). These new interpretations of nationalism have further entrenched the power of the CCP within the Chinese state, but have also opened up a new area of risk. In short, the Chinese party-state was increasingly staking its legitimacy on its ability to continuously provide increasing economic development and better living standards to the Chinese people. As was demonstrated aptly during the May Revolution of 1998 in Indonesia which saw the ouster of President Suharto after his government proved unable to extract the country from the chaos of the Asian Financial Crisis, failing to provide consistent economic goods could result in severe political consequences. Thus, Beijing was forced to develop an understanding and appreciation of the globalization processes in order to keep its side of the pact with the Chinese people.

Since the Jiang period, the CCP endeavoured to demonstrate that adaptation to globalization was not only necessary from an economic viewpoint but also essential to the country's restoration as an advanced state (Moore 2005: 130–1). The 1990s were witness to a great deal of change in China's governance structure in order to better prepare both government and governed for greater international economic engagement. The 1998 governmental reforms saw the number of ministries reduced, others folded into the State Economic and Trade Commission (SETC), and the creation of the Ministry of Information Industry (MII) in order to streamline communication sectors. A follow-up round of restructuring divided the SETC into the State-owned Assets Supervision and Administration Commission (SASAC) and the State Development and Reform Commission (SRDC) which became a central node for development issues similar to the former Ministry of International Trade and Industry (MITI) in Japan (Yang 2005: 37–41; 58–63). Further reforms in 2003 brought about the creation of the Ministry of Commerce (MOFCOM), which has distinguished itself by being more knowledgeable about international institutions and norms when compared to China's industrial ministries (Bell and Feng 2007: 59). However, under Jiang the globalization idea was also approached with varying degrees of reluctance and resistance within the Chinese party-state. It appeared China was being pressured to address this issue while facing many disadvantages in adapting globalization within an international market dominated by great economic powers, particularly the USA.

The need to ensure that the economic reform process would not escape the supervision of the party-state was well encapsulated in Jiang's 'Three Represents' thinking, which was later added to the Chinese constitution as the outgoing president's signature contribution to the debate over the role of the post-Maoist CCP. According to this theory, the Party must always represent the development of China's advanced productive forces, the development of China's 'advanced culture' and the fundamental interests of the majority of Chinese citizens (Jiang, Z. 2002: 7–13). These views underlined the fact that the CCP could and would remain at the vanguard of China's economic development and modernization. Despite the fact that the Three Represents theory can be and has been open to interpretation, its introduction and addition to the Chinese constitution did spark a backlash from party conservatives worried that the concept was a green light for the CCP to develop into a 'bourgeois party,' an impression not dispelled by Jiang's call in 2001 for the

Party to open its doors to private entrepreneurs (Ryosei 2004: 26–8; Dickson 2005: 148–53).

By the late 1990s, China was clashing with the USA over the latter's acceptance of the former into the WTO. At the same time, the 'ring of fire' effect of the Asian Financial Crisis (AFC) had begun, and Beijing saw economies on its periphery fall victim one by one, from Southeast Asia to Northeast Asia to Russia resulting in currency crashes and economic chaos. The AFC served as a stark reminder to Beijing that while economic liberalization could bring great benefits, it also carried its share of risks and unpredictability. Although China was shielded from the crisis largely due to its still-protected currency regime, it nonetheless remained under an international microscope in the years following the meltdown. In Beijing, leaders began to examine the critical questions of greater economic privatization, banking and financial reform, and anti-corruption, cognizant of the fact that a future Asian crisis would be likely to affect China much more directly (Langlois 2002). As well, the political fallout of the accidental May 1999 embassy bombing in Belgrade by the United States and the spy plane incident in April 2001 had become enveloped not only in growing nationalist sentiment but also increasing concerns that globalization was becoming increasingly incompatible with domestic interests and Chinese strategy (Garrett 2001: 411–12; see also Gries 2004: 86–115 and Lanteigne 2005: 33–60). The admittance of China to the WTO did not put an end to these debates but rather transformed them.

Beijing's WTO membership has not only brought about much-needed recognition but has also set the stage for more lucrative trade deals, not to mention further 'locking in' of China's open door policies. Membership, however, also heightened concerns in policy and intellectual circles in the form of the 'new left' movement, seeing globalization as exacerbating socio-economic divisions within the Chinese state and calling for a rethinking of Chinese 'modernity' and its revolutionary legacy (Liu 1996; Zhu 2003; Wang, H. 2003). Although it is uncertain to what degree these ideas are present within the CCP, this example demonstrates the ongoing questions the party-state has had to address when weighing the benefits and costs of economic globalization. The perception of globalization in the Chinese party-state today is far from being universally agreed upon either by external actors or, seemingly, the Chinese Government itself. No debate over the future of Chinese governance can take place without a greater dialogue on China's intentions to address the multifaceted question of globalization in its ongoing reform strategies. Moreover, as the Chinese state has maintained a series of economic controls over key sectors and functions, following a policy of modified developmentalism or 'neo-developmentalism', there is the puzzle of whether the Communist Party is ready to fully accept a retreat of state power over the economy as has been seen in other states embracing globalization.

Developmentalism and China's globalization policies: contradictions?

Not long after globalization formed part of Chinese policy statements, its identification as a source of both economic goods and risks was undertaken by the policymakers. On one side it was seen as a primary method of enriching the state and sweeping aside archaic and ineffectual Maoist economic relics, such as SOEs, but on the other there was the question of what degree of governmental control over the Chinese economy needed to be loosened, keeping in mind the unpredictability of the market as well as lingering 'peaceful evolution' concerns. As well, there are the concerns about the social impact for many labourers forced to leave failed SOEs in search of other work. It was partially for this reason Jiang tended to view globalization as being linked with comprehensive security (Zhang 2004: 292–3). More specifically, the maintenance of a strong economy and trading system has been much more firmly recast since the 1990s as a strategic matter in addition to a developmental one, suggesting not only a re-assessment of state priorities but a greater sense of perceived risk to governance from market disruption.

Today, the adjustment of the Chinese economy to globalization takes place under the twin problems of what Zheng Bijian, author of the initial views on China's 'peaceful rise' (*heping jueqi* 和平崛起) in the international system, termed the 'mathematical propositions'. First, any socio-economic issue related to development, no matter how minor, has the potential to be multiplied exponentially by China's population of 1.3 billion. Second, the country's financial and material resources must be viewed as divided among said great population (Zheng B. 2005: 14–19). This level of economic distortion caused by the population factor raises the country's sensitivity and vulnerability to the potential problems of globalization to great heights in proportion to other emerging markets. At the same time, the 'population factor' underscores the cautious approach the Chinese party-state has taken towards maximizing the benefits of its international opening while seeking to minimize the risks.

It was with these concerns in mind that Beijing under Deng opted to develop a modified developmental economy as it emerged from the no-longer-viable Maoist command system. The post-1978 opening of the Chinese economy has been described as implementing export-oriented policies designed to take advantage of labour and manufacturing, while still retaining degrees of import substitution left over from the late Maoist/transition period (1972–8) (for example, see Wu 2005: 293–4). However, in looking at both Chinese economic strategies and policies during this time, an argument can be made that the economic system being created was not solely a mix of import substitution and export-guided policies but rather a modified developmental system designed to expand China's economic presence while keeping its economic mechanisms under a threshold degree of party-state control. The question here, however, is whether developmentalism will be a 'second stage' in the country's shift from a closed economy to a liberalized one, or will the political and social pressures of globalization assist in the perpetuation of developmental economics for the near term.

Developmental states have been rare in the international economic system, and the debate concerning the degree of developmentalism contributing to the rise of Asia as a strong economic region remains a subject of continued analysis. The Asian developmental model is defined by its observance and respect for market economics and private property, as well as the role of competition in international markets, with growth being seen as the primary goal. However, markets in this system are guided by a small group of highly skilled and educated elites and there are strong links between government and major economic actors, which allow for mutual consensus building on the direction development should take combined with much information sharing. The state bureaucracy has a commanding role in overseeing development, and often there is a 'pilot agency', such as the then-MITI in Japan, to coordinate policymaking and the implementation of new schemes (Öniş 1991: 111–12). The developmental model was studied as an alternative to the neo-liberal model of economic modernization and market engagement for developing states.

Since the AFC, Beijing has been promoting the greater liberalization of trade in East Asia and has agreed to the removal or reduction of tariffs on several goods categories with the ASEAN states while negotiating free trade with Australia, India, New Zealand and South Korea. In December 2005, the first East Asian Summit (EAS) was held in Kuala Lumpur, providing an opportunity for China to assist in the tying together of the various PTAs being negotiated in the region, perhaps even into a regional community. By the time of the follow-up EAS in the Philippines in December 2006, Beijing had abandoned its previous reservations regarding a Tokyo-backed plan to intensify work towards a regional economic partnership agreement and had begun to demonstrate greater support for the plan (Qi 2006; *Kyodo News* 2 December 2006). It would be premature to say, however, that these activities indicate a short-term transition to liberal markets. China, although not adapting all aspects of the developmental model, has created a modified version to account for the still-embryonic private property laws, a still-sizeable agricultural sector, and a considerable percentage of the Chinese economy that remains directly state-owned. According to official figures, SOEs, including those enterprises in which the state is the majority shareholder, represented 44 per cent of gross industrial output and 48 per cent of the labour force in 2001 (Pei 2006: 124). Then there is the straightforward fact that China is much larger, geographically and demographically, than the other 'developmental' states of the recent past, presenting a different set of governance concerns for the party-state and emphasizing the need to avoid economic chaos which could, in turn, spark domestic crisis. China today is on a much different economic footing from the East Asian developmental states of the 1960s and 70s, when they first adopted such policies.

Nevertheless, there are many points of comparison between Asian developmentalism and the modified Chinese version that continues to take shape. As with previous developmental systems, the Chinese state was insulated from external pressures to a sufficient degree for it to implement developmental policies without facing strong domestic opposition. Beijing also had the ability to make changes or repairs during the process, again without significant barriers. As well, the lack of democratic development further allowed the party-state to implement developmentalist policies, as well as to 'capture' emerging actors, which benefited from economic growth and reform, especially business sectors, a process known as corporatism. In the case of China, the often complicated division between SOEs and private and semi-private industries further allowed state oversight of major economic 'players' and sharing of information. Finally, the CCP could and did adopt nationalist agendas designed to increase its legitimacy as the modernization process was underway, stressing the need for economic growth unhindered by potential outside interference (So 2003).

It has been argued that developmental states are not only rare but also appear in very specific cases when state leaders perceive distinct and potentially very harmful challenges to governance, namely the process of 'systemic vulnerability'. A state may seek developmentalist policies if they are facing the threat of economic instability precipitating mass unrest (such as Indonesia in 1998), an increased need for foreign exchange and the wherewithal to fight wars based on national-level insecurity, and constraints on budgets caused by a lack of easily accessible sources of revenue (Doner *et al.* 2005). It can certainly be argued that China falls into these three categories to varying degrees, and this would explain why Beijing would wish to retain developmental features even under globalization pressures. First, the Chinese party-state is painfully aware of the country's history of peasant revolt during the imperial eras, conflicts which often led to the removal of dynasties and, in the case of the fall of the Qing Dynasty in 1911, war-lordism and state balkanization. The legacy of Sun Zhongshan (Yat-sen)'s oft-quoted 1924 comments about China being 'a plate of loose sand' (Goodman 1995: 410) remains relevant in a China still seeking its identity in a globalizing world. Currently, even with China's stunning economic success, strains are appearing in the Chinese countryside as peasants, largely left out of the Chinese miracle, protest their subaltern status. An economic slowdown would magnify these problems and directly challenge the legitimacy of the party-state.

Furthermore, although China is a developing great power, it nonetheless retains many concerns about its economic security in the current reform era. Economics and security, which until the mid-1990s were traditionally considered separately in China, were conceptually fused together largely as a result of the AFC and concerns about a future economic contagion effect on the Chinese economy (see Wang, Z. 2004). It is certainly arguable whether China faces the same severity of threat that Japan, South Korea and Taiwan faced during the Cold War, and it has been noted that China's security situation is more stable today than it was during the Cold War era when China faced concrete state-to-state threats on its borders. Nevertheless, Beijing retains concerns not only about hard security issues such as Taiwan, but also about economic security, including market failures, geographic choke points in its external trade, and its ongoing search for commodities, most especially energy, to continue fuelling its economic growth (for example, see Zweig and Bi 2005; Hale 2004). Economic security has also affected other aspects of China's regional relations, including an increasingly tense diplomatic skirmish towards the end of 2005 between Beijing and Tokyo over exploitation rights to potential natural gas reserves in the East China Sea. The two states have overlapping claims on key underwater gas fields, which both sides, seeking energy sources close to home, are unwilling to concede (Jiang, W. 2006). These incidents call into question whether Beijing can adequately address its concerns about economic vulnerability while continuing its opening process regionally and internationally.

At the same time, while China has been increasingly enthusiastic about regime building in Asia to further stimulate regional economic growth and better coordinate trade policies, Beijing's engagement with international economic regimes has so far favoured those which are consensus-based and informal, lacking a rules-based structure along North American and European lines. Examples of regimes that fit this model include APEC, the ASEAN-plus-three and the nascent East Asian Summit. These types of regimes are consistent with the model of inter-state cooperation known traditionally as the 'ASEAN Way' and more recently as the 'Asia-Pacific Way' (Katzenstein 2005: 142). Despite its increasingly central role in Asian economic development, China has approached economic cooperation warily maintaining its economic sovereignty and ensuring a threshold level of veto power over regional decision-making. The same issues of selective engagement are becoming more apparent within the nascent Shanghai Cooperation Organization (SCO), a Eurasian group within which Beijing has a significant level of influence. Established in 2001 as a primarily strategic regime and featuring a consensus-based structure with equal veto rights among members, the SCO has slowly begun to develop an economic dimension. With some SCO states holding considerable energy supplies, especially Russia, Kazakhstan and Uzbekistan (with Iran as an observer state but possibly a future full member) (Chung 2004; Lanteigne 2006–7), China's interest in seeing the organization increase its trading role becomes more apparent.

Another area of developmentalist policy in China has revolved around its currency, the yuan, which has opened to international markets at a very measured pace since the 1980s and remains under significant government oversight within China's expanding economy. This policy engendered increasingly loud complaints from international critics, especially the USA, that it was highly undervalued vis-à-vis the American dollar due to a currency peg that Washington began to view as increasingly artificial and unfair. In July

2005, Beijing agreed to remove the peg, in place for over ten years, and replace its monetary regime with a managed float, allowing the *yuan*'s value to fluctuate to a wider degree, setting its value against a basket of currencies rather than solely against the US dollar. The directive resulted in a rise in the *yuan*'s value of 2.1 per cent, well below what American policymakers have pushed for (McGregor 2005b). The fact that China had developed into both an economic and trading power was seen as more than enough justification for changes to China's currency policy more in keeping with its global economic status.

The ongoing Sino-American dispute over China's currency rates is a noteworthy echo of similar tribulations between Washington and Tokyo in the early 1980s over Japan's strong economic growth coupled with a weak yen. The end result of that dispute was the Plaza Accords of September 1985, when American representatives met with Japanese and Western European counterparts and agreed to a devaluation of the US dollar, thus not only strengthening the yen but also acknowledging Japan's stronger role in international monetary affairs (Brawley 1998: 361–74). Whether a similar arrangement can be struck on the ongoing yuan controversy is an open question. China's level of frustration with the impasse was well-illustrated by a May 2006 editorial in the *People's Daily* which accused the American dollar of having the characteristics of a 'spoiled child,' unwilling to be a more responsible actor in the international financial community (Ba 2006). These examples have demonstrated a continued preference for measured, developmental reform in the face of economic globalization pressures rather than accelerated liberalization.

The modified developmentalist approach to economic reform has been a key component of China's attempts to adapt to economic globalization while still allowing the party-state to maintain a central role in the ongoing economic reform process. China's large size, market attractiveness, growing economic and political power and foreign policy confidence will likely allow Beijing to maintain its gradualist approach to economic reform for the short term while deterring foreign pressures for more rapid liberalization under anything but Beijing's own terms. Thus, the globalization process for China can be viewed as a process of selective engagement as well as heightened sensitivity on the part of the Chinese party-state. As a result, China's management of the globalization process is becoming increasingly dependent upon its skills in balancing the interplay between domestic policymaking and engagement with international actors and economies.

The question, therefore, is whether Chinese policy will push its economy from a developmentalist model to one more consistent with liberal market strategies and interdependence. It has been argued that this transition is already underway due to both internal pressures (the consistent process of removing regulatory restraints) and global pressures (increased inter-linkage with the global economy and its regimes) (see Zweig 2002). However, with ongoing concerns from the Chinese party-state about preserving stability in its reform process and its concerns about the 'flies' associated with globalization, this process is liable to be slow and measured, at least for the short term. Moreover, analysing the level of resistance from both governmental and non-governmental sources to this process will be an essential part of emerging globalization studies in China.

The glocalization/grobalization question

While globalization as an area of development study continues to mature and find more solid analytical footing, measuring tools are slowly beginning to appear, designed not only to gauge the changes in governance and economic development brought about by globalization but also to demonstrate an actor's success or lack thereof in adapting to globalization processes. Applying these new measuring tools to the Chinese case will be an ongoing process as the state continues to raise its profile in the international economy. Yet it is possible to begin preliminary critiques of Beijing's approach by examining its levels of so-called 'glocalization' and 'grobalization,' concepts with a short research history and processes which tend to complement each other, especially in a developing state.

Glocalization, as the name suggests, involves a coalescing of local and global ideas and materials. Globalization is assumed to be a process whereby cultural ideas and products are spread and universalized around the world, while localization is viewed as the process of selective incorporation, absorption and 'particularization' of global items and ideas (Roudometof 2003: 45). As globalization guru Thomas Friedman phrased it, glocalization was 'more and more local content made global,' adding that in the Chinese case another Cultural Revolution of sorts was forming, not this time with Little Red Books but with 'little white iPods.'(Friedman 2005: A25) An actor benefiting from glocalization is one which utilizes the global and the local in ways which (preferably) are the most beneficial to said actor; the best of both worlds. China, as a large emerging market increasingly desirable to both developed and developing states, is increasingly viewed as adroitly melding global ideas and concepts as its economy grows. In the groundbreaking paper 'The Beijing Consensus,' Ramo describes the process of 'globalization with Chinese characteristics,' as a product of Deng's desire for Chinese ideas merged with Western learning. By combining local Chinese ideas and traditions with beneficial international ones, in everything from economics to architecture to music, he argues that the country is growing not just in wealth but also in confidence (Ramo 2004: 31–5). The Chinese case would appear to be a clear example of successful glocalization contributing to development. However, a consensus is lacking over the degree to which glocalization is winning out over perceived or actual 'Westernization' due to the influx of largely Western products and technologies into the Chinese market. Since the 1990s, concerns were raised about 'de-sinicization' as a result of Deng Xiaoping's reforms (Gittings 2005: 325), yet due to China's size and increasing economic confidence, there is a greater potential for China to adopt a blending of the local and the global to a much more successful degree.

However, this enthusiasm for China's ability to 'glocalize' must be tempered by the fact that the country's economic growth has been accompanied by increasing income inequality and still considerably high levels of poverty in the Chinese interior. This not only leads to the question of who benefits from China's economic rise but also the question of who is driving the glocalization process and does that process remain too centralized? If the answer to the latter question is yes, the next conundrum the Chinese Government faces is how best to ensure that the benefits of glocalization do not move out of its reach, and control.

Grobalization, a more recent term, is described as examining the 'imperialistic ambitions of nations, corporations, organizations and other entities and their desire – indeed their need – to impose themselves on various geographic areas'. The word itself is derived from the need for these actors to expand ('grow') their power, influence and profits on the international level. The original sociological work on the concept by Ritzer further described grobalization as being the spread of 'social forms' with or without 'substantive content', or as he phrased it, 'something' and 'nothing' (Ritzer 2003). It can be argued, however, that the term can be used in the socio-economic context to describe an actor seeking to beat globalization at its own game by introducing not only products and services capable of establishing a global presence but also the 'branding' of ideas which gain a high degree of international attractiveness. Here again the foundations of the Beijing Consensus are relevant, as Ramo argues that the Consensus's three pillars, a focus on innovation, avoidance of chaos via policies devoted to stability, and a theory of self-determination which stresses sovereignty, are becoming more popular in the developing world (Ramo 2004: 11–13). Countries seeking an alternative to the neo-liberal economics of the Washington Consensus and noting Beijing's successes in development are finding this method of economic reform to be increasingly worthy of scrutiny. The ideas underpinning the Consensus, combined with the Hu government's diplomacy and economic engagement, has brought China much political capital, in the form of 'soft power' (*ruanshili* 软势力), in the developing world and has effectively complemented Hu's diplomatic 'charm offensive' (*meili gongshi* 魅力攻势) (see Kurlantzick 2007) in many developing states since the dawn of the new century.

A more concrete, economics-based form of grobalization from the Chinese state has been the aforementioned 'walking out' policy. Begun under Jiang and continued under Hu, the walking-out strategy has resulted in the creation of increasingly 'globalized' Chinese firms now starting to establish an international presence. In addition to Lenovo, other manufacturing firms such as Konka, Haier and TCL were able to expand their regional presence in Asia and beyond after Beijing liberalized laws allowing for the transfer of Chinese materials abroad to assist with out-of-country manufacturing

(Ohashi 2005: 88–9; McGregor 2005a). Like others in East Asia before it, China is actively seeking 'champion firms' and 'globalized' products capable of competing in international markets. On the other hand, however, in economic sectors considered politically or strategically sensitive, such as high-technology and telecommunications, China has actively avoided market liberalization except specifically on its own terms. Beijing's adherence to 'techno-nationalist' policies in protecting key high technological sectors, despite much international pressure, illustrates the distinct methods of China's selective engagement with international markets (Feigenbaum 2003: 200–3). As well, this example further suggests a strong state–industry linkage as well as ongoing developmentalist concerns about having state control over key economic sectors.

There are, however, limits to the use of this term in the Chinese case, especially since the term 'imperialistic' can be widely open to interpretation (as well as conceivably carrying a negative connotation) and suggests a realist focus on power which is arguably not entirely applicable to economic globalization processes. Moreover, grobalization implies that a given actor has a threshold amount of power to actually affect the international system to a great degree with ideas and products, power certainly not available to all actors. As a rising power, Beijing does have the capability of creating global brands out of both its products and its policies, but much will depend on whether the country's economic growth can sustain itself, whether China's internal reforms can be completed, and finally whether the Beijing Consensus idea can be sustained should the country begin to slow down following a period of dizzying growth since the 1990s.

Thus, the ability of China to address the twin challenges to glocalization and grobalization is an area that calls for further measurement as the country continues to immerse itself in the international economy and adjusts not only to the economic but also the socio-political pressures of increased engagement with the global market. So far, an argument can be made that China has successfully developed the structures necessary to handle both challenges simultaneously, and indeed it can be argued that both of these phenomenon are in fact two sides of the same coin when applied to the Chinese case.

What's next? Further areas of study

In a January 2007 article by Chinese Finance Minister Jin Renqing, it was noted that the development of increased economic globalization in the world has coincided with the growth of China's 'comprehensive national power', and that Beijing's growing economic ties have now become the focus of international attention (*Qiushi* 16 January 2007). However, the study of globalization and governance both within China and in the international sphere is still very much in its early stages, due not only to the fact that globalization studies are still in their infancy but also due to the fact that the Chinese party-state is itself still adjusting to the question of how it can best address globalization pressures. Despite advances in Beijing's engagement with many globalization actors, including economic regimes and the overall international market, the party-state's adaptation process to the globalization process continues. Incidents such as the February 2007 'Shanghai Flu' event which saw that city's stock market plunge 9 per cent in twenty four hours, causing aftershocks of similar magnitudes in international trading and further confirming China's growing role in maintaining international financial health (Chung and Dyer 2007: 42), and the more local controversy over the cultural compatibility of the Starbucks coffee store in Beijing's Forbidden City (*Dow Jones Chinese Financial Wire* 12 March 2007), all illustrate the debates both within and outside of China as to what effects the globalization process will have on China's economic development and political direction. It is however, possible to make some preliminary observations of the effect of globalization and its continuing influence on the reforming policies of the CCP in the near future.

First, further study is needed on China's ongoing commitment to adopt more economic globalization policies, including increased liberalization, in line with rules established by the WTO. There are also the questions of the consolidation of property rights, and how they will affect those parts of the Chinese economy still under direct or indirect central supervision. By association, examination is required of sectors which Beijing still oversees in a developmentalist fashion, namely large state-owned enterprises and other economic actors not under direct supervision but still well within arm's reach of the CCP. If the contradiction between the party-state's desire to globalize and its need to maintain a modified developmentalist structure continues to grow, two possible outcomes will be collision or compromise, and either endgame will have a significant effect on many parts of the Chinese economy. A 'collision' may involve an economic downturn or an internal governmental crisis as different actors within various levels of the CCP seek to reconcile the simultaneous needs for economic modernization and liberalization on one side and ongoing state oversight of economic reform on the other. However, a compromise would entail not the retreat of the Chinese state but rather a more selective approach to economic governance, which would likely involve maintaining a modified developmentalist approach, one that is less obtrusive and more flexible.

A second point, connected to the first, deals with strategy development. There is a need to better address the question of how economic security has been grafted onto the subject of globalization in China. Much of China's security thinking has been moved away from traditional, 'state-to-state' strategic concerns. A more current focus is upon how China's delicate economic reform process can best be protected from external shocks and possible malicious interference by outside actors or simple market failures along the lines of the AFC. Indonesia in 1998 remains an important case study for China as to how economic mismanagement and lack of governmental accountability can bring about a deep crisis of governance. As a result of the direct linking between security and globalization, the question of confidence-building, often used in the strategic realm to describe the need to assure a political actor of non-hostile intentions by others, is becoming just as relevant in the economic area from China's viewpoint. China's concerns about developing within an international economy dominated by Western actors, as well as whether Beijing will have to compete for essential resources such as energy, will continue to affect its globalization thinking and will be a major part of the country's still-evolving foreign policy development.

Finally, greater attention needs to be paid to the developmentalism/ globalization question and its effect on the evolving study of Chinese governance. As more and more external economic agents and structures, including regimes, rules and the global market itself, have intruded on various levels of Chinese governance from the local level all the way to the top of the party-state hierarchy, China's economic growth, while remaining impressive, does not negate the requirement for Beijing to continue to seek ways of accommodating external actors and pressures within its economic planning policies. In short, globalization in China can and should be studied from a variety of angles, taking advantage of the slow but steady development of globalization theory to gauge Beijing's progress. Continued engagement with globalization will act as an important test for the ability of the Chinese party-state to adapt to changing internal and external conditions.

Bibliography

'16 East Asia Summit Members to Start Considering Regional EPA', *Kyodo News*, 2 December 2006.

Amalgir, Jalal (2003) 'Managing Openness in India: The Social Construction of a Globalist Narrative', in Weiss, Linda (ed.), *States in the Modern Economy: Bringing Domestic Institutions Back In*, Cambridge and New York: Cambridge University Press, pp. 225–44.

Ba Shusong (2006) 'How to Deal with the US$ as a "Spoiled Child"?', *People's Daily*, 19 May 2006. Available online: http://english.people.com.cn/200605/19/eng2006 0519_267096.html (accessed 30 May 2007).

Baum, Richard (1994) *Burying Mao: Chinese Politics in the Age of Deng Xiaoping*, Princeton, NJ: Princeton University Press.

Brawley, Mark R. (1998) *Turning Points: Decisions Shaping the Evolution of the International Political Economy*, Peterborough, Ontario and Orchard Park, NY: Broadview Press.

Bell, Stephen and Feng Hui (2007) 'Made in China: IT Infrastructure Policy and the Politics of Trade Opening in Post-WTO China', *Review of International Political Economy*, 14(1) (February).

Bueno de Mesquita, Bruce (2003) *Principles of International Politics: People's Power, Preferences and Perceptions*, 2nd edn, Washington, DC: CQ Press.

Chang Ha-Joon (1999) 'The Economic Theory of the Developmental State', in Woo-Cummings, Meredith (ed.), *The Developmental State*, Ithaca, NY, and London: Cornell University Press.

'Chinese Foreign Minister Calls for Building "Harmonious World"', *Qiushi*, 16 January 2007, *BBC Monitoring*/Factiva, 3 February 2007.

'Chinese Lawmaker Urges Removing Starbucks from Forbidden City', *Dow Jones Chinese Financial Wire*/Factiva, 12 March 2007.

Chung Chien-peng (2004) 'The Shanghai Co-operation Organisation: China's Changing Presence in Central Asia', *The China Quarterly*, 180: 989–1009.

Chung, Joanna and Dyer, Geoff (2007) 'China Roars But It's Still Too Young to be Calling All the Shots', *Financial Times* (1 March): 42.

Deckers, Wolfgang (2004) 'China, Globalisation and the World Trade Organisation', *Journal of Contemporary Asia*, 34(1).

Deng Yong (1998) 'The Chinese Conception of National Interests in International Relations', *The China Quarterly*, 154 (June): 308–29.

Dickson, Bruce J. (2005) 'Dilemmas of Party Adaptation: The CCP's Strategies for Survival', in Gries, Peter Hayes and Rosen, Stanley (eds), *State and Society in 21st Century China: Crisis: Contention and Legitimacy*, New York and Milton Park: Routledge Curzon.

Dirlik, Arif (2002) 'Modernity as History. Post-revolutionary China, Globalization and the Question of Modernity', *Social History*, 27(1): 16–39.

Doner, Richard F., Ritchie, Bryan K. and Slater, Dan (2005) 'Systemic Vulnerability and the Origins of Developmental States: Northeast and Southeast Asia in Comparative Perspective', *International Organization*, 59 (Spring): 327–61.

Feigenbaum, Evan A. (2003) *China's Techno-Warriors: National Security and Strategic Competition from the Nuclear to the Information Age*, Stanford, CA: Stanford University Press.

Fishman, Ted C. (2005) *China Inc.: How the Rise of the Next Superpower Challenges America and the World*, New York: Scribner.

Friedman, Thomas L. (2005) 'Chinese Funding Their Voice', *The New York Times* (21 October): A25.

Garrett, Banning (2001) 'China Faces, Debates, the Contradictions of Globalisation', *Asian Survey*, 41(3) (June): 409–27.

Gittings, John (2005) *The Changing Face of China: From Mao to Market*, Oxford and New York: Oxford University Press.

Goodman, Bryna (1995) 'The Locality as Microcosm of the Nation?: Native Place Networks and Early Urban Nationalism in China', *Modern China*, 21(4) (October).

Gries, Peter Hayes (2004) *China's New Nationalism: Pride, Politics and Diplomacy*, Berkeley, CA: University of California Press.

Hale, David (2004) 'China's Growing Appetites', *The National Interest*, 76 (Summer): 137–47.

Hughes, Christopher R. (2006) *Chinese Nationalism in the Global Era*, Milton Park and New York: Routledge.

—— (1997) 'Globalisation and Nationalism: Squaring the Circle in Chinese International Relations Theory', *Millennium: Journal of International Studies*, 26(1): 103–24.

Jiang Wenran (2006) 'East Asia's Troubled Waters, Part I', *YaleGlobal* (25 April). Available online: http://yaleglobal.yale.edu/display.article?id=7302 (accessed 30 May 2007).

Jiang Zemin (2002) 'How Our Party is to Attain the "Three Represents" Under the New Historical Conditions (25 February 2000)', in *Jiang Zemin on the 'Three Represents'*, Beijing: Foreign Languages Press.

Johnson, Chalmers (1982) *MITI and the Japanese Miracle: The Growth of Industrial Policy: 1925–1975*, Stanford, CA: Stanford University Press.

Katzenstein, Peter (2005) *A World of Regions: Asia and Europe in the American Imperium*, Ithaca, NY, and London: Cornell University Press.

Khalip, Andrei (2006) 'BRIC Economies Seen Outgrowing Current Leaders', *Reuters* (26 April).

Kim, Samuel S. (2006) 'Chinese Foreign Policy Faces Globalisation Challenges', Johnston, Alastair Iain and Ross, Robert S. (eds), *New Directions in the Study of Chinese Foreign Policy*, Stanford, CA: Stanford University Press.

Kurlantzick, Joshua (2007) *Charm Offensive: How China's Soft Power is Transforming the World*, New Haven, CT, and London: Yale University Press.

Kynge, James (2006) *China Shakes the World: The Rise of a Hungry Nation*, London: Weidenfield and Nicolson.

Lam, Willy Wo-Lap (2006) *Chinese Politics in the Hu Jintao Era: New Leaders, New Challenges*, Armonk, NY, and London: M. E. Sharpe.

Langlois, John D. Jr (2002) 'Pressures on China from the Asian Financial Crisis', in Ostry, Sylvia, Alexandroff, Alan S. and Gomez, Rafael (eds), *China and the Long March to Global Trade: The Accession of China to the World Trade Organisation*, London and New York: Routledge, pp. 99–119.

Lanteigne, Marc (2006–7) '*In Medias Res*: The Shanghai Cooperation Organisation as a Security Community', *Pacific Affairs*, 79(4) (Winter): 605–22.

—— (2005) *China and International Institutions: Alternate Paths to Global Power*, Milton Park and New York: Routledge.

Liu Kang (1996) 'Is There an Alternative to (Capitalist) Globalization? The Debate about Modernity in China', *Boundary 2*, 23(3): 193–218.

McGregor, Richard (2005a) 'Chinese Companies Count Down to Lift Off', *Financial Times* (London, 30 August): 19.

—— (2005b) 'China Ends Decade-Old Peg to Dollar', *Financial Times* (London, 22 July).

Moore, Thomas G. (2005) 'Chinese Foreign Policy in the Age of Globalisation', in Deng, Yong and Wang, Fei-ling (eds), *China Rising: Power and Motivation in Chinese Foreign Policy*, Lanham, MD, and Boulder, CO: Rowman and Littlefield.

—— (1999) 'China and Globalization', *Asian Perspective*, 23(4).

—— and Yang, Dixia (2001) 'Empowered and Restrained: Chinese Foreign Policy in the Age of Economic Interdependence', in Lampton, David M. (ed.), *The Making of Chinese Foreign Policy in the Era of Reform*, Stanford, CA: Stanford University Press, pp. 191–229.

Naughton, Barry (2007) *The Chinese Economy: Transitions and Growth*, Cambridge, MA, and London: MIT Press.

Ohashi, Hideo (2005) 'China's Regional Trade and Investment Profile', in David Shambaugh (ed.), *Power Shift: China and Asia's New Dynamics* (Berkeley, Los Angeles, CA, and London: University of California Press.

Öniş, Ziya (1991) 'The Logic of the Developmental State', *Comparative Politics*, 24(1) (October).

Pei Minxin (2006) *China's Trapped Transition: The Limits of Developmental Autocracy*, Cambridge, MA, and London: Harvard University Press.

Qi Qianjin (2006) 'China an Opportunity for East Asian Development', *China Daily* (25 March).

Ramo, Joshua Cooper (2004) 'The Beijing Consensus', London: The Foreign Policy Centre.

Ritzer, George (2003) 'Globalization: Glocalization/Grobalization and Something/ Nothing', *Sociological Theory*, 21(3) (September): 193–209.

Roudometof, Victor (2003) 'Globalisation, Space and Modernity', *The European Legacy*, 8(1) (February).

Ryosei, Kokubun (2004) 'Globalizing China: The Challenges and the Opportunities', in Ryosei, Kokubun and Wang Jisi (eds), *The Rise of China and a Changing East Asian Order*, Tokyo and New York: Japan Centre for International Exchange.

Shi Guangsheng (2001) 'China's Foreign Economic Trade in the 21st Century', in Brahm, Lawrence J. (ed.), *China's Century: The Awakening of the Next Economic Powerhouse*, Singapore and New York: John Wiley and Sons (Asia), pp. 119–25.

Shirk, Susan (1993) *The Political Logic of Economic Reform in China*, Berkeley, Los Angeles, CA, and London: University of California Press.

So, Alvin Y. (2003) 'Introduction: Rethinking the Chinese Developmental Miracle', in So, Alvin Y. (ed.), *China's Developmental Miracle: Origins, Transformations and Challenges*, Armonk, NY, and London: M. E. Sharpe, pp. 3–26.

Studwell, Joe (2002) *The China Dream: The Quest for the Last Untapped Market on Earth*, New York: Atlantic Monthly Press.

Wang Hui (2003) *China's New Order: Society, Politics and Economy in Transition*, Cambridge, MA, and London: Harvard University Press.

Wang Yong (2006) 'China in the WTO: A Chinese View', *China Business Review*, 33(5) (September–October).

Wang Zhenyi (2004) 'Conceptualising Economic Security and Governance: China Confronts Globalisation', *The Pacific Review*, 17(4): 523–45.

Weiss, Linda (1999) *The Myth of the Powerless State*, Ithaca, NY: Cornell University Press.

Whiting, Allen S. (1995) 'Chinese Nationalism and Foreign Policy after Deng', *The China Quarterly*, 142 (June): 295–316.

Wilson, Dominic and Purushothaman, Roopa (2003) 'Dreaming with the BRICs: The Path to 2050', *Global Economics Paper No 99* (October), New York: Goldman Sachs.

Wu Jinglian (2005) *Understanding and Interpreting China's Economic Reform*, Mason, OH: Thomson, Southwestern.

Yang Dali L. (2005) *Remaking the Chinese Leviathan: Market Transition and the Politics of Governance in China*, Stanford, CA: Stanford University Press.

Zhang Tiejun (2004) 'Self-Identity Construction of the Present China', *Comparative Strategy*, 23.

Zhao Suisheng (2004) *A Nation-State by Construction: Dynamics of Modern Chinese Nationalism*, Stanford, CA: Stanford University Press.

Zheng Bijian (2005) 'A New Path for China's Peaceful Rise and the Future of Asia' Bo'ao Forum for Asia, 2003, in *China's Peaceful Rise: Speeches of Zheng Bijian, 1997–2005*, Washington, DC: Brookings Institution Press.

Zheng Yongnian (2004) *Globalization and State Transformation in China*, Cambridge and New York: Cambridge University Press.

Zhu Xueqin (2003) 'For a Chinese Liberalism', in Wang Chaohua (ed.), *One China, Many Paths*, London and New York: Verso.

Zweig, David (2002) *Internationalizing China: Domestic Interests and Global Linkages*, Ithaca, NY, and London: Cornell University Press.

Zweig, David and Bi Jianhai (2005) 'China's Global Hunt for Energy', *Foreign Affairs*, 84(5) (September–October).

Index

Printed in the United States
by Baker & Taylor Publisher Services